Romancing the Business Loan

Romancing the Business Loan

Getting Your Banker to Say "Yes" in the 1990s

Gary Goldstick

LEXINGTON BOOKS
An Imprint of Macmillan, Inc.
NEW YORK

Maxwell Macmillan Canada
TORONTO

Maxwell Macmillan International
NEW YORK   OXFORD   SINGAPORE   SYDNEY

Library of Congress Cataloging-in-Publication Data

Goldstick, Gary.
  Romancing the business loan: getting your banker to say "Yes" in the 90s/Gary
Goldstick.
    p.   cm.
  ISBN 0-02-912398-4 (pbk.)
  1. Commercial loans—United States. I. Title.
HG1642. U5G65 1994
658.15'244—dc20   94-10603
                                                  CIP

Lexington Books
An Imprint of Macmillan, Inc.
866 Third Avenue, New York, N. Y. 10022

Maxwell Macmillan Canada, Inc.
1200 Eglinton Avenue East
Suite 200
Don Mills, Ontario M3C 3N1

Macmillan, Inc. is part of the Maxwell Communication Group of Companies.

Printed in the United States of America

printing number

1 2 3 4 5 6 7 8 9 10

To the memory of my parents, Margaret and Louis Goldstick

—They are sorely missed

Contents

Acknowledgements

Every writer knows that there is a huge gulf between the ideas you carefully nurture and the several-hundred-page book that eventually appears on booksellers' shelves and, hopefully, in readers' homes. I want to express my appreciation to J. Brandelyn "Brandy" Collins for her major contribution in bridging that gap. Her research efforts, along with the meticulous analysis, editing, and correcting of my drafts and preparing the final manuscript, were invaluable in bringing this book to fruition. I also want to thank my Lexington editor, Beth Anderson, for helping me organize, clarify, and tighten the presentation of many of the concepts.

Finally, I want to express my sincere appreciation to my friends, clients and colleagues who took time from their very busy schedules to review the draft of the manuscript and provide candid criticism and suggestions for its improvement. Thank you to Steve Adamson, Bill Birnbaum, John Burtchael, Leslie Cohen, Larry Fox, Bill Hall, Lana Hansen, Harold Hansen, Russ Hindin, Dan Jimenez, Dave Lampe, Rue Lund, Ted Mitchell, Mike Nave, Dick Pinsker, Wally Upton, and Gary Wimberly.

Introduction

Several months ago, when I was traveling on an assignment, I received a call from my wife with a message to call a prospective client. "He sounded very anxious," she said. "He gave me several different numbers where he could be reached. He said it was very important."

I phoned the client—I'll call him Sam—shortly thereafter and briefly reviewed the basics of his business problem. Sam was in the business of growing vegetable plants (such as tomatoes and bell peppers), which he sold to farmers for transplanting in their fields. He owned approximately ten acres of climate-controlled greenhouse area. He received orders from farmers to grow transplants of various types to an agreed maturity, then deliver them to the fields where they would be planted. According to Sam, he'd been in business for more than twenty-five years and was a recognized and respected expert in the transplant business.

Sam said that his bank, which had been providing him with a line of credit for more years than he was able to recall, had decided not to increase the line of credit and, in fact, was no longer interested in having him as a client. He had previously exhausted his cash reserves, had tapped every other source of available funds, and was desperate. Sam didn't need to point out that an inventory of growing plants is materially different from that for steel, garments, or computers. If you don't care for the plants every day, they'll die, and your inventory will disappear both physically and financially.

We made arrangements to meet the next day, which was Saturday. During our three-hour meeting Sam provided the details to his story of the previous day. The more Sam talked, the more I began to see the bank's point of view. Of course, I didn't reveal that to Sam—at least, not yet.

Sam had met with the bank the previous Wednesday, the date on which his line of credit expired. Without providing any prior notice to his loan officer, he advised her, her supervisor, and the regional manager of the following information:

- He expected to show a substantial loss for the fiscal year just ended. He estimated the loss as being in the neighborhood of two to three hundred thousand dollars, but it would take him several weeks to come up with the exact figure because he had terminated his controller and was now handling that job himself.
- He needed an additional two hundred and fifty thousand dollars on his line of credit to get through the current crop year.
- He couldn't provide any cash flow projections to give the bankers any indication as to how he planned to pay off the line of credit.
- He felt that a recent appraisal of his assets, which indicated a loan/asset ratio of approximately 50 percent, provided the bank with adequate collateral.

The bank apparently thought otherwise; the loan officer called Sam on Friday morning to advise him that the bank would not provide additional funding. This had created the current crisis.

Sam was visibly agitated. The business he had built over a twenty-five-year period was hurtling to an imminent demise. He had not met the payroll on Friday, and the power would be turned off in three days unless he found some money to pay the previous month's bill. He was doing a balancing act with his critical suppliers, who would soon cut him off if he couldn't satisfy them during the next few days.

I had sat through scenes like this many times. An anxious and depressed entrepreneur, with his back against the wall, catalogs the various plagues that have occurred or are about to occur. He criticizes the bankers for their lack of compassion, empathy, and business judgment, as well as for their faint heart in not providing him the capital he so desperately needs. Anyone in their right mind could see that the banker was not assuming any significant risk in providing it!

But this time it was slightly different. I found myself feeling quite ambivalent about Sam's problem. Sure, I was attentive and was ready to give him the best professional help I could. At the same time, though, I saw Sam's predicament as a parable—the inevitable denouement of the immature business and financial strategy of the prodigal businessman.

The underlying question that continued to churn in my mind was this: why was he so surprised by the bank's decision? Sam was no fool. He was educated and had twenty-five years of experience dealing with various credit grantors, including bankers, vendors, and lessors. Most of the businesspeople that Sam dealt with (such as his suppliers, customers, competitors, and members of the Rotary Club to which he belonged) considered him a professional. But by the bank's standards, Sam was an amateur who didn't inspire confidence, merit additional loans, or warrant further consideration.

As I pondered the dichotomy between Sam's view and that of the bank, I realized his situation was similar to that of many of my clients and, in fact, to my own when I had been the president of a struggling electronics manufacturing company. I reflected on the times I had raged and ranted over the insensitivity of my bankers and their blindness in not being able to see that the prosperity of my company was guaranteed. The only ingredient lacking was their loan.

At some point during that meeting with Sam I experienced an epiphany. I saw Sam's present situation, my previous experience with bankers and investors, and the unsuccessful relationships of many of my clients with their bankers as manifestations of a common malady that affects a majority of entrepreneurs and CEOs. Simply put, they lack—in fact, they are unaware of—the skills and attitudes that are necessary for achieving success with credit grantors and credit-granting institutions.

This lack is at the heart of the problem and is why business owners like Sam, who are skilled in conducting the affairs of their companies and respected by the communities, are viewed by their bankers as being unsophisticated and lacking business acumen.

There are three ingredients in a successful business:

1. *The dream.* The business concept, the idea, the products, the service, the project, or the deal that promises to provide the wealth and success the entrepreneur craves.

2. *The management.* The people, organization, systems, policies, and procedures that together allow the dream to be implemented.
3. *The finances and financial management.* The money and the controls on the money that provide the fuel to run the engine of business.

If any one of these three legs (which together form the basis of every successful enterprise) is inadequate, the enterprise either doesn't get off the ground, fails after a short and unsuccessful flight, or lumbers along for years without providing any wealth, security, fulfillment, or comfort for the entrepreneurs. The last group of businesses are known by venture capitalists as "the living dead."

A dream is a necessary condition for creating a new business; but it is not sufficient. You must also have the means to implement the dream—namely, the management team to make the dream happen, and the money to finance it. The operating equation is this: Dream + Management + Money = A Business.

A dream without adequate money remains a fantasy, something you can tell your grandchildren about in retirement. But the equation above is somewhat incomplete, because we haven't distinguished between what it takes to create a business that is doomed to failure and a business that has a reasonable probability of success. A more accurate equation is as follows: A Good Dream + Competent Management + Adequate Money = A Potentially Successful Business.

A good dream gives a business a reason to exist. It has a distinctive competence (something it does very well—hopefully, better than its competitors) or valuable resources (location, patents, trade secrets, and so on) that allow it to distinguish itself from its competitors. It has a competitive advantage over the other businesses that serve its markets, so a sufficient number of customers will choose to purchase its products or services over those of the competition, and it has the potential to generate sufficient profit to sustain operations and grow to meet the volume demands of the marketplace.

Competent management means that the entrepreneurs have attracted to their business individuals with the education, training, and experience to carry out the operational tasks that are required to implement the dream. The various line and staff functions of a business include sales, production, purchasing, accounting and finance. For a large business with many employees, these tasks are carried out by different persons; in a small business, one manager may be responsible for several management jobs. Whether the company is large or small, however, the employees who are responsible for managing the various aspects of the business must be competent to do the jobs they are assigned. Otherwise, the dream will never get a fair chance to be realized.

Adequate money means that the business has access to the capital necessary to finance its activities and assets until the dream is financially self-sustaining. Obtaining financing for a business has never been easy, but in the past it was a good deal easier than it is in the 1990s. The banking and savings and loan industries, which have been primary sources for business loans, experienced cataclysmic changes during the mid-1970s and the 1980s. These changes resulted in policies, procedures, regulations, and a lending environment that substantially increased business owners' difficulty in obtaining and maintaining reliable financing. The failure rate of new businesses is in the range of 50 percent to 60 percent during the first five years, and statistics show that ultimately 94 percent of new businesses formed will either fail or be discontinued because they are not able to meet the goals the owners have formulated.

In my capacity as a management consultant, I have often been called upon to pick up the pieces of a failed enterprise and explain to the creditors and the bank what happened and why. In a large percentage of instances the failure could be directly attributed to a lack of adequate financing or financial management. The dream underlying the business was viable, and the operating management competent—but the failure of the entrepreneurs to provide adequate funds to the business, or to manage what funds they had, killed the enterprise. This type of business tragedy doesn't have to happen. It is my hope that this book will help you successfully obtain and manage the funds for your business.

—Gary Goldstick

1

Bankers Are Just Like Anybody Else, Except Richer

This is a song to celebrate banks,
Because they are full of money and you go into them and all you hear is clinks and clanks,
Or maybe a sound like the wind in the trees on the hills,
Which is the rustling of the thousand-dollar bills.
Most bankers dwell in marble halls,
Which they get to dwell in because they encourage deposits and discourage withdrawals,
And particularly because they all observe one rule which woe betides the banker who fails to heed it,
Which is you must never lend any money to anybody unless they don't need it.
I know you, you cautious conservative banks!
If people are worried about their rent it is your duty to deny them the loan of a nickel, yes, even one copper engraving of the martyred son of the late Nancy Hanks;
Yes, if they request fifty dollars to pay for a baby you must look at them like Tarzan looking at an uppity ape in the jungle,
And tell them what do they think a bank is, anyhow, they had better go get the money from their wife's aunt or uncle.
But suppose people come in and they have a million and they want another million to pile on top of it,
Why, you brim with the milk of human kindness and you urge them to accept every drop of it,
And you lend them the million so they have two million and this gives them the idea that they would be better off with four,
So they already have two million as security so you have no hesitation in lending them two more,
And all the vice-presidents nod their heads in rhythm,
And the only question asked is do the borrowers want the money sent or do they want to take it withm.

1

> *But please do not think that I am not fond of banks,*
> *Because I think they deserve our appreciation and thanks,*
> *Because they perform a valuable public service in eliminating the jackass-*
> *es who go around saying that health and happiness are everything and*
> *money isn't essential,*
> *Because as soon as they have to borrow some unimportant money to*
> *maintain their health and happiness they starve to death so they can't*
> *go around anymore sneering at good old money, which is nothing*
> *short of providential.*
>
> —Ogden Nash[1]

Virtually every business, at some point in its existence, will experience a need for cash. It will come down to this: either the business gets the needed cash or

1. a potentially vigorous business will be stillborn,
2. the growth of a potentially profitable business will be curtailed,
3. the pursuit of a promising business opportunity (such as a merger, or a new product or service) will be frustrated, or
4. a previously thriving business that has fallen on hard times will fail and cease to exist.

The birth, growth, and life of most business enterprises depend on the ability of their senior management to get a lender or investor to say "yes" and agree to provide the needed financial support.

Unfortunately, every year thousands of deserving businesses in search of capital are cut down in the prime of their existence with a chorus of "nos" from the bankers and investors to whom the CEOs and CFOs have pitched their story. Many are healthy, moderately profitable companies with products and services that have achieved respectable market shares, and with management teams that are committed and competent.

Poor communications between business owners seeking a loan and bankers who control their access to funds characterize the relationship. The common lament of business owners who have been denied loans is that bankers only lend money to people who don't need it. Bankers are often reluctant to level with an applicant as to the real reasons for rejecting a loan. They want to avoid offending their customer, who in many cases is a person of some influence in the community; they don't want to lose the customer's deposits or drive him or her into the arms of another banker. So the exit interview between a banker and a recently rejected applicant is made up of mealy-mouthed homilies stressing the need for more capital, improved financial statements, and a hoped-for better lending climate when those damn regulators won't be so tough.

Yet the managers of companies who have been denied financing see other businesses whose relationships with financiers and lenders are thriving. These other firms don't appear to be doing anything spectacular; they seem to have market prospects, balance sheets and historical profitability that are comparable to the managers' own. So what do these financially favored businesses know that their unfortunate colleagues do not?

These companies have learned that before a banker makes the conscious and apparently rational decision to commit cash to a project, that project—and the managers and promoters behind it— will first have to win his or her heart. Highly successful borrowers have cultivated a shrewd understanding of how a banker gets emotionally committed to a deal, and they have honed the skills required to further that process to a successful conclusion.

It is the ability to anticipate and respond to a banker's spoken and unspoken needs, aspirations, desires, and fears, and the heightened awareness to exploit opportunities to deepen a banker's commitment, that distinguishes the firms that get loans from those that don't. I'll be discussing these essential skills briefly in the next chapter and then in much greater depth in Part II of this book. But before I do, it behooves us to develop some deeper insight into the banker's mind.

Bankers Have Been Given a Bum Rap

Banks are OK. In fact, the marble, granite, and glass edifices that house banks are regarded with reverence and awe by most members of the community. They are a symbol of stability, of conservative values. We need their apparent security when we want to store the few baubles our great-aunt Sarah left us when she died.

But we don't like bankers. We grudgingly deal with them when we need something from them—like a loan to buy a new car or house, a loan to finance receivables when our business is growing, or a loan to finance our seasonal inventory during the lean period between Christmas seasons. We regard them in much the same way that we view undertakers: we're happy to know they are available to perform their necessary service in those rare instances, but we'd just as soon not socialize with them.

Our attitude toward bankers is not surprising when you consider how bankers have been portrayed in history, in literature, and in the cinema. Two thousand years ago a religious revolutionary by the name of Jesus of Nazareth led a mob that drove the Jewish bankers from their traditional markets in the temple. Jesus was merely implementing the precept of Psalm 15:5 that "[he] who does not put out his money at interest shall sojourn in [the Lord's] tent and shall dwell on [the Lord's] holy hill." Martin Mayer, in his book *The Bankers*, points out that much of the poor image of the banker reveals the fear and hatred felt historically by the productive worker (such as the farmer, tradesman, or craftsman) for the moneyed man who profits by the misfortune of others, "appropriating to himself the fruits of the fields he has never tilled—and ultimately, often enough the fields themselves."

The archetype for the grasping, greedy, unscrupulous banker was created by William Shakespeare in *The Merchant of Venice*. In the play, the banker Shylock agrees to lend three thousand ducats to Bassanio, a friend of the merchant Antonio, secured by a pound of Antonio's "fair flesh, to be cut off and taken in what part of your body pleaseth me." When business reversals prevent Antonio from paying, Shylock is determined to have his pound of flesh and insists on the letter of the law. He is prevented from liquidating this human collateral only by the clever intercession of Portia, Bassanio's betrothed.

Then there's the greedy Mr. Potter, the character played by Lionel Barrymore in the perennial Christmas movie *It's a Wonderful Life*. Mr. Potter, the owner of the town's major bank, wants to take over the building and loan company run by George Bailey (played by Jimmy Stewart). Potter recovers several thousand dollars of the loan company's money and fails to return it. The shortage is discovered by the bank examiner, who threatens to close the building and loan company and prosecute George Bailey. Bailey contemplates suicide, but his guardian angel intercedes and helps him understand just how important his life is. The townspeople rally around George's family and make up the missing money, saving the building and loan company and thwarting the evil Mr. Potter.

Probably the most well-known banker in literature is Charles Dickens's covetous and stingy Ebenezer Scrooge. In *A Christmas Carol*, Scrooge exults in his mean-spirited nature. He is insensitive to the feelings and needs of his employees, his relatives, and the community at large. His metamorphosis from a tightfisted banker to a good Samaritan who uses his position and wealth to help his fellow man is a miracle of the Christmas season.

Finally, in his classic *The Grapes of Wrath*, about the migration of displaced tenant farmers from Arkansas and Oklahoma to California, John Steinbeck places the blame for the calamity squarely on the bankers:

> The bank—the monster has to have profit all the time. It can't wait. It'll die. . . .
>
> The banks is something else than men. It happens that every man in a bank hates what the bank does and yet the bank does it. The bank is something more than men. I tell you. It's the monster. Men made it, but they can't control it.[2]

In real life, newspapers frequently describe farm foreclosure auctions where the family sits out on the lawn watching their possessions being sold off by a sheriff, all under the watchful eye of the banker. Is it any wonder, with this type of press, that bankers as a group are not held in high esteem?

This is an unfortunate situation, especially as it affects business owners and entrepreneurs, because for the great majority of businesses in the world the banker is an essential ingredient for formation and growth. I believe that the general antipathy toward bankers stems in part from the fact that most businesspeople have no idea just how risky and difficult a business banking has always been, and how much more difficult it has become since bank deregulation. I will explore this issue in some depth in the balance of this chapter.

A Christmas Carol (Slightly Revised)

Ebenezer Scrooge groped his way home through a dark, grimy warehouse district of London. He felt quite satisfied with himself and even allowed ever so faint a smile to light about his countenance. He had meticulously kept the Christmas spirit (at least his version of the Christmas spirit). He had rejected his nephew's invitation to Christmas dinner, impolitely and without explanation, and shouted down his nephew's "Merry Christmas!" greeting with "Bah, humbug!" The businessmen who happened into his shop seeking contributions for the poor were summarily dismissed without extracting so much as a farthing from him. He was confident that he had been successful in making his miserable clerk, Bob Cratchit, feel guilty over being paid a full day's wages for Christmas without having to do one stitch of work.

Scrooge was about to open the door of his miserable flat when he noticed that in the very spot the door knocker was accustomed to occupy, was a visage which bore a striking resemblance to that of his dead partner, Jacob Marley. Scrooge had scarcely thought about Marley in the seven years since his death—except for the one time a year he reviewed the accounts in Marley's estate. As executor and trustee he dutifully determined the earnings of the various trusts and sent off the checks and his report to Marley's heirs.

Marley's face had a dismal light about it, like a bad lobster in a dark cellar. It was not angry or ferocious, but looked at Scrooge as Marley used to look, with ghostly spectacles turned up on its ghostly forehead. As Scrooge looked fixedly at the visage it was a knocker again.

Scrooge slowly ascended the stairs and opened the door to his small flat. But before he shut the door he walked through his rooms to see that all was right. He had just enough recollection of the face to desire to do that.

Several minutes later Scrooge heard a clanking noise deep down below, as if some person were dragging a heavy chain over the casks in the wine merchant's cellar. The cellar door flew open with a booming sound, and then he heard the noise much louder on the floors below . . . then coming up the stairs . . . then coming straight toward his door.

"It's humbug still!" said Scrooge. "I won't believe it."

His color changed though when, without a pause, it came through the heavy door and passed into the room before his eyes. The same face; the very same Marley in his pigtail, usual waistcoat, tights, and boots. The chain he drew was clasped about his middle. It was long and wound about him like a tail and it was made of cash boxes, keys, padlocks, ledgers, deeds, and heavy purses wrought in steel. His body was transparent so that Scrooge, observing him and looking through his waistcoat, could see the two buttons on his coat behind.

"How now!" said Scrooge, caustic and cold as ever. "What do you want with me?"

"Much!"—Marley's voice, no doubt about it.

"Who are you?" asked Scrooge.

"Ask me who I was."

"Who were you then?" said Scrooge, raising his voice.

"In life I was your partner, Jacob Marley."

"Mercy!" cried Scrooge. "Dreadful apparition, why do you trouble me?"

"I am very unhappy, Ebenezer, and therefore I cannot rest."

"Why so?" asked Scrooge.

"You have not done right by me, Ebenezer. The trusts that you have managed for my heirs since my death have, by my calculations, paid a mere 2.87 percent compounded over the seven years since my death. Since inflation has averaged 3.42 percent per year, my heirs have lost an average of 0.55 percent per year. This has caused me great dismay, Ebenezer, since I had always considered you a very shrewd banker."

Scrooge's face turned crimson. He attempted to stammer a reply, but the ghost held up his hand and clanked his chains.

"I had thought that the considerable sum I left for my wife and children should have maintained them in the lifestyle they enjoyed while I walked the earth as a mortal. But that assumed you would earn a yearly return of 3 percent over the inflation rate, which was less than you and I did during the twenty two years we were partners. Your poor performance, Ebenezer, has caused my wife to take in lodgers in order to maintain the household and pay for our children's education, and this has caused me much humiliation."

"Jacob," said Scrooge, "times are different. It's hard to find good borrowers. There is terrible competition. Our operating costs have increased. I do the best . . ."

The ghost let out a wail that chilled Scrooge to his bones.

"And," continued the ghost, "you have made yourself into a miserable, cantankerous misanthrope, which has brought both discredit and calumny on your head. Is it any wonder that you cannot find "good borrowers" but must scour the back alleys for the thieves, pimps and whores who often do not pay back the loans? Why, Ebenezer, would any self-respecting citizen who can obtain a loan from one of the many respectable houses in London do business with you?"

Scrooge started to reply, but the ghost held up his hand. "Hear me. My time is nearly gone. You will be haunted by three spirits. Without their visits you cannot hope to reverse the relentless decline in your business, your social interactions, and your humor and health. And I cannot expect that my trusts will earn at least 3 percent over the inflation rate. Expect the first tomorrow when the bell tolls one. Expect the second the next night at the same hour. The third will come the next night when the last stroke of twelve has ceased to vibrate. Look to me no more; and look that, for your own sake, you remember what has passed between us."

Scrooge was soon visited by the Ghost of Christmas Past, who transported him back in time to the month following Marley's death. He found himself in his office watching a seven-years-younger Scrooge shouting angrily at a young, apparently clean-cut eager tradesman asking for a loan to purchase inventory for a men's apparel store.

Scrooge looked at the ghost and stated, "That young man looks vaguely familiar. Do you know him, honorable shade?"

"I do," replied the ghost, "and so do you, Ebenezer. He is Thames E. Frank, proprietor of a number of very successful haberdashers in England, Wales, and Scotland. The entire royal family purchase their wardrobes from his stores, and that sets the fashion trend for the country. He has a line of credit of five million pounds at 5 1/2 percent with your competitor, Warburg and Co."

"My God," exclaimed Scrooge, "and I threw the gentleman out. Why, he could have been my customer."

The ghost nodded in agreement.

The ghost took Scrooge to later times and different places. Each scene bore a striking similarity to the previous one: Scrooge refusing to lend and, in fact, abusing a then-aspiring, now highly successful entrepreneur who was presently a valued customer of a Scrooge competitor.

The following night Scrooge was visited by the Ghost of Christmas Present. It took Scrooge by the hand to the port of London, where he observed a vivacious and curvaceous, beautifully dressed young woman about to board a steamer. She was accompanied by a portly gentleman of middle age, who was smoking a rather large cigar.

"Do you have my box of jewels, dearie?" she cried.

"Yes, luv."

"And do you have the money from the sale of the furniture?"

"Yes, luv."

"And the hundred thousand pounds Mr. Scrooge gave you yesterday?"

"Right here in m' pocket, luv," he said, patting his left breast.

Scrooge's face was ashen. The portly gentleman was his new client, Mr. Gark; the woman, a notorious music hall singer. He had just loaned Gark one hundred thousand pounds to purchase and remodel an industrial building, yet the implication of the scene he was observing was clear: Gark was fleeing the country with his mistress, and the couple's affair was to be financed by Ebenezer Scrooge.

Scrooge looked sheepishly at the ghost. "Mr. Gark had an excellent reputation. My correspondents stated that he was a successful real estate investor who had completed many profitable projects. I had no reason to suspect . . ."

Scrooge's voice trailed off. He was mentally reducing the capital account of Marley's trust by the one hundred thousand pounds. He turned to the ghost and asked, "Does Marley, or rather, does Marley's ghost know?"

The Ghost of Christmas Present nodded.

Scrooge held his head in his hands and sobbed, "I have no way to ascertain the character of my borrowers. My colleagues and friends deceive me. They send me all the crooks and swindlers and they keep for themselves the bright, honest businessmen. They laugh at me behind my back. They all wish me ruin."

When Scrooge looked up, the ghost was gone, and he was again back in his bedchamber.

The next night Scrooge was visited by the Ghost of Christmas Yet to Be. It took Scrooge to a courtroom, which Scrooge recognized as being Old Bailey. The ghost motioned to Scrooge to observe the proceedings. It became quickly apparent to Scrooge that there was a trial in progress. The prisoner in the dock was old, wizened, and disheveled. He stood holding on to the rail, his reddened eyes unfocused, wandering. Scrooge could not help but feel sympathy for such a forlorn and unhappy person.

"Who is the prisoner?"

The ghost made no reply.

"Please, venerable spirit, do I know the unfortunate wretch?"

The ghost nodded.

"I cannot place him, spirit; tell me his name and his business affiliation. Perhaps I might do something to lessen his misery."

The ghost pointed to one of the attorneys, who was about to question the prisoner.

"Mr. Scrooge," stated the attorney, "do you understand the charge against you?"

"Yes," whispered the prisoner.

"You are charged with mismanaging and squandering the assets of the estate of Jacob Marley, your former partner who died seventeen years ago. How do you plead, guilty or not guilty?"

"I did my best," cried the prisoner. "There were just no good borrowers. My colleagues deceived me. Cutthroats and scoundrels took advantage of me. I'm not to blame . . ."

"The prisoner will confine himself to answering the question," cried the judge pounding his gavel.

"Your answer, Mr. Scrooge," said the attorney.

"Not guilty," whispered the prisoner, lowering his eyes.

Scrooge was incredulous. He now recognized that the prisoner was he, older by a decade, and from appearances a rather hard and unhappy decade at that. And he was on trial for mismanaging Marley's trust. It was horrible, horrible, to end his career in the dock of Old Bailey.

"Good spirit, answer me this one question. Are these the shadows of the things that *will* be, or the shadows only of things that *may* be?"

The ghost pointed to the prisoner.

"Men's courses will foreshadow certain ends to which, if perse-vered in, they must lead," said Scrooge. "But if the courses be de-parted from, the ends will change. Say it is thus with what you show me!"

The spirit was unmoved.

"Good spirit," Scrooge pursued, falling on his knees and clutch-ing the spirit's robe, "assure me that I yet may change these shad-ows you have shown me by an altered life."

Holding up his hands in a last prayer to have his fate reversed, he saw an alteration in the phantom's hood and dress. It shrunk, collapsed, and dwindled down into a bedpost.

Yes! And the bedpost was his own. The bed was his own, the room was his own. Best and happiest of all, the time before him was his own, to make amend in!

"I will live in the past, the present, and the future!"

Scrooge repeated as he scrambled out of bed. "The spirits of all three shall strive within me. Oh, Jacob Marley! Heaven and the Christmas time be praised for this! I say it on my knees, old Jacob, on my knees!"

And Scrooge was true to his word. He immediately arranged to send a large turkey to Bob Cratchit so that the family could enjoy a proper Christmas feast. He then put on his best clothes and went to his nephew's for dinner, where he was so witty, charming, and such enjoyable company that his nephew's wife chastised her husband for failing to invite Mr. Scrooge to dinner before.

The following morning he told Bob Cratchit he was raising his salary and was making arrangements to see that Tiny Tim, Bob's in-valid son, would get the best medical attention money could buy.

Scrooge lived Christmas every day. He became as good a friend, as good a master, and as good a man as the good old city of London knew, or any other good old city, town, or borough in the good old world. And, to his surprise, his business improved—first slightly, then gradually, and eventually enormously. Good business prospects soon engulfed him. His income increased, his loan write-offs dwindled to nil, and his prosperity became the talk of the Lon-don financial circle.[3]

Business Owners Versus Bankers: The Source of the Misunderstanding

Many of the problems business borrowers and their bankers experience in dealing with each other arise from the fact that they approach the borrowing/lending of money from two entirely different perspectives. In his book *How to Borrow Money from a Banker*, Roger Bel Air identified eleven areas in which broad chasms exist between the entrepreneur and his or her banker. The most significant ones are summarized in Table 1-1.

An entrepreneur is a gambler, a risk seeker. He makes an investment and takes actions based on a set of assumptions about how his world is presently structured and how it is likely to behave in the future. He seeks opportunities in the marketplace and invests his own money and that of his creditors to achieve personal gain. He enjoys the challenge and the excitement of pitting his wits against those of his competitors, customers, and suppliers.

Bankers are intermediaries who are charged with the awesome responsibility for prudently investing their depositors' money. Banks attract employees who want order, who are by nature careful and cautious, and who tend to be conservative in their judgment and demeanor. Their primary concern is not to deplete the assets

TABLE 1-1

How Bankers and Entrepreneurs Differ

Issue	Entrepreneur	Banker
Attitude toward risk	Risk seeking	Risk avoiding
Worldview	Optimistic (focuses on upside)	Pessimistic (focuses on downside)
Decision-making authority	Has authority to make most decisions	Authority very limited
Previous experience	Usually production and sales in single industry	Finance
Regulatory	Usually operates in unregulated environment	Banks highly regulated

under their trusteeship, which implies that they make very prudent loans.

Entrepreneurs are eternal optimists. In many ways, Wile E. Coyote is the archetype for the entrepreneur, and his scheming to dispatch the Road Runner is a metaphor for the entrepreneur's quest for financial success. Each ingenious plan that fails gives rise to another—and another. There is no end to the creative energy Wile E. Coyote expends in his perpetual chase; he always looks at the upside possibilities, and he invariably forgets to protect himself against the downside. Wile E. Coyote rarely reads the fine print.

Bankers, however, must focus on the risks in the enterprise. They want to avoid being surprised. Their responsibilities obligate them to assess the probability of every potential horror that might befall the business and cause their loan to be at risk.

The CEO is, in most matters, the ultimate decision maker in her company. In a transaction involving the purchase or sale of products or services, the CEO can deal directly with her counterpart and arrive at a mutually acceptable contract. Banking is organized in a highly bureaucratic manner, though, and no banker—including the president of the bank—has the decision authority comparable to that of the CEO of a nonfinancial firm. Policies, procedures, and checks and balances are designed to limit decision authority in a bank and force every loan commitment through multiple reviews. There simply is no one person in a bank that the business owner can "look in the eye" and make a deal.

Entrepreneurs usually have a sales, production, or engineering background. Moreover, their experience is usually limited to the single industry in which their current business competes. Bankers, however, have financial backgrounds and have been involved with many industries. As a result, bankers are able to understand a business from its "numbers" (financial statements) alone and discern many of its weaknesses without having to walk the production floor—something very few business people can do. The business owner will want to talk about orders, shipments, and new product releases. The banker will be interested in these things, but she will want to focus on the financial history and projections.

Finally, most business owners have never worked in a highly regulated industry where officials of the local, state, and federal government have the power of life and death over the business. Therefore they have little empathy for the banker, who must constantly be aware of the laws and regulations that govern the bank's operation and the regulators who can and will scrutinize her every action.

Thus it should not come as any surprise that the business owner and the banker often have a great deal of difficulty in dealing with each other. But deal with each other they must, since they have a symbiotic relationship. Each needs the other to survive.

How Bankers Make Their Money: An Introduction to the Banking Business

If you are going to be a serious competitor in the quest for financing, it is important that you have a clear understanding of what motivates bankers. And to understand what motivates bankers in the marketplace, you have to know how they make their money. Bankers make money in three distinct ways: executing and processing financial transactions, participating in such transactions as a principal, and rendering advice on these transactions.

In executing and processing financial transactions, the banker acts as an agent for other parties to the transaction. Some of the activities that make up this component of the business include check processing, managing assets (for example, collecting rents), custody and safekeeping of documents, and executing purchases and sales of stocks. Bankers view most of the processing activities (such as check processing) as cost centers or necessary evils to attract customers or low-cost deposits, while the execution activities (such as brokerage and operating safe depositories) are viewed as profit centers. Economics of scale are at work in all of these activities, and profitability depends on large volume because human decision making is not required to any great degree. Although the executing and processing businesses aren't very glamorous and are highly competitive, they often provide an opportunity for the banker to access their customers' other needs.

Participating as a principal is the most visible and highest-risk aspect of the financial services industry. Some elements of this part of the business include deposit taking, borrowing, lending, leasing, trading securities, providing performance guarantees, and investing. The common denominator of these activities is that they involve the institution's balance sheet and therefore its capital. In performing these types of transactions the bank is operating as a business, providing products and services and risking its capital just like any manufacturer, wholesaler, or retailer. In fact, the acceptance of risk is a large part of the product or service the bank is providing.

Rendering advice on financial transactions includes merger and acquisition activity, securities underwriting, corporate finance, financial restructuring, personal financial planning, investment advice, and investment management. These activities are the glamour areas of the financial services industry; they are the areas in which Michael Milken, Peter Lynch, and other lesser-known financial engineers made their fortunes. In all of these activities the customer pays the banker a fee for the advice provided. It is the banker's brains and contacts—rather than the risk she is willing to accept, or the people and computer and facilities she controls—that determine how much money she will earn.

Prior to 1933, a bank could engage in all three major phases of banking. In the last half of the nineteenth century big-city banks (especially in New York, Chicago, and San Francisco) became active in bond markets, and American banks performed all the functions now normally performed by investment banking firms. In the early days of this century a number of banks formed "securities affiliates" to play in the stock market, a development that was a natural outcome of the federal government's reliance on the banks to sell the "liberty bonds" of World War I. These securities affiliates could branch away from the home city of the bank, and their charters gave them very broad powers.

These organizations engaged in highly speculative activities fueled by the funds available from their banking affiliates and their ability to manipulate the public trust. For example, one firm, National City Company, bought Latin American bonds before studying their quality. Those that later appeared to be good investments were placed in the bank's portfolio; those that appeared to be marginal were sold to the public. The banks ran real estate syndicates through their securities affiliates, and still others manipulated their own stocks.

In 1933 Congress passed the Glass-Steagall Act, which forbade commercial banks to own common stock or to underwrite and sell stock or corporate bonds to their customers or depositors. Implicit in the Glass-Steagall Act was the idea that investment banking and commercial banking are pursued to their respective different ends with substantially different risk/reward criteria by very different types of bankers.

Since that time there has existed a major division in the banking business between the commercial bankers (who operate depository institutions, process checks, and make loans) and the investment bankers (who perform the transactions in the securities market, engage in brokerage activities, and provide the bulk of advice on financial transactions). Between the early 1970s and early 1990s court decisions and actions by regulatory bodies have allowed both commercial and investment bankers to invade each other's traditional turf on a very limited basis, and further deregulation is inevitable because of the pressures of global competition.

Chino Valley Bank is a midsize California bank with sixteen branches and 330 employees; in 1993 it was listed among the sixty most profitable banks in the United States. The distribution of Chino Valley Bank's three major sources of revenue for the year ended December 31, 1992, is summarized in Table 1–2, and the bank's key operating performance ratios for Chino Valley Bank are calculated in Table 1–3. Table 1–3 also compares these key operating ratios to those of the top five California banks.

On the basis of the data presented in the figures, you will expect your banker to be focused on maximizing the interest rate on your loans and the fees charged for the various bank services and accommodations. He will want to avoid situations that will consume the management time of the bank's executives, because this will tend to

TABLE 1–2

Chino Bank Revenue Sources, Year End 1992

	Revenue	Percentage
Loans and leases	40,491,000	72.5
Investments and federal funds sold[a]	8,549,000	14.9
Noninterest income	7,038,000	12.6

[a]Since 1933 banks have not been allowed to buy corporate stock, and they rarely buy corporate bonds; but they can buy notes and bonds issued by federal, state, and local governments.

TABLE 1-3

Chino Bank Performance Ratios for Year End 1992
Chino Bank versus Five Largest California Banks

	Chino	Bank of America	Wells Fargo	First Interstate	Union Bank	Bank of California
Operating cost (% of assets)	4.2	3.7	5.9	4.34	4.58	3.97
Loan charge-off rate (% of loans & leases)	0.48	1.12	1.97	1.36	1.19	1.8
Net interest margin (%)[a]	5.75	4.75	5.70	4.89	5.00	3.74
Earnings (% of assets)	1.62	0.90	0.54	0.57	0.62	(0.21)

[a]Defined as $\dfrac{\text{Interest income} - \text{interest expense}}{\text{assets}}$

increase operating costs. He will also want to avoid any situation where he believes repayment of the loan may be in doubt; if he cannot find sufficient borrowers that he is comfortable with, he always has the option of investing his deposits in risk-free government securities.

From fairytales to literature and Hollywood movies, the stereotype of the banker has been set in the public mind. In the following chapters, though, I would like to reintroduce you to the banker. We will delve inside her world, see what makes her tick. You may be surprised to find that she is much like the tailor down the street or the dry cleaner on the corner. And through understanding her and her method of operation, you'll discover that she is the one necessary friend you need to be able to count on to make your good dream a reality.

2

Whatever Happened to That Friendly Neighborhood Banker?

We [bankers] determine who will succeed and who will fail.
—Attributed to John Bunting, former president of First Pennsylvania
Bank and Trust

The Ballgame Has Changed

In the 1980s the headlines of newspapers, magazines, and the evening news focused on the tales of change, success, and failure in the U.S. financial system. We learned about corporate raiders such as Irwin Jacobs, Carl Icahn, and T. Boone Pickens, the savings and loan debacle, and the hundreds of billions of dollars it would take to bail out the system; the failures and mergers of major commercial banks, and the projected shrinking of the commercial banking system; the insider trading scandals involving Ivan Boesky, Michael Milken, Dennis Levine, and Martin Siegel; and the concern that the nation's insurance system was undercapitalized. These big-money boondoggles affected not only Wall Street tycoons, though, but every small business or entrepreneur who needs a loan today.

In the summer of 1990 Big-O Tires, a Denver-based distribution firm with sales of $107 million and a 1989 profit of $1.6 million, was informed by its bank, Central Bank of Denver, that its line of credit would not be renewed when it matured in April 1991. Steven Cloward, the CEO of Big-O Tires, was astonished. Here was a profitable company that was paying interest and fees on $16 million in loans and credit lines, and had never been late or missed a payment, being invited to leave the bank. (Although profits were expected to be down to $0.7 million in 1990 because of the Gulf War, management was predicting profits would recover in 1991.) The company retained an investment banker; six months and a $150,000 fee later, Central Bank was replaced by a commercial finance company at a slightly higher interest rate.

What's going on here? Normally, you would expect a banker to walk over his own grandmother in order to preserve an account like Big-O Tires, yet here Central Bank of Denver was driving it out the door. After all, wasn't Big-O Tires an earning asset on Central Bank's balance sheet? Didn't the interest and fees it was paying contribute to Central Bank's income stream?

The explanation Central Bank gave Big-O Tires' management was disingenuous: "We don't feel comfortable with the tire business". While we cannot be privy to the decisions of the bank's loan committee, Big-O's experience was typical of that of thousands of small and midsize businesses in the early 1990s. There was substantial anecdotal evidence that the "credit crunch" many healthy businesses were subjected to was a manifestation of major structural changes in the U.S. business credit system.

Since the mid-1970s the banking industry, along with the savings and loan industry, has undergone a series of crises that have affected the very structure of the industry and changed the way financial institutions do business. These developments will continue to have serious consequences for small-business and middle-market borrowers (companies with annual sales between $5 million and $75 million) and their access to capital.

At a private gathering in 1973, Arthur Burns, chairman of the Board of Governors of the Federal Reserve System, reminisced about the "old-time fatherly banker" who was concerned with his community, put service to customers above other considerations, did not bother about comparing his earnings with those of some other banker down the street, and never gave a thought about the price/earnings ratio at which his stock was selling. There is little doubt that the events between then and the early 1990s have exterminated what "old-time fatherly bankers" still survived in the mid-1970s, and they have taken their place in history with the polyester leisure suit and the rotary dial telephone.

A Brief Recent History of Banking Institutions

In the mid-1970s bankers still joked about operating by the 3-6-3 rule: take money from depositors at 3 percent, lend it out at 6 percent, and be on the golf course by three o'clock. Looking back at it from the mid-1990s, that philosophy of banking looks as ancient as the early nineteenth-century medical technique of bleeding with leeches.

Starting in the mid-1970s many of the country's largest corporations—which had provided the banking industry with a reliable and secure income stream—found that they could borrow less expensively by going to institutional investors (such as pension funds, insurance companies, and mutual funds) and nonfinancial institutions with idle cash. The financial instrument used to implement this transaction is called *commercial paper.* Commercial paper is a liability of the issuing corporation; its maturity may range from 2 to 270 days. The borrower, who is generally a large multinational corporation with exemplary credit (such as General Electric or Ford), pays an interest rate below the bank prime lending rate but generally 0.25 to 1 percent above Treasury bills; the rate is therefore attractive to investors. The economic advantages to corporations of issuing commercial paper resulted in the commercial banking industry losing a large portion of its previously secure interest income.

About the same time, the money market fund was created; this allowed a depositor to invest indirectly in government securities and earn substantially higher interest than the banks were permitted to pay. In addition, Merrill Lynch began competing with the banks via their Cash Management Account, a checking account that pays money market rates. Other brokerage houses soon offered similar services. As interest rates rose in the 1970s, large depositors began shifting their deposits out of savings accounts and into these money market accounts, where they received 6 percent to 7 percent higher interest. Although the banks were ultimately allowed to raise their rates and sell their own money market funds and certificates of deposits in order to compete for deposits, balances in banks' checking accounts—their primary source of low-cost funds—barely grew during the 1980s. Thus the major effect of the deregulation that created the money market fund was that the bank's cost of money increased.

In their search for new business to replace this income, banks pursued three markets that were inherently more risky. In doing so, they brought to an end their forty-year history of low credit losses. The banking industry's problems in the 1980s resulted from loan losses in these three credit categories:

- Loans to developing countries (LDCs)
- Highly leveraged loans to commercial corporations to finance buyouts
- Financing commercial real estate

What these three categories of loans had in common was that they offered high yields, they were easy for banks to originate, and they had a previous history of low loan losses.

Loans to LDCs

Led by New York banks, U.S. and foreign banks lent heavily to developing countries between the mid-1970s and the early 1980s. The opportunity to lend to these developing countries was created by the surge in oil prices in 1973: the oil-rich states placed their newly acquired riches in the banks, and the banks needed to find borrowers for the funds in order to create the profits to pay for the deposits. Who better to lend to than the nations that were building their infrastructure to service the oil demand, as well as those who were struggling to pay for the oil at the newly inflated prices?

The developing countries were willing to borrow all the money that was offered, and the bankers—who were in competition with each other—offered generous terms. When the second oil price shock occurred in 1979, though, interest rates shot up, with the prime rate going up to 21 percent. This caused an immense problem for the LDCs, who had borrowed when floating rates were at 7 percent and were now forced to pay three times the original interest rate. The LDCs were not able to service the debt they had accumulated; the bankers, wanting to avoid seeing their large loan portfolios defaulted, began lending the LDCs the funds they needed to pay the interest and added the amount to their outstanding debt.

By 1984, U.S. banks had lent an aggregate of $375 billion to corporations or governments in countries such as Argentina, Brazil, Chile, Mexico, Peru, Poland, and Zaire. The theory underlying these loans was that countries could not go bankrupt. For many years the major banks and the U.S. controller of the currency maintained the fiction that these loans were sound even though the banks had to continue to lend funds so the debtor countries could pay their interest. Eventually the banks had to face up to the fact that a large percentage of the money they had loaned to developing countries would never be repaid, and between 1984 and 1986 they wrote off an aggregate of $116.9 billion.

Highly Leveraged Transactions

This type of lending includes the funding of leveraged buyouts, leveraged corporate recapitalization and restructurings, and leveraged mergers and acquisitions. In a typical leveraged buyout transaction, the stock of a profitable public company is purchased by an investment group which uses primarily borrowed funds to effect the purchase. The transaction is structured so that the profits of the company (which will be owned entirely by the investors) can service the interest and principal payments of the loan.

Leveraged buyout (LBO) lending was pioneered in the 1970s by specialized investment banking firms such as Kohlberg, Kravis and Roberts (KKR) and Forstmann Little and Company. The number of LBO transactions grew from thirteen a year in 1981 (representing $1.6 billion) to an average of more than three hundred a year in the peak years of 1986 through early 1989; in 1989, deals with a total value of $66 billion were completed. Bankers loved these transactions because the up-front fees were very large (1 to 2 percent of the transaction), as were the interest spreads. As with any new area of business, though, at the peak of the LBO frenzy there was too much money looking for too few good deals. As a consequence, many of the loans that financed transactions in the late 1980s were inherently more risky than those in the first half of the decade. Several of the firms involved in these later loans ultimately wound up in bankruptcy court, and the banks lost millions on the loans.

Commercial Real Estate

Banks (and savings and loans) all across the country financed the real estate boom of the 1980s, which filled up the downtowns of America with empty office buildings and suburban communities with unsold condominiums and sparsely rented strip centers. The Garn–St. Germain Act, signed into law in October 1982, eliminated restrictions on the percentage of loans in a bank's portfolio that could be used for real estate ventures and—for the first time in banking history—allowed banks to lend to developers who had virtually no equity. During the 1980s bank portfolios of commercial real estate grew 300 percent and helped create approximately one-third of America's office space.

The folly of the overbuilding caught up with the banking industry in 1990, by which time some regions of the country had an estimated ten-year oversupply of office space. Between 1948 and 1982, the year the Garn–St. Germain bill was passed, the cumulative loan charge-offs of the entire banking industry were $28 billion. Between January 1986 and October 1990, however, banks wrote off $75 billion in troubled loans, nearly three times the total for the previous thirty-four years. A large portion of this was attributable to real estate. For example, when the Bank of New England (the twenty-first largest bank in the United States) failed, 37 percent of its loan portfolio consisted of warehouses, office buildings, and shopping centers. In an interview in *Financial World*, former Chase Manhattan chairman David Rockefeller admitted that as competition from other institutions increased, the profits banks made on loans to their traditional business borrowers decreased, and the pressures to lend funds inevitably resulted in declining credit standards.

The tough banking environment that has prevailed since the 1970s is evidenced by the accelerating failure rate of banking institutions. In the forty six years between 1933 (the year in which federally backed deposit insurance was created) and 1979 (the year before Ronald Reagan was elected), 558 insured banks failed, an average of slightly more than twelve a year. From 1980 to 1990, though, a total of 1,245 banks failed or were restructured by the FDIC—an average of 125 per year, approximately ten times the rate of the previous forty six years.

The Savings and Loan Scandal

"Ever since the first Florentine loaned his first ducat to his first Medici, it has been one of the most shopworn clichés of the financial industry that the best way to rob a bank is to own one. This maxim, like all maxims, is rooted in a basic truth about human nature: To wit, if criminals are given easy access to large sums of money, they will steal, and under such tempting circumstances even honest men may be corrupted."

—L. J. Davis[1]

Any discussion of the current state of the commercial banking industry and how it will affect the ability of business to borrow money would be incomplete without a discussion of the savings and loan (S & L) debacle of 1987. Banks (and savings and loans) are not like any other business, in that the federal government insures bank deposits up to $100,000 per depositor. Therefore, the bank's problems ultimately become the public taxpayer's problems.

The current estimate of the cost to the taxpayer of the savings and loan bailout is $180 billion, not including interest. In order to appreciate the calamity that this debacle represents to future generations of American taxpayers, I have in Table 2–1 compared the cost of the S & L bailout to other major obligations that have fallen on the taxpayer; I have calculated the values in current dollars in order to properly compare their cost.

TABLE 2–1

Comparison of the S & L Bailout to Wars and Financial Debacles

War/Financial Scandal	Date	Cost	Cost in 1993 Dollars
S & L Scandal[a]	1993	$180 billion	$180 billion
TeaPot Dome Scandal	1924	$0.2 billion	$1.7 billion
Vietnam War	1973	$150 billion	$510 billion
Korean War	1953	$67 billion	$362 billion
World War II	1945	$1 trillion	$8 trillion

[a]As reported by the *Wall Street Journal*, May 14, 1993.

The cost of the S & L bailout is about 35 percent of the cost of the Vietnam War, and 50 percent of the cost of the Korean War. It is either a testimony to the strength of the American democracy or a manifestation of the passiveness of the American population that the populace did not riot and bring down the government.

The U.S. banking system is divided into two parts—the commercial banks, and the savings and loans (also called thrifts). The main business of the commercial banks is to gather deposits and make short-term loans or investments. Because their loans generally mature in less than one year, the banks have been able to weather many turbulent situations and swings in the business cycle. Although banks do issue long-term mortgages (fifteen to thirty years), this is a relatively small portion of their business, and many of the mortgages they do write are sold off to other institutions.

The savings and loan companies, and savings banks, had a different purpose—namely, to promote long-term savings among the populace and finance the purchase of single-family homes and small apartments. Overseeing their activities was the Federal Home Loan Bank Board. In return for accepting this supervision, the S & Ls, like the banks, received federal deposit insurance; the maximum insured amount per account in the 1970s was $40,000. Federal deposit insurance meant that the return of the depositors' money (up to the maximum per account) was guaranteed by the full faith and credit of the U.S. government, independent of the fortunes of the thrift who owed the depositor.

As long as interest rates remained stable, which they did from the 1930s well into the 1960s, running a thrift was an undemanding task. By the late 1970s, however, with inflation running at 13 percent and money market funds paying interest at 8 percent, the thrifts could no longer attract depositors at their 5.5 percent rate (0.25 percent greater than the commercial banks were authorized to pay) and saw their cheap source of funds dry up.

In early 1980 the thrifts were given permission to pay market rates for deposits and so compete with commercial banks and money market funds; however, they were not allowed to raise the interest rates that they charged for mortgages. Since there was a substantial unbalance between the interest rates the S & Ls had to pay to attract deposits and the rates they could charge for a thirty-year mortgage, the S & Ls were guaranteed that whatever mortgages they did write would be unprofitable; as a result, very few mortgages were written. At the same time that the thrifts were given the ability to pay market rates for deposits, Congress raised the insurance coverage on deposits from $40,000 to $100,000. The combination of these events opened the floodgates to "hot money": deposits in $100,000 increments that were placed by brokerage houses in those institutions that were offering the best deal on any given day. The brokers moved their money from S & L to bank to bank, depending on who was offering the best rate. The loyal S & L depositor base that George Bailey relied on was replaced by Wall Street brokers representing wealthy investors or Arab sheiks.

It should have come as no surprise that by 1982, two years into the regulatory "reforms," the S & L industry—representing 3,300 thrifts—was broke. Its collective net worth had deteriorated from $32.2 billion in 1980 to $3.7 billion by December 1982. The industry "discovered" that if your business is restricted to providing loans for mortgages that cannot pay more than 6 to 7 percent, and you have to pay 12 to 13 percent for the money you lend, *there simply is no way to be profitable.*

Rather than let commercial Darwinism allow the weak thrifts to either fail or merge with their stronger competitors, though, the Federal Home Loan Bank Board and Congress decided to help the S & L industry grow out of its problems. They passed new laws and regulations that changed the industry accounting practices so that marginal thrifts would appear more profitable; certain state legislatures followed suit. The effect of these changes was to authorize the S & L industry to gamble with other people's money. And since the return of this money to depositors was effectively guaranteed by the federal government, the risk of the gamble was foisted upon the ignorant taxpayer.

In addition, the restrictions that had ensured that S & Ls would be owned collectively by members of the local community were changed; now anyone who had the money could buy or start a thrift. The Garn–St. Germain Depository Institutions Act of 1982 gave the thrift owners the ability to virtually abandon the business of financing home mortgages, the very business thrifts were chartered to engage in. In California, Texas, and Florida, laws were passed to permit state-chartered thrifts (which were still eligible for federal deposit insurance) to invest 100 percent of their deposits in any venture they chose—junk bonds, shopping centers, motion pictures, and so forth.

Most of the legislators and bureaucrats who formulated and voted for these changes tended to think of the S & L lobby as representing the likes of George Bailey of *It's a Wonderful Life*. If Frank Capra had never made the movie, this latest generation of lawmakers wouldn't have gotten such a mistaken impression. In fact, many of the Jimmy Stewart–type owners of S & Ls were bought out by the Willie Sutton types, who realized that the changes in the rules made owning a bank (or an S & L) the easiest way to rob one. (As Willie Sutton said, "it's a rather pleasant experience to be alone in a bank at night.")

The newly unfettered thrift industry that emerged was flush with cash and characterized by incompetence and corruption. The thrift industry executives who were experienced in running an institution that specialized in single-family loans were certainly not competent to engage in the businesses that had been the province of the commercial banker, the investment banker, and the venture capitalist.

In the mid-1980s I had a client that had borrowed approximately $35 million for the development of condominiums and a shopping center in a resort community. The client's education and training qualified him to be either a ski instructor or short order cook; armed with a modest net worth (thanks to a well-divorced and newly acquired wife) and grossly inflated appraisals of the project's value, however, he was able to extract several times the thrift's legal limit for loans to a single borrower for the ill-conceived and guaranteed losing development. He paid an egregious 10 percent fee for the loans he received, which may have been the vigorish the loan officer needed to fund the loan.

One of the most troubling aspects of the deregulation of the thrifts that occurred in the early 1980s was that so many (up to 60 percent by some estimates) were looted by the crooks who purchased or controlled them. Lincoln Savings' Charles H. Keating, Jr., Vernon Savings and Loan's Don Dixon, and Sunbelt Savings and Loan's Ed McBirney III are examples of thrift owners who engaged in the pattern of deceit and corruption that contributed to the huge bailout bill. They paid themselves lavish salaries, lived imperial lives on their company expense accounts, made loans without any commercial justification in order to earn huge fees for themselves and their cronies, ignored every implicit or explicit requirement for professionalism and prudence, and—until they were indicted, tried, convicted, fined, and jailed—enriched themselves and their associates at the expense of many of their investors, their depositors, and U.S. taxpayers.

Lowell L. Bryan tells the story of a real estate developer in Texas who approached one of the aggressive thrifts with plans to build a $15 million building. Why not a $25 million building? the developer was told. All we need from you is an up-front commitment fee of 4 percent of the loan so that we can book the fee immediately as profit; that way we will have the capital we need to make the loan. Of course, we will loan you the money for the commitment fee, and we will want to build into the loan the interest payments needed to keep it current for five years, just in case you have trouble leasing space in the building. We can also give you the name of a good appraiser for your property, and we will not require you to guarantee the loan personally. The building will be our sole collateral.

Thus the S & L loaned him $1 million, which he immediately paid back as a commitment fee for the $25 million loan. The S & L recorded the fee payment as profit, which increased their capital by $1 million. Since the S & L could accept deposits in the amount of 33.3 times its capital, this new profit allowed it to accept up to $33 million in new additional deposits. The S & L then loaned the developer the $25 million he needed.

The very generous accounting rules masked the fact that many of the projects the thrifts invested in were failures. Many of the buildings that were funded by the thrifts sat empty for years after construction was completed; however, the loans were kept current because the developers typically borrowed sufficient funds to prepay interest for several years. If the prepaid interest was exhausted before the buildings were sold or leased, the loan went into default. Since the market values of the properties were far below the loans that had been accumulated for the projects, loan charge-offs were taken, and the S & L financial statements eventually had to reflect substantial losses.

How could this happen? Weren't the thrifts under the supervision of the Federal Home Loan Bank Board? Didn't bank examiners regularly review the thrifts' loans and investments? And where were the thrifts' independent auditors—the Arthur Andersens, the Ernst and Youngs, and the rest?

As the story of the S & L debacle unfolded it had become clear that while the signs of the growing disaster were apparent to Ed Gray soon after he was appointed head of the Federal Home Loan Bank Board in June 1983, the antiregulatory philosophy of the Reagan administration and the substantial support for the thrift industry among key legislators in the House and Senate (who had received substantial campaign contributions from Keating and the others) effectively kept the lid on the problem until the 1988 elections were over, Ronald Reagan was safely out of Washington, and George Bush had won the presidency.

In February 1989, President Bush unveiled a S & L bailout plan; in August of that year the bailout plan was signed into law. The Federal Home Loan Bank Board was abolished, as was the FSLIC (the now-bankrupt insurance fund that insured thrift deposits), and a new entity specifically devoted to solving the thrift mess—the Resolution Trust Corporation—was created.

Paying the Piper: The Fallout

There is the story of two trout that were swimming in the lake and just happened to jump at the same time (which I understand is rare behavior for trout). One trout pointed to the lake below him and said to the other, "Now that's the stuff I was telling you about." The story illustrates the universal truth that it is difficult to appreciate the significance of changes in one's environment when one is part of the changes that are occurring. So it is with the banking industry. The consequences of the crises that have befallen the banking industry, and the forces that have been set in motion to rebuild and strengthen it, will make it more difficult for small and midsize businesses to obtain financing. Let's briefly examine some of these forces.

1. SMALLER ASSET POOL.

I previously discussed how the banking industry has been affected by the introduction of commercial paper and the creation of money market funds. The banking industry has also seen its share of the financial asset market eroded by the growth of pension funds and

TABLE 2-2

Percentages of Assets Held
by Different Types of Institutions

	1970	1980	1990
Commerical banks	52.5	44.8	36.3
Thrifts	21.8	25.9	15.9
Pension funds	22.5	25.9	34.8
Mutual funds	3.2	1.5	7.9
Money market mutual funds	0.0	1.9	5.1

stock and bond mutual funds. Table 2–2 shows the changing share of financial assets held by various types of financial companies in the United States since 1970. This figure shows that the market share of the depository financial institutions (the commercial banks, and the S & Ls) have been declining, and the market share of the nondepository institutions (pension funds, mutual funds, and money market funds) has been increasing.

Small businesses and middle-market businesses that cannot issue investment-grade securities will have increasing difficulty gaining access to funds. These companies have traditionally been funded by commercial banks, thrifts, and insurance companies, all of which ideally have the marketing, systems, and management skills to operate on a risk/return policy that can access and service this market. The nondepository institutions, such as mutual funds and pension funds, have very limited operating budgets in the best of circumstances and traditionally purchase only investment-grade securities. To put it simply, the fatherly neighborhood banker referred to by Arthur Burns, if he exists at all, will have less money to lend.

2. CENTRALIZED PROCESSING.

The effort to maximize their efficiency in originating loans caused the large banks to centralize the decision process and streamline the way loan products are offered to small prospective borrowers (those with less than $5 million in annual sales). Lenders in the typical business loan centers located throughout a state don't have the time to work on small deals, and they are not allocated much credit to originate them. Therefore these smaller loans are approved or declined on the merits of the financial statements and related information that the owner can present—an area where small businesses are traditionally weak.

3. TIGHTER REGULATION.

Another response to the S & L crisis and the tenfold increase in bank failures between 1980 and 1990 was the creation of a regulatory environment that was substantially more critical and restrictive than that of the 1970s. Lending officers are required to provide far more internal documentation, a costly and time-consuming process for the banker and one that will tend to discourage her from making small loans. Bankers are more demanding in terms of the collateral they require to back up the loan since the deterioration of collateral below the face value of the loan may result in the loan being considered technically in jeopardy even if the borrower is current with the payments. Personal guarantees of the loan by the company's principals were often requested but not universally demanded before the 1990s; they are now a standard requirement on all loan agreements.

Bank examiners are charged with the responsibility of ensuring that the laws under which the institution operates are followed. This is accomplished by a periodic review of the bank's loan and investment portfolios and an analysis of its operating methods.

The central function of the bank examiner is to classify problem loans using his or her best independent judgment. A bank typically is examined at least once a year by state and federal regulators; seven thousand bank examiners oversee twelve thousand banks and the remnants of the thrift industry. If an examiner classifies a loan—that is, finds it deficient in some way—the bank can be asked to set aside reserves for a possible loss. This in turn can reduce the institution's earnings and capital.

Regulators have life-and-death power over a bank. In an April 27, 1993, *Wall Street Journal* article, Fred Bleakly wrote, "Regulators can decide whether a bank fails or is shackled with operating restrictions, whether management should be shown the door and whether bankers are surprised at their homes with letters asking for an accounting of their personal assets."[2]

In 1992 Congress passed the FDIC Improvement Act, which

provided a $70 billion loan to shore up the depleted deposit insurance fund and granted new sweeping powers to regulators. Regulators are now authorized to become involved in the management of a bank in the event its tangible equity falls below 2 percent of its assets. By the end of 1993 regulators were allowed to set executive compensation standards and earnings guidelines of poorly capitalized banks.

With this kind of power in the hands of the bank examiners, bankers can be expected to be very conservative as they strive to keep loans that are prone to classification off their balance sheets. David S. Bizer, in an article in the March 1, 1993, *Wall Street Journal*, estimated that the tougher asset rating standards instituted by examiners in 1989 resulted in a 6 percent decrease in outstanding loans by 1992.

4. CAUTIOUS LENDERS.

In a July 5, 1991, *New York Times* article, Louis Uchitelle wrote the following:

> Just as bank failures in the Depression years bred a generation of conservative bankers, the new banking crisis is creating a cautiousness among lenders that bankers themselves say may slow the flow of loans long after the recession [of 1990–1992] ends. Many factors affect a banker's willingness to lend, from the health of the bank to the size of the underlying capital base, but none are as important as the mind-set of the bankers themselves.[3]

There is wide evidence that the traumas of the banking and S & L crises have greatly affected the mind-set of lenders and made them much less willing to accept risks that they would have eagerly competed for a few short years ago. Bankers report in surveys that in all types of lending, interest rates will be higher, terms will be tougher, loan-to-equity ratios will be lower, and the funds made available in a given situation or to a given borrower will be a lower percentage of the bank's tangible capital than in the past.

In testimony before Congress in February 1993, Alan Greenspan, chairman of the Federal Reserve System, acknowledged that a wave of new bank regulations passed in the wake of the S & L crisis made it prohibitively costly for banks to make loans to small businesses. Mr. Greenspan criticized impediments to what used to be called character loans, where a bank could basically make a loan of a modest amount to an individual based on its knowledge of that individual and its full expectation being repaid without going through a number of formal documents, without collateral, and without various appraisals. In the 1990s, such character loans are effectively dead.

5. THE BASEL AGREEMENT.

In the 1970s, bank regulators from the industrialized nations formed a group—the Basel Committee—to coordinate bank supervision throughout the world. In 1988 the committee implemented the International Basel Agreement, which completely changed the way financial institutions calculate the capital they are required to have to support their portfolios of loans and investment. Prior to the Basel Agreement, banks in most countries were required to maintain a percentage of other deposits on hand to deal with any sudden demand for the return of their funds. The Basel Agreement changed the methodology for calculating capital requirements from percentages of deposits to percentages of assets. This stemmed from the discovery by the regulators that depositors never line up outside a bank looking for the return of their money unless a bank has an asset problem first; in other words, banks fail because their assets have deteriorated, not because their depositors have become fickle.

The rules require banks to maintain capital equal to 8.0 percent of their business and most consumer loans. Other categories of bank assets, such as single-family mortgage loans, were assigned lower capital requirements on the theory that they involved less risk. Certain types of government bonds were assigned a risk weighting of zero and therefore require no capital.

These new rules completely changed the manner in which bankers determine in whom to invest their assets. A loan to a business will require them to maintain 8 percent capital, will carry the risk of default, and will cost substantial management time to set up, administer, and monitor. Government bonds, meanwhile, require between 2 percent and zero capital, need no management, and do not incur the risk of default. Bankers are primarily economically motivated beings; unless the potential profit from a business loan is substantially greater than what they can earn on a government bond, they will choose investing in government bonds over making business loans.

Richard C. Breeden and William M. Isaac, writing in the *Wall Street Journal* in November 1992, noted that between March 1989 (when the new capital rules went into effect) and the date of the article, U.S. bank holdings of government bonds increased 68 percent, their holdings of real estate loans—primarily single-family loans that required 4 percent capital—increased 27 percent and their holdings of all other securities and loans remained flat or declined.

6. LIABILITY CONCERNS.

The investigations that unraveled the S & L debacle resulted in approximately three thousand civil and criminal actions against bank directors and officers, accountants, and attorneys. As of November 1992, $825 million in fines and restitutions had been collected. An unintended consequence of this rash of litigation against bank directors and officers is that financial institutions found it increasingly difficult to attract and keep well-qualified directors. Moreover, the fear of personal liability for bad business judgments (evaluated in hindsight) has caused bank officers and directors to impose lending policies that tolerate only the lowest levels of risk. These policies are, of course, absolutely contrary to the needs of small-business and middle-market borrowers, loans to whom are inherently risky.

Effect on Businesses

As the amount of total funds available to small businesses and middle-market companies shrinks, the competition for the available funds will escalate. As a result, banks, insurance companies, and thrifts will be able to fill their loan portfolios with borrowers of a substantially higher average grade than was the case in the 1970s and 1980s.

This means that the business owners who need financing in the 1990s are going to have a more difficult time and will have to go to substantially greater lengths to make their businesses and themselves attractive to their prospective bankers.

In addition, because of this new environment, the businessperson can never assume that the financing she has is permanent, or that she will be able to depend on the bank to fulfill her financing needs into the distant future. Factors outside of either party's control can cause problems in financing a business. Banks ride with the tide of their success and failure, and they can change direction and policy depending on shifting circumstances.

The financial strength of your bank is very important to you. A weak bank that is being carefully monitored by regulators will be under tremendous pressure to improve the quality of its loan portfolio. This can result in the bank's cutting back on the amount of credit it allocates to your industry and attempting to improve the quality of its loan portfolio by culling its weakest loans. These actions could have a very adverse affect on your ability to maintain or increase your credit line. In the worst case, your bank may be taken over by the regulators, who may sell your loan on the open market. And you can be certain that the buyers of loans of failed banks or S & Ls are definitely not your avuncular neighborhood banker.

As George Dawson, an author and consultant who specializes in acquiring loans for small businesses, states: "To get a loan (the business owner) must separate himself from all the hopeful borrowers who look like losers to the bank. He must excite the loan officer. He must stand out from the crowd. He wants the loan officer to know that he is different from the typical unprofessional and unprepared business person." He will have to romance the loan, as opposed to requesting it or waiting for it to come calling.

3

Trolling for the Money

If you don't know where you're going, you're likely to wind up somewhere else.

—Yogi Berra

The borrower is servant to the lender.

—Proverbs 22:7

A start-up or growing business needs money for a variety of reasons: to purchase capital assets, to buy inventory, to carry receivables, to cover losses during a downturn in sales or profits, and to pay for new marketing and research and development programs. Banks (thrifts and commercial institutions), finance companies, insurance companies, factors, mortgage bankers, venture capitalists, and private investors—all of whom can be grouped in the generic class of "banker"—earn their profits by servicing these needs. The problem for the business owner is to discover the particular lender who can be motivated to provide the needed financing.

As a businessperson, you must follow seven steps:

1. Determine how much money you need.
2. Determine how much the financing will cost to obtain and to service.
3. Determine how and when you will be able to pay it back under the assumption that your plan for the business works out.
4. Determine how and when you will pay it back under the assumption that your plan for the business does *not* work out.

5. Identify the organizations and institutions that provide the type of financing you require for your type of business.
6. Prepare a loan proposal that tells your story and will persuade your lender why investing in your business makes sense for him.
7. Take your show on the road and see how it plays.

The steps outlined above will, I'm sure, appear to be eminently reasonable. If you have never sought financing, you are very fortunate to be reading this before you develop bad habits. You'll be surprised to learn that the vast majority of businesspersons do not understand the loan acquisition process; as a result, their businesses rarely have the financing required for the company to achieve its full potential.

The balance of this chapter will discuss the above steps in sufficient detail to give you a clear idea what is involved in each step, even if you don't possess the skills to perform the tasks yourself. (I will address the issue of outside help at the end of the chapter.)

First, a story that illustrates what happens if you don't follow the process. Several years ago I was retained by a young couple who had invested their savings (and then some) into a business that appeared to have broken the record for the shortest period from formation to liquidation—less than four months. What intrigued me was how they had come to invest so much of their money and themselves in a futile effort to establish a marginal business during a recession, in a competitive industry with inadequate capital and absolutely no competitive advantage.

The husband's father had been very eager to see his son advance in life. The son was a competent mechanic who had developed an excellent reputation in the small city in which they lived as being "good with a wrench." But he was at the top of his pay grade at the large truck repair facility that employed him, and at only thirty-five years old didn't believe he had much growing room. His father, a former owner of a very successful automobile dealership, decided the city could support a distributor of after-market diesel truck parts (parts manufactured by someone other than the maker of the original equipment, performing the same function but at a much lower price). The father speculated that as trucking companies continued to cut costs in order to remain competitive, it was inevitable they would ultimately shift their purchases from the original equipment manufacturers to "clones." He reasoned that clones could become as big a factor in the trucking business as they had in the computer business.

The son was enthusiastic but cautious; he was reluctant to give up his job, with its medical and retirement benefits. He felt he would have a very difficult time replacing the job at a comparable level of pay. But the father pushed and hounded, and for every concern the son raised, the father was quick to reassure him, frequently citing his own experiences and successes. The father was supported in his promotion efforts by the wife, whose need for money far outstripped her husband's salary. She saw the new business and the "large profits it would generate" as the answer to her prayers. Little by little the father prodded the son into considering starting the new business. The son was finally pushed over the edge when the father agreed both to finance the business and to help manage it.

Since the son had never been in business, he did not realize that his father's offer to help manage the operations was quite unrealistic: the father lived approximately 250 miles from the intended location of the business, and he enjoyed a rigorous retirement schedule of golf, church, charity, and social activities. In addition, neither the father nor the son had any conception of what the father meant when he said he would finance the venture. It would later develop that the father's total experience and understanding of financing a new business was based on his experience twenty years before when he started his automobile dealership.

The father had been a very successful salesman and sales manager with the largest Ford dealership in the small city in which he lived. Based on that experience, a belief that Japanese automobiles had a competitive advantage over what was being produced by Detroit, and $10,000 in savings, he decided to start a Toyota dealership. A local banker whom he knew from the Rotary Club agreed to provide a $20,000 unsecured character loan. Inventory was consigned by Toyota, who charged interest at prime; when the cars were sold, financing was provided by either the purchaser's bank or one of the large automobile financing concerns. The father's dealership prospered with the growth in market share of the Japanese automobile industry and particularly Toyota. Twenty years later he was able to sell it for $2 million and enjoy a very prosperous retire-

ment. Thus the father's reality was that you can start a very profitable business with $10,000 of savings and $20,000 from a friendly banker. The father was the prisoner of his own successful, but
very limited business experience.

Bizarre as it may seem, the father determined that the $30,000
he had started his business with in 1970 was worth $50,000 in
1990, and he agreed to provide his son with that much in either
cash or bank financing that he would personally guarantee. Armed
with this $50,000 and the $10,000 proceeds of a second mortgage
on his home, the son quit his job, rented warehouse space, built
shelves, and hired (with the aid of his father) two salesmen, a coun-
terman, a parts runner and a bookkeeper-secretary. With the aid of
the personal guarantees his father provided to the parts suppliers,
the son was able to stock the newly built shelves with tens of thousands of dollars of diesel truck parts. The champagne glasses were
clinked, flyers were printed and mailed, ads were placed in the
local newspapers, and the salesmen were unleashed on the targeted
customer base. The only financial plan, project, or target that existed was the estimate of the daily sales required to break even and
the dollar volume of inventory necessary to keep them from running out of stock.

During the first month sales were at 25 percent of the break-even
level; during the second month sales were at 55 percent. An 80 percent of break-even sales level was reached during the third month.
Sales were hovering around 105 percent of the break-even level
during the first two weeks of the fourth month when, without
warning, the bank account went dry. After several days and nights
of frantic meetings and several requests from the son and his wife
that the father provide more money, and an equal number of tear-
ful refusals by the father, all three agreed that the business could
not survive. Shortly thereafter they announced the termination of
the business to their employees, customers, and suppliers.

When the liquidation of the assets was completed, the father had
lost his entire initial investment of $50,000 and had to make good
on guarantees of approximately $55,000, for a total loss of
$105,000. The son was not able to get his job back and had to set-
tle for a lesser one at a 25 percent pay reduction. And the wife had
to get a job to replace the husband's lost income and pay the addi-

tional secured trust deed on their house. Even more difficult for her, she had to give up her dream of a wealthy life-style.

The saddest aspect of the story is that none of the participants in the drama understood why the venture had failed. The father believed that it failed because the market was not as big as they had estimated. The son believed it failed because the father lost his nerve and wasn't willing to put in the few extra dollars it took to "get over the hump." The wife believed the business failed because her husband was not a very good manager.

While all of these diagnoses had some basis in reality, the major reason the business failed was that it was grossly undercapitalized. I performed an analysis of the operating capital the business needed to achieve the sales and profit levels projected and support the losses that the business would sustain until it achieved break-even operation. The analysis indicated a capital requirement of between $160,000 to $180,000—at least $100,000 more than was available.

The tragedy of this story is that the debacle could have been avoided. The amount of capital required to fund a business plan is easily determinable; a CPA or management consultant could have formulated the plan and told the father that the required investment was four times the amount he was offering. The father then would have had the choice of either declining to go forward, thus saving himself the loss of capital and his son the loss of a job, or providing the $160,000 in funds that were necessary to give the business a fighting chance. Unfortunately, the father never had those alternatives so he bought the worst case: he lost his money without giving the business a realistic opportunity to be successful.

1.   How Much Money Do You Need?

The process of determining how much money you will need requires that you create, first in your mind and then on paper, your vision and expectations for the business over the ensuing months with regard to the following key issues. (Note that when I write *you* and *your* here and elsewhere in this book, I am referring to the collective you that consists of your company's owner/CEO, key senior executives, professional advisors and other partners, and shareholders.)

- What capital assets will you need to implement your plan? Capital assets can include land, buildings, vehicles, machines, tools, or the like. These acquisitions should be listed on a schedule along with the date the items are required and an estimate of the cost of the items.
- What are your optimistic, target, and pessimistic sales forecasts by month for the following one- to two-year period, starting with the date your plan is to be initiated?
- What are your optimistic, target, and pessimistic estimates as to what your cost of goods will be over the following two years? (*Cost of goods* refers to the aggregate of the labor, material, and indirect costs that are required to provide the products or services purchased.)
- What is your anticipated budget for selling expenses to achieve the sales forecast you estimated above? Selling expenses will consist of all expenditures you anticipate making to create orders for your products or services. They include sales representatives' salaries and expenses, commissions, advertising, travel to trade shows or to see customers, promotions, exhibit costs at trade shows, public relations, and the like.
- What is your anticipated budget for general and administrative (G & A) expenses? G & A expenses include those expenditures that will be made to establish and maintain the business independent of the volume of sales. They include rent for the facilities you occupy, salaries and expenses of the company officers, the costs of the accounting and financial functions, the costs of outside professionals (such as attorneys, accountants, and consultants), telephone expenses, and casualty insurance.

As you can now appreciate, the forecasting of revenue and expenses for future periods is not a trivial problem. But unless entrepreneurs understand the industry they are operating in and the related costs for their method of operation, and are able to quantify their vision of the future, determining the financing needs of a business will be impossible.

Once you have a series of sales and expense forecasts you are comfortable with, you will be able to develop profit and loss projections for various levels of sales, along with balance sheets and cash flows. This process will require the assistance of a competent accountant or consultant who can use existing computer programs that eliminate much of the time-consuming drudgery of the calculations. The questions propounded above will result in nine separate sales forecasts (three estimates of sales and three estimates for sales costs), nine balance sheet projections, and nine cash flows. The result of this analysis will be a series of estimates (one for each sales forecast/balance sheet/cash flow) of the financing that will be required to avoid the company's cash balance falling below some agreed minimum.

One aspect of financial forecasting that often confuses entrepreneurs is the difference between a profit and loss forecast and a cash flow forecast. The underlying assumption of a profit and a loss statement is that revenues and expenses are placed in the same reporting period in which they occur independent of whether revenues have actually been received or expenses have actually been paid. A cash flow forecast is a projection of what the company's checkbook balance will be. In summary, revenues and profits are not to be confused with cash receipts; expenses are not to be confused with cash expenditures.

These estimates of financing requirements will provide you with the first reality check as to how much money your business plan will require. As you proceed through the other steps of the process, you will modify and refine this estimate until you have a firm proposal you will present to lenders.

2. How Much Will the Financing Cost?

The cost of financing is composed of the front-end costs required to obtain the loan and the continuing costs of servicing it. The front-end costs typically include loan fees, appraisal fees, filing fees, and professional and accounting fees required to negotiate and document the loan agreement. The servicing costs will include the interest costs of the loan and the periodic financial audits that the lender may require.

The total cost of financing will be a function of four major factors: the history of and prospects for the business, the entity or institution that provides the financing, the type of financing provided, and the financial strength of the business. The primary sources of financing for a business are as follows:

- *Equity* includes all funds invested in the business that don't have to be repaid in accordance with a specific timetable. Equity is typically provided by owners, friends and relatives, wealthy individuals who like to dabble (also known as "angels"), restructuring firms or "vulture capitalists" (investors who seek out distressed companies), venture capitalists, and the public.
- *Debt* includes those funds provided to the business in accordance with a contract that spells out how the funds are to be repaid. Debt is provided by commercial banks, insurance companies, commercial finance companies, leasing companies, and real estate lenders. Obviously, all of the equity sources could also be sources for debt.
- *Government agencies* guarantee or provide both debt and equity.

Owners, friends, relatives, and "angels" are the primary sources of equity of a new company, a company in crisis, or a company with poor prospects. Occasionally, a venture capital firm will fund a start-up on the basis of the reputation of the founders and the prospects of the product or service being developed.

Venture capitalists are primarily interested in firms that have superior management, some track record, and a product/service that can carve out a significant niche in a growth market. Venture capitalists are very focused on how they will recover their investment, and they don't go into an investment unless they see a high probability of a public offering of their stock or a sale to a strategic investor (an investor who wants to be in that business).

Restructuring firms (sometimes known as "vulture capitalists") are interested in businesses that are involved in or just emerging from a turnaround. They earn high returns for their investors by being able to "bottom fish" intelligently. The public, meanwhile, is a source of financing for firms in excellent condition with good track records and promising prospects, or in "high-flyer" situations that can be promoted to the public by an aggressive investment banker.

The cost of acquiring equity from any of these sources will depend on the extent of the legal, accounting, and due diligence work the equity provider and/or the investment banker requires. These amounts are not insignificant; they can range from a few thousand dollars when dealing with friends and relatives to several hundred thousand in the case of a private placement investment or a public offering.

Commercial banks will provide financing for businesses that have some history, are in sound financial condition, and have reasonable prospects of competing profitably in their industry. Commercial banks are a major source of financing for small business, providing approximately 90 percent of short-term loans and 70 percent of their long-term loans. As I discussed in the previous chapter, commercial banks have become far more conservative in evaluating prospective credits. Commercial banks will provide the lowest cost of debt financing, typically charging a rate equal to prime (the rate they charge their largest and best customers) plus 1 to 3 percent floating with the prime rate; however, commercial banks won't lend unless they believe the borrower can repay the loan as agreed, without pain, and without the bank having to liquidate the collateral. Insurance companies, being regulated, have lending criteria that are also very conservative; moreover, they traditionally finance larger, mature companies with a track record of consistent earnings.

Since commercial finance and leasing companies are unregulated, they are typically the next most attractive source of financing for a business that cannot qualify for bank credit. Finance companies generally make loans secured by the company's assets (accounts receivable, inventory, real estate) and, in order to cover the increased risk of financing a nonbankable borrower, typically charge an interest rate 3 to 5 percent above that of a bank. In addition, they monitor their clients' operations very closely and position themselves to seize their collateral and liquidate the assets if serious problems develop. The company will also pay more in closing costs than it would through bank financing. At the end of 1992, commercial finance companies' share of commercial and industrial lending was 34 percent.

Leasing companies provide funding for specific items of equipment (such as computers), machines (automatic machine tools), vehicles (cars, trucks, and trailers), airplanes, farm equipment, and many other items. The rates charged by the leasing companies will be a function of the nature of the item being leased, the financial strength of the lessee, and the duration of the lease. The advantage of leasing capital equipment over buying it is that leasing requires less money down, and you can often get a reduction in the interest rate if the equipment still has value at the end of the lease term. Since leasing is always an option in arranging for the financing of a purchase, lease financing can be very competitive, and it is one area of financing in which even a weak borrower (perhaps with barely enough funds to open the business) can obtain relatively low-interest financing. Certain foreign-owned banks that are not regulated like domestic banks may also be a source of financing for borrowers who are not "bankable."

A major part of the analysis and due diligence that commercial banks, insurance companies, and commercial finance and leasing companies perform is focused on the ability of the company to pay back the loan from its net cash flow (operating profits plus noncash expenses). They must always be prepared to force the company to liquidate assets in order to repay the loan, but they won't make the loan if there is a reasonable probability they will have to liquidate assets.

Hard money lenders is the appellation given to firms that lend to the riskiest borrowers and, therefore, often make loans when they fully expect to be paid back via liquidation. Two prominent hard-money lenders are factors and mortgage bankers (real estate lenders). Factors lend on receivables—the most liquid of company assets, after cash and securities. They typically advance 50 to 80 percent of the receivable amount and charge interest rates of 8 to 25 percent more than the prime rate. The factor actually purchases the receivables from the company; depending upon the agreement, the company may be obligated to repurchase uncollectible receivables from the factor.

Real estate lenders will advance 50 to 75 percent of the value of the land and improvements; loan periods range from five to fifteen years, and interest rates will be 1 to 10 percent more than the prime rate. The interest rate may either vary with the prime rate or be fixed at the time the loan is funded. Loan fees can range from one point (1 percent of the loan) to ten points depending upon the size of the loan, the financial condition of the borrower, and the nature of the institution or individuals providing the funds.

Government-sponsored sources of financing or financing guarantees may be available on the federal, state, or local level. They exist as part of all governments' desire to create and expand businesses to improve the availability of jobs within their jurisdiction and to enhance the gross domestic product of the area. Government agencies also provide financing to help particular groups (such as minorities, women, workers with disabilities, and veterans) start and expand businesses and to assist businesspeople in solving particular problems (complying with environmental regulations, reducing hazardous waste, coping with foreign competition, recovering from a natural disaster, conserving energy, and so on).

These sources of financing typically provide loans at below market rates to borrowers who often cannot qualify for bank financing. As a consequence, they deserve very serious consideration in any financing strategy. Information on the various government and community programs are available through the Small Business Development Centers, a network of locally based centers that link the resources and information of federal, state, and local governments with those of the educational community and the private sector. Table 3–1 (which was prepared by Bruce Barren, chairman of EMCO/Hanover Group, a Los Angeles–based merchant banking company) is a summary of the likely availability of various capital sources at the several stages in a company's life cycle.

3. How and When Will You Pay Back Your Loan If Your Plan for the Business Works Out?

Let's briefly review what you know at this stage of the process. On the basis of the work you did to answer the first question, you have determined a range for your required financing that may be composed of both debt and equity. The answer to the second question has provided you with a menu of alternative sources of financing, each of which has its own idiosyncracies, requirements, and costs.

To answer this third question, you have to be prepared to perform a series of analyses to project the company's balance sheet and cash flow assuming alternative financing mixes (and costs) that management believes will be available. Then you can determine whether these forecasts will achieve the paybacks the various lending organizations will require. In the jargon of the trade, this is called a *what-if analysis.*

The prerequisites for performing such an analysis are as follows:

TABLE 3–1

Sources of Capital Funding Potential

	Business Life Cycle Stage			
	Start-Up	Operation	Growth	Initial Maturity
Equity				
Individual investors	1	1	2	3
Corporations	3	3	2	1
Employee stock ownership plan (ESOP)	3	3	2	1
Venture capital	1	1	2	3
Small business investment corporation (SBIC)	2	2/1	2/1	1
Public offering	3	3/2	1	1
Personal and business associates	2	1	2	3
Debt Finance				
Commerical banks	2	1	1	1
Savings & loan associations	3	2	3	3
Life insurance companies	3	3	2	1
Commercial credit companies	2	2	1	2
Factors	3	2	1	2
Government programs				
Small Business Administration	2	1	1	3
Community Development Corporation (CDC)	3	3	1	1
Economic Development Commission (EDC)	3	3	1	1
Small Business Investment Corporation (SBIC)	2	1	3	3
Private Limited Partnership	1	2	2	3
Other				
Research development grants	2/1	1	2	3
Tax shelters	2/1	2	2	2
Private foundations	2	1	2	3
Corporate Annuities	3	3	2	1
Joint Ventures	2	1	2	3
Licensing agreements	3	3	2	1
Vendor financing	3	3	2	1

Note: 1 = most likely source; 2 = possible source; 3 = unlikely source.
Source: Bruce Barren, the Interface between the Accountant and the Turnaround
    Specialist. Los Angeles: EMCO Group, 1991

1. The results of the work performed to answer Question 1.
2. The determination of the most likely sources of financing that will be available to the company and the costs of this financing.
3. The Robert Morris[1] financial statement statistics for the generic company being analyzed.
4. A knowledgeable and realistic analyst (a CPA or management consultant) who has experience in both formulating financial plans and in implementing them.

As the analysis proceeds, the CPA or consultant will make various reality checks with the owners (to see if they can live with the risks inherent in the level of borrowing), with the management (to see if the plan is operationally feasible), and with the potential lenders (to see if they can live with the balance sheets and cash flows the various alternatives will generate). When the analyst discovers one or more financing alternatives that appear to work, Question 3 has been answered—at least for the time being.

4. How Will You Pay Back the Loans If Your Plan for the Business Doesn't Work Out?

The usual first response I get to this question is, "Why wouldn't the plan work out? The forecasts show it will!" And now I am faced with a dilemma. Having espoused the benefits and importance of planning and forecasting—and having badgered my clients with tales of businessmen who refused to plan and forecast, then wound up penniless in bankruptcy court—how can I now tell them they should view their working financial plan with a healthy dose of salt? The answer is found in the concept of risk.

Your calculations of the cash the business will require and its ability to pay principal and interest on its loans are made up of various estimates as to what sales, costs, expenditures, and receipts will occur at various times in the future. Your ability to estimate these items accurately will vary greatly. For example, you can estimate with a high degree of accuracy what the rent for your facility is likely to be for several years in the future, since this amount will be fixed in the contract between the landlord and the chief executive. Likewise, you can predict with almost similar accuracy the salaries, benefits, and perks of the executive staff, since they will all have to agree to compensation packages as a prerequisite to going forward with a business plan.

Estimates of shipment volume (the number of items shipped within a given month), selling price, and inventory turns are invariably more speculative, however, and these will be characterized by broad probability distributions. The other variables that compose the forecast will fall between these extremes in terms of your ability to estimate their future values with any degree of certainty.

That there is no certainty regarding the future is both trite and true. Therefore the entrepreneur must never fall in love with her plan to the extent that she forgets just how easily poor estimates or unplanned events can cause a business plan—and frequently a business—to fail. A banker understands this concept thoroughly, and as a consequence he will want to understand what plan you have to repay his loan if the business plan you have proposed does not prove out in reality.

Loans to secured creditors are usually repaid from three sources: (1) the liquidation (that is, conversion into cash) of the receivables, inventory, equipment, and real estate securing the loan; (2) the liquidation of other collateral that has been pledged as security; and (3) the calling of the guarantees that the principals signed when the loan was initiated. Bankers know all too well that the euphoria business owners experience when a loan is funded and a business enterprise is launched has a mirror image of depression, despair, stonewalling, and litigation when a business plan fails and the banker must foreclose on collateral. You can therefore expect your banker to be very focused on the loan-to-collateral ratio under worst-case conditions; the lower this number is, the more comfortable your banker will feel. It should now be clear that a very critical aspect of any financing program is the formulation of this worst-case plan.

5. Identify the Organizations and Institutions That Provide the Type of Funding Your Business Requires

At any point in time there are literally thousands of lending and investing institutions and individuals who are willing and able to fund projects. The executives who manage these institutions are always looking for worthy borrowers with projects that match the lending criteria that have been established for their particular institution.

From this vast galaxy of potential lenders and investors, the entrepreneur seeking to fund a business plan must identify the most likely prospects. This is by no means a simple task. It frequently frustrates even the most dedicated chief financial officers, because for any given deal the company will be fortunate to interest even a handful of prospective lenders.

Each lending institution operates in accordance with lending policies that are established by its board. These policies are designed to allow the institution to achieve its volume and earnings objectives at an acceptable level of risk. They reflect the experience, skill, and prejudices of the senior executives of the institution. These policies, however, are not static. Institutions frequently plunge into a "hot" business area and find that they greatly underestimated the inherent risks. A major business expansion in a specific industry is followed by a retreat from that industry, and lending policies are changed to reflect the new reality. Pendulums in the banking industry swing very widely, as was exhibited by the gluttony/starvation cycle of the lending forays into the oil industry, Latin America, and commercial real estate. A policy of "fund any deal you can get without offending the regulators" is followed by "don't fund any deal under threat of instant termination."

In addition, institutions frequently find themselves in a situation where they are unable to "write" new business because of problems with their regulators, a balance sheet problem, a pending or recent merger, or a pending or recent management change. Therefore the landscape of prospective lending institutions is often very fuzzy and is in a constant state of flux.

The characteristics of a company that limit its universe of potential lenders/investors are as follows:

• The type of business that it conducts as characterized by the company's Standard Industrial Code (SIC) classification.
• The size of the business, as measured by its annual gross revenue.
• The financial condition of the business, as measured by some of its key ratios (such as current assets to current liabilities, debt to equity, and profits to sales).

- Where the business is in its life cycle (that is, is it a start-up? An adolescent? A mature business? A turnaround?)
- Its recent history, as manifested by past sales, profits, and return on investment.
- The amount of funding required, the time horizon needed to pay back the loan, and the collateral available to secure it (receivables, inventory, capital equipment, real estate, patents, or licenses).
- The location (city, county, state, country) of the company's primary business operations and assets.

Each of these factors can be viewed as a filter that sifts lenders whose policies can accommodate the company's particular situation from the universe of available lenders. As each filter is brought to bear, the list of prospective lenders is further diminished; it is a fortunate chief financial officer who, after working the telephones and fax machines for a month, can identify several prospective lenders who will look seriously at the company's business plan.

The company's challenge is to identify this elusive handful of prospects as quickly as possible. It's not an easy job. Usually it is accomplished in a haphazard manner, with the company's senior executives relying primarily on existing contacts and relationships within the community and industry where the company does business. This is unfortunate, since it is in the company's interest to cast as wide a net as possible and create interest in a large number of lending prospects. That is because a large percentage of prospects that express initial interest fall by the wayside after the business plan is presented and the due diligence process progresses. Senior executives are often reluctant to call prospective lenders "cold" and believe an introduction is essential to being taken seriously by the prospective lender. This is highly unproductive behavior on the part of management, since it will limit the company's options.

I recommend that the chief financial officer or chief executive officer enlist the resources necessary to identify the maximum number of prospective lenders. These resources may include investment bankers whose business it is to know at any given time what institutions are actively in the market, what situations these institutions are primarily interested in, who the key contacts and decisions makers are, and what lending policies are operative. The fees charged by the investment banker (which are a percentage of the funds being raised) become part of the up-front financing costs of the project and are paid when the project funds. A competent investment banker often makes the difference between funding and not funding a difficult project.

Seeking capital—whether debt or equity—requires a great deal of the time of senior management, most of whom will be called upon to meet with prospective lenders, make presentations, and answer questions about the company's operations and strategy. It is up to the CEO to ensure that the staff is not overly distracted from their main responsibility: to operate the business.

6. Prepare a Loan Proposal That Will Persuade Your Lender To Invest in Your Business

Having identified your prospective lenders and created some interest, your company's next task is to prepare a detailed loan proposal. The loan proposal is the vehicle by which the company presents itself to the lending institution. Senior executives of the institution who must approve a loan will never see the company, or its products, executives, or employees; they will only know the company through its loan proposal and the reports that the lending officers prepare about the company and the proposal. This is why the loan proposal is critical to achieving funding. It must be accurate, thorough, and prepared in a professional and interesting manner. The more understandable and exciting you can make your industry, products, and business to the bankers who will be evaluating your request, the higher the probability is of your winning converts for your cause.

A typical outline and organization of a loan proposal is as follows:

INTRODUCTION.

Describe the deal, including the amount needed, what you intend to do with it, why the funds requested will help the company, how you will pay it back, and the collateral you are offering to secure the loan.

BUSINESS DESCRIPTION.

Describe the business, the products and services you offer, how your products and services are priced, the composition of your revenue stream, your industry and your company's position in it, the key ingredients for success in your industry and the degree to which you possess them, your market share, your competitive advantage, and how you intend to sustain that advantage.

Then describe your customer base and the structure and customer concentration of your revenue stream by customer type, your marketing/advertising strategies for creating customers, and your distribution system.

Also describe your competitors and how they compare to you in terms of sales volume, financial strength, market share, and product line.

Finally, describe your key suppliers and how they contribute to your strengths and weaknesses.

ORGANIZATION.

Describe the manner in which the company is organized, the key management personnel (include resumés) and their compensation, and the labor force (including turnover rate, pay scales, benefit package, and labor relations history).

PLANT AND EQUIPMENT.

Describe the physical facilities in which the business operates, whether those facilities are owned or leased, and, if leased, the key terms of the lease; the major items of capital equipment used in the business; and the extent to which the current physical facilities and capital equipment limit the company's production volume.

Since real estate and capital assets will serve as collateral for the loan, detailed listings of these should be prepared, along with a description of how they are being financed and their most recent appraised or estimated value.

HISTORICAL FINANCIAL PERFORMANCE.

The financial history of the company for the last three to five years should be presented in spreadsheet format; the company's past annual financial statements and the most recent interim statement will also be included. Describe any anomalies or significant financial events in the company's history (such as extraordinary profits, losses, major financings, acquisitions, divestitures, the introduction or abandonment of major product lines or services, seasonal variations, and changes in accounting policies). Any aspect of the financial statements that undermines their continuity or comparability must be explained.

Discuss the historical values and variations of the critical ratios, and explain why any trends or significant changes in the ratios have occurred. If your ratios differ substantially from those of your industry, explain why.

Discuss the systems, policies, equipment, and procedures that are employed to manage the finance and accounting department and how senior management ensures that the financial information it receives is timely, relevant, accurate, appropriate, and consistent.[2] Discuss also any major changes that have occurred or are planned in the accounting system.

This section should include a number of the underlying schedules of your current financial statements, such as aged accounts receivable (including a discussion of the history of your relationship with your major customers, plus your credit approval, invoicing, and collection policies and procedures), aged accounts payable (including a discussion of your historical relationship with and the extent to which you are dependent on your major suppliers), a schedule of all debt and leases (including lender, origin of the debt, interest rate, terms, and collateral pledged, plus a discussion of whether you have ever been in default on a particular obligation and why), and a schedule describing the composition of your inventory (broken down where appropriate by raw material, work in process, and finished goods, including a discussion of the major items that account for the bulk of the dollar value and how inventory is valued and controlled).

FINANCIAL PROJECTIONS AND REPAYMENT.

This section will be comprised of the model and its underlying assumptions that were created to answer Questions 1 and 3 (How much do you need? How will you pay it back?) modified to reflect the policies and terms of the highest probability lenders (the answer to Question 5). When preparing this section you should keep the following key points in mind:

- The financial projections, consisting of profit and loss, balance sheet, and cash flow statements for your most likely target scenario, should be on a monthly basis for the first two years of the plan and a yearly basis for the following three years. A statement of sources and uses of funds should be presented on a yearly basis.
- Ensure that you have an underlying rationale or justification for every revenue element, cost element, and relationship that appears in your model. Your senior management will be asked to explain these assumptions.
- Organize and present all your assumptions for the plan in such a manner that they tie in with and refer to the historical material about the company that has been presented in the previous sections.
- Clearly describe how the loan proceeds are to be used (for example, if a major item of capital equipment is to be purchased, show when that purchase is planned to take place).
- Use the model to describe the sensitivity of the company's cash flow and its ability to service debt to variations in values of the most critical and speculative variables.
- Take care to ensure the projections are not overly optimistic. They should be conservative yet not pessimistic, since bankers will always be skeptical of the projections and tend to "haircut" the numbers anyway. Presenting an overly aggressive forecast is virtually guaranteed to turn off a prospective lender.
- Describe any current or threatened litigation, including a brief analysis of the issues involved, an assessment of the company's risk, and an estimate of the resources that will be required to fund the litigation to its conclusion.
- Include as appendices any material you believe will help the banker understand your industry, business, products, and future prospects. Sales literature, market analyses, surveys, and newspaper and magazine articles about the company, major competitors, or the industry are all appropriate.

7. Take Your Show on the Road and See How It Plays

Having completed the loan proposal and satisfied yourself that you are prepared to defend it, contact your handful of lending prospects and ascertain that they are still interested in hearing your story. Send out the proposals to those who are willing to talk and begin to prepare yourself mentally for the most grueling and excruciating parts of the process: the bank's evaluation and due diligence.

4

Running the Gauntlet

The Loan Request Evaluation

The Golden Rule of borrowing: He who has the gold makes the rules.
                              —Anonymous

Behind all its global responsibility and impersonal style, banking is still a people business. . . . It may be the most personal business of all, for it always depends on the original concept of credit, meaning trust. However complex and mathematical the business has become, it still depends on the assessment of trust by individuals with very human failings.

                              —Anthony Sampson[1]

The purpose of this chapter is to make you a believer—to convince you that the process for preparing the loan request, as described in the previous chapter, is not an academic exercise you may do or not do as you please. It is an absolute necessity if you're serious about acquiring a loan. Failure to prepare and be able to defend a comprehensive loan package will substantially lower the probability of your being successful.

In the lending profession, a good loan is one that gets paid back. The dilemma of the banker is to discover among the many potential borrowers those few "good loans" to fill up the institution's loan portfolio. Bankers who make good loans get raises, win promotions, and are considered for senior management positions. Those who make bad loans are passed over at review time, are terminated, and often drop out of the banking industry.

The credit evaluation process is based on what bankers refer to as "the five Cs of credit." These five code words are universally understood in the banking profession, and each stands for an area of credit investigation that will contribute to the final loan decision. They are *character*, *capacity*, *conditions*, *capital*, and *collateral*. These elements are in the forefront of the banker's mind when she is evaluating a proposed loan. If you're going to be successful in obtaining credit, you had better learn to think like a banker, and if you're going to think like a banker you must understand the five Cs of credit.

I will now discuss what the banker understands each of these code words to mean.

Character

In the banker's mind, character (which I will have more to say about in Chapter 6) refers to the integrity and fortitude of the borrower and is the most important evaluation criterion. If the banker doesn't believe the borrower will do what he promises and has the mettle and persistence to see a business through difficult times, the banker will not even look at the other evaluation criteria. This is based on the theory that even if the borrower faces daunting business problems, a determination to pay his debts will see the credit transaction through to a successful conclusion. In contrast, the borrower who lacks character and comes up against hard times will not have the resolve to make the sacrifices necessary to repay the loan.

Bankers prefer not to lend money to strangers because the banker doesn't know anything firsthand about the character of the borrower. Historically, depositors and lenders did their banking business within the community where the directors and lending officers of the bank lived and worked, thereby ensuring that the bank did not have to deal with strangers.

Unfortunately for bankers, character is an inner quality of an individual that reflects the sum total of their history from birth to the date the loan proposal is submitted, and it is not amenable to direct measurement. Although the banker will undoubtedly base her evaluation to some extent on her interviews with and observation of the borrower she will also rely on reports as to the reputation of the borrower, what mutual friends and business associates think, and comments that she can garner about other relationships the borrower has had with bankers and business associates. The litigation history of the borrower and the reports of various credit reporting agencies will also contribute to her evaluation.

Simply stated, the banker wants to know if you, the borrower, can be trusted with the bank's money. Unfortunately, though, there is no litmus test for character. Bankers say that a borrower's character is like a tea bag: you don't know its strength until you test it in hot water. The following are twelve questions a banker would probably ask you if she believed she could expect you to answer truthfully.

- Are you a legitimate businessman who is requesting the money for the reasons outlined, or are you a crook in a business suit who is using the loan proposal as a subterfuge to steal the bank's money?
- Do you intend to use the money as outlined in the loan proposal, or are you easily diverted to new projects and will use the money any way you see fit once you get your hands on it?
- If your company or project gets into trouble, can I depend on you to use your best efforts and make personal sacrifices to resolve your business difficulties and repay the loan?
- Can you be trusted to protect the bank's collateral until the loan is paid, or will you divert it as you see fit when your cash flow gets tight?
- Do you intend to steal from your company in order to avoid taxes (that is, remove cash, product, or other assets from the corporation without accounting for it)?
- Do you intend to use the company as a welfare office to employ or provide income for relatives and friends who don't contribute any substantive value to the business?
- Will you pay yourself so well in salary and perks that you deplete the working capital of the business and prevent it from realizing its potential—or, worse, cause it to default on its obligations to creditors?
- Do you plan to have the company purchase expensive toys for your imperial use, such as luxury cars, boats, airplanes and vacation condominiums?

- Do you gamble, and do you intend to rely upon the business to cover your losses?
- Are you on drugs, and do you rely on the business to pay for your habit?
- Do you plan to take frequent vacations, so that the company will have to operate without the benefit of your presence for large periods of time?
- Is the information you have provided in the loan proposal complete, relevant, and accurate to the best of the ability of you and your staff, or have you fudged it just a little bit to make the presentation more convincing?

I have analyzed my own client base to determine the percentage of cases in which the CEO would have had to provide answers opposite to what the banker wanted to hear. My results showed that this would have been necessary in 40 percent of the cases.

As stated above, the evaluation of character is the most important and most difficult part of the loan evaluation process.

Capacity

Capacity refers to the ability of the business to pay back the loan in accordance with the terms of the contract. It also refers to the ability of those who are managing the business to manage it successfully, to make prudent business decisions, and to anticipate, avoid, and manage risk. To use a nautical analogy, the banker who is asked to finance a ship's cargo is not interested only in whether that cargo can be sold for a sufficient profit to repay the loan. He also is very interested in the education, training, and experience of the senior officers who will manage the crew and navigate the treacherous waters the ship must sail.

The two dimensions of the capacity evaluation are the professional stature of the senior managers and the company's business plan. The senior managers act as trustees for the funds invested in the company. If the money loaned is dissipated as a result of the inexperience, ignorance and/or stupidity of the senior managers, the banker suffers the same loss as if the borrower simply stole the money.

The banker will want to see a management team that has the skills and experience to fill the essential technical and administrative functions the company needs to operate (sales, production, finance, administration, and so forth). A key position that isn't filled by a competent manager will invariably undermine the business and prevent it from achieving its potential—or, even worse, from paying back the loan.

The previous experience of the managers will be very important. The banker's underlying assumption is that past performance is an excellent indicator of future performance: a management team that can sport an array of impressive resumés will help persuade the banker that the company can carry out the business plan it submitted. In contrast, if the company's financial history is spotty and cannot be explained away in a manner that doesn't reflect adversely on the competence of the senior managers, the banker is likely to conclude that the company lacks the capacity to carry out its business plan. There are times, however, when a banker falls in love with a deal and funds it despite management's previously exhibited incompetence.

Venture capitalists tend to place a higher value on the quality of the management in their evaluation process than do bankers. They recognize that a business plan is only a very rough guide for the future performance of the firm, and that unforeseen circumstances will threaten to derail the plan; only a first-class management team will have the skill, intelligence, and experience to regroup and bring the company back on track.

A key aspect of the banker's evaluation of the company's capacity to pay back the loan will be her assessment of the reality and feasibility of the business plan. She will want to understand the threats to your plan and the events that could disrupt it. She will need to understand thoroughly the assumptions underlying the plan and financial forecasts, and to convince her that they are conservative and appropriate. The combination of a competent management team and a conservative, realistic business plan will go a long way in persuading a banker that the company has the capacity to perform as promised.

Conditions

Conditions refer to the factors and events beyond management's control that can adversely affect the probability of the loan being repaid. They constitute the banker's "nightmare" or worst-case scenarios—malevolent combinations of events that appear to have conspired to destroy the banker's investment.

A few years ago I was involved in attempting to refinance a agricultural enterprise located in California. The business was vertically integrated and engaged in growing, harvesting, packing, processing, marketing, and transportation. In the process of evaluating the plan, the banker posed the following questions:

- What will be the effect on production rates and costs if the drought continues? (California was in the fifth year of a drought cycle.)
- What will be the effect on production rates and costs if the major pesticide in use is suddenly banned by the EPA?
- What will be the effect on your market share if your major competitor decides to increase its production capacity by 50 percent?
- What effect will a 50 percent increase in the price of diesel fuel have on profits, and could you pass the cost increase on to your customers?

When the lender asks "what if," he is probing the subject of conditions. He will want to be assured that management is aware of the events and trends that could either help or hurt the business, and that it has plans to respond to negative events.

In evaluating conditions, the banker will focus on what is happening in the industry in which the company competes. For example, if the industry is operating at overcapacity—with too many sellers running after too few buyers, declining prices, and high business failure rates—the loan will be rated low on this dimension. Conversely, if the industry is expanding, with consumer demand and prices increasing, the banker will tend to give a high rating to conditions.

Capital

The concept of the banker's perspective of capital can best be understood from the following vignette. Tom and Mary are very good friends of yours; you've known them for many years and believe they have excellent character. Tom, an aerospace engineer, has been out of work for several months, and job prospects in his area of the state are not bright. Fortunately, Mary is a teacher, and her salary is just adequate to support the family while Tom is looking for a job.

Tom approaches you for a loan for $10,000. He offers you a second trust deed on his house, which has a first mortgage of $85,000 and has recently been appraised at $104,000. Tom tells you that he's tried all the conventional lenders but can't qualify because he's out of work. He appeals to your friendship and your compassion, refreshes your memory of when he helped you bring in a sixteen-inch brown trout, and convinces you that you will incur very little risk in financing a second trust deed on the house.

Fully prepared to provide the funds, you casually mention the loan to your wife. Fortunately for you, she's a bit more objective, and her judgment isn't clouded by the experiences you and Tom have shared in Little League, Boy Scouts, and junior college. She looks at this as if you and she were bankers—which in this case, you are. She quickly reviews the terms of the proposed loan and is satisfied that the duration (five years), interest rate (current fixed mortgage rates plus three points) and principal payments (interest only for first year, then fully amortized over the following four years) are acceptable. She then asks the banker's question: what if Tom gets a job out of state, and he and Mary move? What motivation do they have for continuing to make the payments on the first trust deed and the second trust deed you're about to fund?

You smile, with that self-assured smile only husbands can create when they're talking finance to their wives. "Tom and Mary wouldn't just walk away from their investment in the house. I'm sure they'd rent it and continue to make the payments." Fortunately for you, your wife is an avid reader of the real estate section of the paper. She says, "Well, how much investment capital will they have in the house after we provide the $10,000?"

You quickly add the amount of the first trust deed ($85,000) to that of the proposed second trust deed ($10,000), then subtract the sum ($95,000) from the appraised value ($104,000). With that self-assured smirk returning to your face, you announce triumphantly, "Nine thousand dollars. Tom and Mary won't walk away from $9,000."

You're on the verge of signing the $10,000 check when your wife grabs the pen out of your hand and says, "OK, let's think worst case. Tom and Mary decide to get a divorce, and each hires a lawyer to punish the other so that all their savings will be dissipated and they won't be able to support themselves, let alone the house. What do we do then?"

"Easy," you say, "we'll sell the damn thing and get our money back." You study your wife carefully, confident that the argument is over and you can provide the $10,000 to your friend Tom (which you desperately want to do), all the while telling yourself that this is a good business deal.

You look over at your wife, who is smiling broadly, and you know you're in trouble. "Let's assume that we want to sell it," she says. "The only way we can do that is to foreclose. If we foreclose we have to refinance the first. That will cost us foreclosure costs, refinancing costs, escrow fees, points for the new loan, and so on. Let's say we can get everything done for $3,500. Then we have to sell the house. Assuming we can sell the house at market, we'll have real estate commissions and closing costs of about 8 percent, or $8,320. That means we'll net, if we're lucky, $104,000 minus $3,500 minus $8,320, which is $93,180. After we pay off the $85,000 first, we'll recover $8,180 of our $10,000 investment—a minimum loss of $1,900."

You are stunned. "How can that possibly be?" you say. "What happened to Tom and Mary's $9,000 equity?"

"It's simple," says your wife, trying not to be too condescending. "It got eaten up in the foreclosure, refinancing, and seller's expenses. When you figured out how much their investment was worth, you ignored all of the transfer costs that occur when a deal goes bad. Tom and Mary simply do not have enough *Capital* in the deal to make it a good investment for us. We'd better pass."

You look at her closely and see finality in her eyes. You rip up the check.

The banker's analysis of capital will focus on two primary financial parameters. First, how much capital does the business owner have at risk in comparison to the funds the bank will risk in making the loan? Second, once the prospective loan is made, what is the estimate of the worst-case (highest) debt-to-worth ratio of the business over the duration of the loan, and will the business have adequate liquidity to carry out its activities?

The capital you have in the project for which you're requesting financing satisfies two needs of the banker. Her first is for an equity cushion between the amount of her outstanding loan and the net proceeds from the sale of collateral in the event of a liquidation. Her second need is that you, the borrower, have sufficient assets at risk in the project so you cannot afford to "walk away" or abandon it. Otherwise she will recognize that if the going gets tough, you, more likely than not, will get going—to your next project, leaving to the banker the distasteful (and very expensive) process of asset recovery and liquidation.

The issue of debt-to-worth ratio and the liquidity of the assets is central to the financial stability of the firm and its ability to weather reversals without becoming insolvent. A business is operationally insolvent if it cannot meet its obligations as they mature; it is terminally insolvent once its balance sheet liabilities exceed its assets (that is, it has no net worth). Either situation creates a problem for the banker, since it will result in the loan being classified by the bank examiner as being in jeopardy. An operationally insolvent business cannot continue to operate without restructuring or compromising its obligations with all of its creditors—or, failing that, seeking the protection of the bankruptcy system. A business that has no net worth or a negative net worth means that in the event of a liquidation, some of the company's debt will not be paid.

The ratio of debt to worth in a business is referred to as its *leverage*. Highly leveraged firms have high ratios of debt to worth; slightly leveraged firms have low ratios of debt to worth. The higher the leverage of a firm, the higher the risk that the banker will not be paid in full in a liquidation.

The debt-to-worth ratio of a business is to a large extent under the control of the owners and managers. The amount of leverage that is appropriate for a business is a function of the industry in which it competes, the historical trends in the particular business, the risk tolerance of the owners, and the requirements of the company's bank. In many situations, a company cannot arrange the financing for expansion unless it makes the risk more acceptable to the bankers by increasing the equity base of the company and lowering the debt-to-worth ratio. Table 4–1 is a table of the median debt-to-worth ratios for companies in several different industries.

Whereas the debt-to-worth ratio provides an indication of the risk that the business will not be able to pay its debts if and when it is liquidated, the ratio of sales to working capital is the financial in-

TABLE 4–1

Ranges of Ratios of Debt to Worth
and Sales to Working Capital
for Selected Industries

Industry	Sales Supported by $1 of Working Capital($)	Debt/Worth
Manufacturing		
Bread and bakery products	12–15	0.8–1.1
Drugs and medicine	2.3–2.7	0.3–0.4
Electronic components	2.9–5.1	0.4–0.6
Wholesalers		
Dairy products	9.6–13.1	0.9–1.1
Electronic parts and equipment	4.4–8.3	1.0–1.2
Sporting goods, recreational goods and supplies	5.5–5.9	0.7–0.9
Retailers		
Stationery and office supplies	6.1–8.6	0.6–1.0
Computers and software	8.0–11.9	1.2–2.1
Department stores	3.4–4.7	0.5–1.4
Service organizations		
Computer programming and other services	3.8–5.9	0.5–1.0
Insurance agents	4.3–19.1	1.6–2.1
Physicians	6.3–8.0	0.8–1.1

Note: Debt-to-worth ratios are those of companies within the upper quarter of their industry with sales over $5 million per year.

Source: Robert Morris Associates, *Annual Statement Studies,* Philadelphia: Robert Morris Associates, 1992.

dicator of the company's ability to meet its obligations as they become due. Working capital is defined as current assets minus current liabilities. The unique way business is conducted in an industry gives rise to a different sales-to-working-capital ratio required to maintain operating solvency. Industry examples of the average sales volume that can be supported by a dollar of working capital are also shown in Table 4–1.

If the ratio of sales to working capital in your business plan is significantly greater than the industry average for your industry, the banker will be concerned that you are operating your business on a precipice and you will not be able to maintain solvency when problems that affect your working capital arise. Typical problems are unexpected late payments from a major customer, a key supplier going out of business, or delays in the receipt of inventory due to inclement weather.

Collateral

The "fifth C" refers to *collateral*, the assets that are available for liquidation in the event your plan doesn't work out and the banker has to foreclose on the loan. How much collateral does a banker want in order to feel comfortable about the loan? As much as he can get. Why? Because the value of collateral is ephemeral; it changes all the time, and it rarely sells for the same price at which it has been appraised.

The collateral that supports the loan is the banker's risk reducer, his safety net, his escape hatch. He does not want to see any of his loans classified or in foreclosure, but if events conspire to bring about that situation, he will rest easily if the collateral can be quickly and easily sold for more than the amount of the loan. This is what bankers mean when they say a loan is "well collateralized." The collateral can consist of all the assets of the borrower that are not specifically pledged for any other purpose (in which case the loan is referred to as unsecured), or it can consist of identified assets that are specifically pledged to secure repayment of the loan.

The assets that appear on the balance sheet are recorded in accordance with generally accepted accounting practices. The book values that appear, though, may have no relation to the market values that might be achieved if the assets were sold. Some assets (such as real estate or depreciated vehicles) may be sold for much more than the book value; others (such as specialized equipment that was manufactured specifically to your needs) may be sold for much less. The banker will want to understand thoroughly the assets you own and the values he could achieve if he had to liquidate them.

The assets that are typically offered as collateral are certificates of deposit, marketable securities, notes receivable, accounts receivable, inventory, vehicles, production equipment, real estate, licenses, trademarks, and customer lists. The amount of the collateral value assigned by the bank will be some percentage of the appraised value of the asset that reflects the anticipated liquidation costs of the bank and the discount from market that type of asset commands. Typical collateral values that are assigned to various assets are shown in Table 4–2.

The personal guarantee from the owner of the business is viewed as an alternative source of repayment of the loan. There's a substantial difference, however, between collateral that the banker can foreclose on and sell and a guarantee on which a collection suit can be brought. The problem with guarantees for the banker is that she only has a sketchy idea, at best, of the ability of the guarantor to pay the loan until she brings suit, obtains a judgment, and institutes collection action. By the time the bank gets around to suing on a guarantee, the guarantor frequently has dissipated or hidden his or her assets or placed them beyond the bank's reach.

Virtually all banks require personal guarantees for loans to closely held or private corporations. Attempting to avoid signing a guarantee if you are the sole shareholder of a closely held corporation is usually an exercise in futility, and it can create uncertainty in the banker's mind as she wonders whether your avoidance is indicative of some hidden agenda.

Asset Quality Rating: Where the Rubber Meets the Road

You now have some insight into the philosophy underlying the manner in which the banker will go about the process of evaluating

TABLE 4–2

Collateral Value of Various Types of Assets

	Collateral Value as % of Market Value
Accounts receivable (less than 90 days past due)	70–85
Accounts receivable (greater than 90 days past due)	0
Inventory	
Raw material (not manufactured by firm)	10–60
Work in process	0
Finished goods (manufactured by firm)	10–70
Capital equipment	20–60
Real Estate	50–75

your loan. Hopefully, that process will have a successful conclusion: you'll receive your funding, and your loan will become an asset in the bank's portfolio. Once your loan is in the bank's portfolio, it will be periodically rated in accordance with an asset quality rating (AQR) scale to assess its risk. As the banker is reviewing and evaluating your loan proposal, she will undoubtedly have in mind the AQR scale and be estimating the rating that will be assigned to the loan if it is funded. The AQR scale used by a major bank is shown in Table 4–3.

AQR scores determine whether the borrower's relationship with the institution will continue. If the loan is assigned an AQR of 4 or better, the bank will probably continue the relationship unless the institution decides that either the borrower or the industry in which the borrower competes is no longer attractive.

If the loan is assigned an AQR of 5, the company will be carefully scrutinized until the bank management can decide whether they feel the loan is an acceptable risk (and lower its AQR to 4) or not an acceptable risk (and assign it a rating in the range of 6 to 8). If the score stays or goes above 5, the bank will want to see the loan repaid sooner rather than later. The responsibility for managing the loan will be moved from the loan officer "on the line" to the so-called workout or special-assets department, where bankers who specialize in problem loans will use their very considerable skills in reducing the bank's risk and ultimately bringing about the conversion of the loan to cash.

Since the borrower in this case can no longer depend on a continuing banking relationship, he or she is obligated to pursue one or more of the following courses of action, which are listed in decreasing desirability:

1. He or she can negotiate an agreement with the bank to pay down the loan over some certain period; this accommodation is usually referred to as a "workout plan."
2. He or she can seek out a new lender to buy out the existing obligation. Since it is very rare that a new bank will have any interest in extricating a troubled borrower's bank from its problem loan, new lenders will typically be institutions whose policies allow them to take greater risks—and, of course, charge higher interest rates and fees. Commercial finance com-

TABLE 4–3
Asset Quality Ratings

Asset Quality	Rating	Liquidity	Risk	Comments
Prime	1	High	Very Low	Firm in existence for a long period, having strong equity with many years of consecutive profits and unblemished history; firm can access public equity markets to raise capital. Rating also applies to reasonably strong borrower supported by a strong guarantor and/or fully secured by liquid collateral and/or assets fully guaranteed by approved governments and banks.
Prime	2	Good	Low	Self-liquidating loan with an unquestioned secondary source of repayment to borrowers of local, regional, or national stature. Borrower has proven management, shows consistent earnings, strong equity, and well-defined growing market. Firm has limited access to public equity markets to raise capital.
Standard	3	Acceptable	Low	Borrower has probable secondary source of repayment, proven management, good equity, and well-defined market; however, the firm does not have the ability to access the public equity markets to raise capital.
Acceptable	4	Acceptable	Acceptable	Borrower has adequate earnings and debt service capacity but not strong enough to sustain a major setback. Company is relatively new or liquidity or equity is not strong, profitability is volatile or trend related, statement analysis reveals unexplained variances. The firm doesn't have the ability to access the public equity markets to raise capital.
Special mention	5	Questionable	Questionable	Asset has potential weaknesses that deserve close attention. If left uncorrected, these potential weaknesses may result in deterioration of the payment prospects of the asset.
Classified: substandard	6	Unacceptable	Unacceptable	Assets are inadequately protected by the net worth and liquidity of the substandard borrower exhibits well-defined weakness or weaknesses that jeopardize the liquidation of the debt
Classified: doubtful	7	Unacceptable	High	Collection in full of this asset is improbable. Possibility of loss extremely high, but not exactly determinable.
Classified: loss	8	None	Loss	Assets are considered uncollectable and of little value. Asset will be written off.

panies, factors, hard-money lenders (who take primarily real estate as collateral), venture capitalists, and vulture capitalists all can operate in higher-risk plateaus than banks can.

3. He or she can bring in an equity partner to shore up the balance sheet, which may make the company's financial situation attractive to a greater array of lenders.

4. He or she can arrange to sell the company in order to achieve some return over the liquidation values of the business.

5. He or she can liquidate the company—sell the inventory and capital equipment and real estate, collect the receivables, pay off the bank loan, and pay off the unsecured trade creditors (to the extent that adequate funds are generated).

6. He or she can mail the keys for the building to the bank, abandoning his or her interest. Though very attractive, this action is usually precluded by the fact that the borrower has personally guaranteed the obligations.

With this insight as to how your loan will be evaluated once it is in the bank's portfolio and the consequences of it receiving an AQR of 5 or worse, you can appreciate why your loan officer is so cautious. His nightmare is to have one of his client's loans placed in the special mention on its very first rating. That kind of performance will not move a banker up the hierarchy of the institution.

This chapter has been concerned with giving you an understanding of the underlying philosophy that guides the loan evaluation process. In the next chapter I will examine the process the bank typically follows and how your participation in that process can be a significant factor in whether your loan is ultimately approved.

5

Defying the Odds

Proving Your Company Is the Exception

As the banker embarks on the loan review process in the hopes of "putting some new business on the books," she cannot forget what she knows about company failure statistics. Your job of getting a loan will be considerably easier if you know what she knows and can empathize with her concerns and prejudices.

Your loan officer will be thinking that the statistics for the survival of a business are not particularly promising. Fifty percent of all new businesses fail within the first five years of operation, 75 percent fail during the first ten years, and ultimately 94 percent of new businesses fail or are terminated without having earned a decent return for the owners. Of the 6 percent that survive, fewer than one-third will survive to see a second generation of management, and only half of those will successfully make the transition to a third generation. From the vantage point of the loan officer, even if she is considering a company with a ten-year track record, there's roughly a 76 percent probability the company will get into financial trouble and fail.

Failure strikes at all levels of business. Highly visible and successful business executives have led their companies to disaster. Large corporations have ignored warning signs and collapsed. Even the outstanding companies chronicled by Peters and Waterman in *In Search of Excellence* are not failure free; of the 14 exceptional companies glowingly featured in the book, 8 at the most could claim that stature ten years later. For example IBM, which for years was among the most favored stocks in the portfolios of investment managers and the darling of the management consultant gurus, reported an operating loss in 1992 of $4.97 billion, the largest loss in American corporate history.

With the low success rate of businesses, it is surprising that banks ever loan them money! Yet to make money, banks must make loans. Therefore bankers have developed very strict guidelines to lead them through the minefield of bad risks. There are several aspects of the loan approval process that the average businessperson finds markedly different from the normal process of purchasing or selling goods and services. Unless you understand these differences and accommodate your behavior to the unfamiliar and often nerve-racking process, however, you will be at a substantial disadvantage competing for a scarce resource—funds.

Loan Processing Frustration: No One to Face Off With

1.   The ultimate decisions about whether an institution will fund your loan will often be made by people you never meet. Financial decisions are made in a hierarchical framework where, for example, a $50,000 loan can be approved by the loan officer, a $250,000 loan can be approved by the senior vice president, a $1 million loan can be approved by the executive vice president, and anything larger must go to a committee of the board of directors.

This means the CEO usually never gets a chance to tell her story directly to the decision maker but must rely on an intermediary, such as the loan officer, to "sell" the story. This barrier between the customer and ultimate decision maker(s) is intentional and is designed to prevent well-positioned and wealthy borrowers from exerting influence over bank officials who have fiduciary responsibility for the depositors' money. The consequence of this policy is that the prospective borrower must not only persuade her loan officer that the loan is an acceptable risk for the institution, but also make sure that the loan officer has enough knowledge to persuade the ultimate decision makers of this conclusion.

2.   During the process of the loan evaluation, the loan officer will "build a file" on the prospective borrower. The file will consist of all of the information the bank obtains about the owners, directors, and officers of the prospective borrower, as well as the indus-

try in which the business competes. The bank will include in the file all information it has available from its previous relationship with any of the principals, the company, or any of the company's competitors. Bank files provide considerable data about present and past customers, including deposit activity, past borrowing records, and anecdotal material on the bank's relationships with any of the individuals or entities involved in the current application.

In addition to its own files, the banker can be expected to build its file from (1) credit reporting agencies, (2) other lenders with whom the banker may have a personal relationship, and (3) customers, competitors, and suppliers of the prospective borrower who are also customers of the bank. These sources can be expected to supply valuable insight into the past and present performance of the applicant and will be fully utilized in the loan evaluation process.

3. Members of the bank's staff will take the information contained in your loan proposal and reorganize and restructure it into a format that is familiar to the middle and senior managers who will have to make the ultimate decision on the loan application. It is axiomatic for a banker that a borrower's past financial performance is highly predictive of future performance; consequently, financial analysis is a cornerstone of the loan evaluation process. The staff will "spread the financials"—that is, present the historical and projected financial statements for the time periods covered in the loan proposal—and will calculate the critical ratios for each time period. The staff will then analyze and attempt to explain the variation of the ratios and look for evidence of weakness in the key areas of liquidity, solvency, and profitability. In addition, the staff will compare the company's ratio with those of companies in the same industry, using sources such as the Robert Morris *Annual Statement Studies* reports. The analysis of trends and the comparison of the prospective borrower's financials with those of other companies in the industry will tell the banker whether the proposed loan fits within the bank's current financial criteria for new loans.

4. If the credit is still considered viable after the staff has completed its analysis, the bankers will initiate the due diligence process, during which the banker investigates the principal, the management team, and the company.

The due diligence process is the first serious "date" with the banker. Up until this point you've had general conversations, shared anecdotes, and provided reams of information on your business, yourself, and your plans. But now you're going to find out whether you and your banker have the common goals, interests, and values that are the basis for a marriage.

As is the case in any date where you are exploring a relationship, you realize your behavior is going to be scrutinized minutely. You don't know exactly what your date will focus on, so you worry about everything and prepare for all contingencies. You shave extra close, make sure your nails are clean, purchase a new suit and tie, get a haircut, shine your shoes, and brush and floss your teeth for the third time that day. You should prepare for the due diligence process with similar thought and care, recognizing that this is your very best opportunity to persuade your banker he wants to do business with you, and hopefully to sweep him off his feet with the exciting opportunity you've provided him.

It is essential that you understand everything in the business plan. The banker needs to believe you are in control of the firm and have an appropriate depth of knowledge about the key aspects and operations. A banker performing due diligence on a loan can be likened to a detective performing an investigation of a crime. Both are searching for the truth, both need to test people's stories to separate fact from fantasy, and both have a lot riding on making sure they do not fail to uncover or misinterpret some important fact. Neither can afford to be misled or defrauded by any of the persons who are material to the process.

The banker has two major objectives during the due diligence phase: to evaluate the deal, and to evaluate the CEO/borrower. The banker needs to understand the business and the business plan. He has to understand what is in management's mind so that he will be able to make an effective presentation to the decision makers, answer their questions, and make an effective defense of his recommendation. He will want to check out the assumptions, statements, and projections in the plan to see if they are realistic. He will want to challenge the CEO and her key subordinates to see if they are in agreement and whether the plan represents a true consensus of the management team, has been stuffed down their throats by the CEO, or represents the fantasy of a strategic planner or loan packager. Is the plan optimistic? If so, what is the basis of the optimism? Is the optimism shared by all the key managers? If not, why not?

In preparing and advocating a business plan, executives invariably tend to emphasize strengths and opportunities on which their company's strategies are based and to downplay or even neglect threats and weaknesses. The banker, therefore, will have to ferret out these threats and weaknesses and determine and assess how they may affect the company's forecasts. The banker's basic question to the company will be this: what supportive elements, if suddenly taken away, might seriously damage or even destroy this business? These elements are the underpinnings upon which the firm depends for its continued existence. Eight such underpinnings are shown in Table 5–1.

The banker will attempt to identify which underpinnings, if disturbed or disrupted, constitute a threat to the business, and what the worst-case effect would be on the company if that threat materialized. For example, if one underpinning of the business is a particular government regulation, would a modification or elimination of that regulation adversely affect the company's business plan?

Failure: It's Always on Their Mind

By engaging the management in a discussion of worst-case scenarios, the banker gets a feel for the potential impact of the threat on the business. She will then rank this threat, perhaps using a simple scale from zero (no impact) to ten (catastrophe). She will want the management to estimate the probability that a particular threat will materialize, to explain what steps—if any—they have taken to reduce that probability, and what contingency plans they have for dealing with the problems if the threat materializes.

She will focus on whether the CEO and his team have really thought through the weaknesses of the company and its vulnerability to threats, whether they are realistic in their assessment of the probability of such threats occurring, and whether they have prudently invested the company's resources to minimize its vulnerability. These discussions provide the banker with an invaluable insight into the thinking, management styles, and risk profile of the CEO and his management team, and they will have a substantial effect on how she writes her report and whether she recommends the loan.

As the banker plows through the checklists she must complete as part of her due diligence, she is carefully searching for information and clues that will enable her to understand the borrower, his motivation, and his strengths and weaknesses. She will be looking for unrealistic assumptions or assumptions that appear to contradict the company's experience, errors in the model that has been used to project the financial performance, errors in the calculations, and any hint of absence of candor or misrepresentation. During meetings with the CEO and the members of the management team, she will scrutinize the CEO's behavior with the thoroughness and intensity of a doctor performing a proctological examination, and the behavior she observes will be part of the file that the banker will rely upon in making her recommendation.

Due Diligence Meeting: Showing Your Stuff

Several years ago I was performing consulting services for an industrial firm that had a history of erratic earnings. The company's secured lender decided it wanted the company out of the bank, and I was enlisted to help the company woo a new lender. Notwithstanding the poor history, the firm had a number of very attractive features to recommend it. It was in a consumer products industry that was both recession proof and inflation proof; the industry was controlled by an oligopoly of which it was a member. The company had been in business for in excess of forty years, so its brand names were well recognized and enjoyed wide consumer acceptance. Most important, it was in the process of bringing to market a new product line that had excellent profit possibilities.

That, however, was the good news. The bad news was that the CEO/owner (whom I will call Fred) enjoyed the dubious reputation of being an autocrat who made precipitous decisions, abused his management verbally, was prone to repeat management errors endlessly, and had great difficulty attracting and retaining competent, professional middle and senior management personnel. My interactions with Fred confirmed that his reputation was well deserved. While he was well-read and had a keen intellect, he was frequently unable to accept facts that were at odds with his emotional perceptions.

We prepared a very comprehensive loan proposal and submitted it to a number of institutions. Unfortunately, our timing could not have been worse, since the country was engulfed in its most severe credit crunch in a decade. We persisted, though, and eventually a major bank expressed interest in the loan and was eager to talk.

Shortly after 9:00 A.M. on the appointed morning the bankers' contingent filed in with bulging briefcases, dressed in classic dark business suits. The five-person bank group consisted of the local contact from Los Angeles, a senior credit analyst and a senior vice president from Chicago, a consultant from Dallas who specialized in our industry, and his assistant, a marketing specialist. The company group consisted of Fred; his father, Sam, who had founded the firm, the chief financial officer; the vice presidents of marketing and manufacturing; Bill, the director of research and development; and myself.

The first half hour was consumed by introductions, coffee, and placing everyone in their appropriate context in terms of the commonality of business associates, places lived, sports participated in, and so on. When that mine was exhausted, Richard, the senior credit officer, looked at Fred and said, "We're very impressed by what you've accomplished with this company. The size of the group we've brought together and the distance we've come should give you an indication of how serious we are. This is what we hope to accomplish today."

And then he outlined and elaborated on the agenda. The introductory meeting, which was in progress, would be followed by a number of breakout meetings where the various members of the bank group would meet individually with the senior managers of the company in order to probe the various aspects of the company. Then there would be a brown-bag lunch around noon to review progress, a plant tour in the early afternoon, and finally a group meeting at around 3:30 P.M. to review what had been accomplished, summarize outstanding concerns, and describe the subsequent tasks and schedule in order to complete the loan evaluation process. It was mutually agreed that the meetings would adjourn promptly at 4:30 P.M. to allow the out-of-towners to make their flights.

I hadn't met Richard prior to this meeting, and I was very pleased by the enthusiasm he expressed for the deal. I knew we had a long way to go to close this loan, but I allowed myself the luxury of mentally computing the incentive I was scheduled to earn on closing. My delightful reverie was rudely terminated by Fred; he had a previous luncheon date he said, so he would have to forgo the brown-bag meeting. He wouldn't be back, either, since he was scheduled to fly to San Francisco for an important customer meeting. But he had great confidence in his senior management and his "very, very expensive consultant," he said while nodding at me, so he was confident the bankers would "be well taken care of."

"Shit," I thought to myself, "not a good sign."

Richard smiled weakly and said something insipid about the importance of customers, but I could see his mental computer starting to tally up the score on Fred. I remembered Kenny Rogers singing something about "never count your money when you're sitting at the table" and promised myself not to think about my incentive again until after the closing, if there was one.

The coffee was cleared away, bathroom breaks were taken, and the group reassembled for business about 9:50 A.M. Richard turned to Fred's father, Sam, and asked him to give a brief outline of how the company got started and its progress up until Fred took over as CEO nine years ago.

Sam was sixty-five years old, robust, six foot two inches tall, and broad shouldered with a large beer belly. He wore a constant wide smile and spoke enthusiastically about every activity he was involved in. Golf was his passion, and he prided himself on having played with several pros that were on the PGA tour. Sam's personality was so engaging that his presence lit up every gathering. He responded enthusiastically to Richard's request: sitting at the end of the table, he flashed his big smile at the group and with the style of an experienced storyteller described how he started the business in his garage in order to minimize expenses and didn't move into an industrial building until sales exceeded $50,000 per month. He spoke nostalgically about how he made his first sale to a Fortune 500 client.

After about five minutes, Fred became quite agitated and said, "OK, Dad, no one is interested in a pageant; let's speed things up a little. We've got a lot of ground to cover." The bankers fidgeted, revealing their embarrassment. I looked over to Fred, trying to send him a signal to back off. Sam appeared to be stunned. He looked over to Richard as if he was seeking permission to continue. Richard smiled and said, "Please go on, Sam. We've got plenty of time. I'm fascinated." Fred shrugged his shoulders and slumped down in his chair.

"That's two," I thought. Sam quickly recovered his stride and told several anecdotes on the theme of how he repeatedly overcame tremendous odds to build the company to its position of market leadership. Richard then asked me to summarize the salient points of the business plan and to describe the most critical assumptions and my primary areas of concern. I opened the large black notebook that contained the business plan and launched into my well-rehearsed discussion of the company's strengths and weaknesses, the key success factors for the industry, and the company's future prospects.

A few minutes into my presentation, Fred interrupted and said, "Gary and I don't necessarily agree on our sales forecast. I'm convinced we can grow at a much faster rate, and I expect to push in that direction."

The room became very silent. Richard glanced over to me, puzzled. I smiled wanly. Fred then went into a long tirade on how "the people who wrote this plan just don't understand what the company can do" and how "I'm going to show my managers what's possible just as soon as this financing is complete and I get that —ing bank off my back."

An ominous silence pervaded the room. I started to pick up on my presentation but was again interrupted by Fred. "Hey, Bill," he said, motioning to the director of research and development, "go get those prototypes of that new drill design." Bill replied that he had sent them up to a major customer for approval, and they wouldn't be back until Saturday. Fred did not mask his anger: "You and I will talk about that immediately after this meeting. You obviously weren't listening to me when we met yesterday."

"That's three," I thought, "or was it four?"

Fortunately, Richard realized he couldn't control the large group meeting with Fred in attendance, and he suggested that we immediately break into the smaller groups. Jan, the marketing specialist, was to meet with Fred and Bill to review the R & D program, the status of the new product line, and marketing in general. The CFO and I met with the bankers. The consultant from Dallas met with the vice presidents of sales and production.

Shortly before 12:30 P.M. people started to drift back into the conference room, where sandwiches, drinks, and cookies were available. Jan and Bill were in the conference room when I arrived. They appeared to be engrossed in a serious conversation, so I was reluctant to intrude. Jan looked up at me, and I saw that her face was very flushed, with her eyes teary and her make-up smeared: it was obvious she'd been crying, and Bill was trying to comfort her. Bill quickly stood up, grabbed my arm, and led me out the door.

When we were out in the hall, Bill said, "Things got a little animated in there. Jan asked Fred a few questions about the last new product fiasco—you know, the six small power tools with interchangeable motors—and Fred got very defensive. He railed at the marketing and product development departments and said that things got screwed up because he was spending all his time fighting with the bank and didn't have the time to closely monitor the progress of the program. Then Jan asked him about the apparent discrepancies between the written business plan and 'Fred's plan,' and he got abusive and yelled at her and said that she 'obviously doesn't understand the business,' and the meeting went downhill from there."

"Where's Fred?" I asked.

"He left for lunch about a half hour ago. I've been trying to calm her down. She's embarrassed at not being able to deal with him."

Lunch went well. Sam entertained everyone with his golf stories, and it occurred to me that this deal would be a lot easier if Sam could replace Fred as CEO. Following lunch the visitors were given a plant tour and shown a promotional video for the new product line. The tour concluded about 3:30 P.M., and the entire entourage reconvened in the conference room. Jan had recovered her composure and spoke enthusiastically about the R & D laboratory and the quality control systems.

Richard reconvened the meeting and—addressing me as the apparent authority figure, Fred and Sam being absent—reviewed what he felt had been accomplished. He then asked each of the members of his team to share their primary concerns about the proposal and encouraged myself and the other members of the management team to respond. He said it was his style to be very candid and direct in due diligence meetings, since he found that the process was substantially accelerated that way. He expressed regret that Fred was not around to participate in the discussion.

"Another nail in the coffin," I thought.

The ensuing discussion was animated, intelligent, and very positive and went a long way to restore my confidence that this was indeed a doable deal. The two major concerns of the banker's group were whether the financial systems and controls (which had been very marginal) were adequate so management could make timely and effective decisions, and whether the new product line would have sufficient penetration to drive the 15 percent compounded sales growth that we projected in the business plan. I knew we'd be able to persuade the bankers that both concerns posed very little risk.

I was much less confident that I would be able to convince them that another major concern—Fred, who had not been explicitly discussed—didn't constitute a serious risk. I believed that it did. I certainly wouldn't lend any money to any company run by Fred, including a hot dog cart.

At the agreed breakup time, the briefcase-closing and jacket-retrieving ritual occurred, and good-byes were exchanged along with telephone and fax numbers. I was anxious to speak with Richard privately to get his candid assessment of the company's prospects, so I offered to drive him to the airport. He accepted, and during the twenty-minute drive we talked about a wide range of related subjects. I liked Richard and sensed that he liked me. I decided to broach the heretofore unmentioned issue—namely, Fred.

"You know," I said, "you've probably seen Fred at his worst. He isn't usually that oppressive and argumentative."

Richard thought for a moment and responded, "I certainly hope so."

Richard called me a few days later to say that although he liked the company and the industry, and was very impressed with the turnaround the management team had accomplished, the bank had decided not to consider the credit further. He didn't have to say why; I knew, and he knew that I knew. Fred, by his unseemly and inappropriate behavior, had sabotaged his own deal.

Twenty Questions—and Then a Lot More

The banker may want to inquire in depth about almost anything, including your background from high school and college days to the present, how you did academically, your level of involvement in community affairs, and your personal life. Questions representative of the type you will be asked appear in Table 5–2.

You don't want to either oversell or omit important information about yourself, your management team, your products or services, the market, the competition, your previous successes and failures. You should make your presentations during the due diligence meetings as accurate as possible, since candor and full disclosure are highly valued currency to a banker.

But the due diligence process does have its hazards. If the banker detects misrepresentations, discrepancies, evasion, omission of critical information, uncalled-for optimism, dissension among members of the management team, or a lack of professionalism on the part of the CEO or members of the management team, it is likely that although the banker will appear to complete the process, he or she will quietly drop the deal.

TABLE 5-2
Typical Due Diligence Questions

How was the business started?

How and when were some of the major products or services created? What was the source of the idea?

What is unique about the product or service? Why do your customers purchase from you rather than your competitors?

What are the barriers to other competitors entering the market?

Do you have any patents, trademarks, or licenses that will help you protect your competitive position?

What are your competitive advantages in each of the products or services you offer?

Who are the owners of the company and in what percentage? Which owners are active in the business?

What banks and finance companies have you previously done business with? How did those relationships evolve? Why are you not continuing to do business with them?

What is your basis for your predictions of market growth?

Describe the present structure of your market in terms of market shares, competitive advantage, and plans of your customers and competitors.

Describe the major threats to your business, your assessment of the probability and impact of these threats, and your efforts to minimize their impact on the business.

Do your employees belong to a union? Describe the relationship with the union.

How do you evaluate the members of your management team? Are you planning to replace any of these executives in the near future? Where are the major weaknesses in your management team?

What are your own strengths and weaknesses? Do you believe you are the best person to manage this company as CEO?

What is the status of your personal life? What are your hobbies? How do you spend your spare time?

What do you plan to do with the business over the next five years?

Having stressed the importance of full disclosure and candor on the part of the CEO/businessman in dealing with a banker, I must now admit that the pressures of business and the extreme need for financing, coupled with the very human desire to avoid issues that might cause the banker to shy away from the deal, often cause the CEO to bury the dirty laundry and hope for the best. It's similar to not wanting to tell your hoped-to-be significant other that the real reason you are now divorced is because your wife caught you in a very compromising position with your secretary.

On the other hand, the banker, who is supposed to delve into every material nook and cranny to discover any negative information about the company or the CEO, is often reluctant to inquire about sensitive personal matters that might offend a potential customer and drive him or her into the arms of another banker. Therefore, some very critical issues may never see the light of day because the CEO and the banker have both tacitly adopted a "don't ask, don't tell" policy on certain subjects.

The unfortunate result is that unless the CEO volunteers information on these subjects, the banker will conclude his due diligence investigation without fully resolving some serious questions about the CEO and the business. If the loan is a close call, such unresolved questions on the part of the banker could undermine the case for approving the loan.

Some of the questions your banker would like to ask are as follows:

"We are concerned that your brother-in-law, Joe, is your sales manager. The meetings we've had with some of your senior mangers indicate that, to be kind, he's not universally admired. It smells like blatant nepotism."

"Jane, I see from your loan proposal that your business owns a vacation condo in Maui, an airplane, and a thirty-eight-foot sailboat. My calculations show that your out-of-pocket cost to date for these items and activities is $350,000, and your annual cost to support them is about $75,000, which is almost 5 percent of last year's pretax earnings. Do you really believe this firm can support these toys? And wouldn't you and the company be better off selling them and investing the funds in the business? After all, it would reduce your loan request and improve your debt service coverage."

"Dave, we're concerned about the number of community organizations and charities you're active in: Boy Scouts, Cancer Society, Lung Association—of which you're a regional director—Rotary, and a half dozen more. I could understand all this community involvement if you were a banker, because that's a major way we make our contacts. But you're a manufacturer of a product that's distributed worldwide. How can you afford to spend so much time on charity and community affairs?"

"I understand that you were in the hospital last fall. What was the problem, and what is the current situation?"

"Bob, I understand that you and your wife separated last spring. What effect has that situation had on the business?"

If these issues are not addressed in a forthright manner, the banker might complete his due diligence investigation with an uncomfortable feeling that may cause him or her to reject your loan application. Therefore, even if these questions are not asked directly, you should address them.

Some Key Issues to Keep in Mind

1.   Some borrowers believe they can wait to see if the banker is going to make a commitment before they determine how much money they really need to borrow. Wrong! Every commitment issued by a banker is an offer to lend funds based on a set of assumptions that come directly or indirectly from the potential borrower's loan proposal. If your loan proposal has been prepared in a haphazard manner and you determine after the loan approval process begins that your project really needs more funds or a different financial structure, you can expect two things to happen with certainty. First, the banker will have to retrace his steps and repeat much of the loan approval process; second, your credibility with the banker will sink like a rock. The banker and his staff have invested time and effort on the basis of the requirements you stated and the projections to support those requirements. If either the requirements or projections turn out to be the result of a less than thoroughly serious effort on your part, the banker's time and that of his staff will have been wasted.

You know how you feel about customers who are "shoppers" or

"tire kickers." The banker feels the same way—don't waste his time!

2. The evaluation of the loan application and the due diligence investigation will often take longer than you anticipate or plan for. As a consequence, financial results and projections, operating results, and backlog compilations that were current when the loan application was submitted may be stale when the banker is ready to lend. The last thing you ever want to see is the look on your banker's face when you deliver updated financial information that reflects a major shortfall in anticipated performance after the funds have been deposited in your bank account. Continuously update your financials and projections and provide them to your bankers; don't appear at a loan closing conference until you've satisfied yourself that the information you've presented to your banker is the most accurate and most current the company can produce.

3. I've discussed at length the importance of candor, honesty, and full disclosure when dealing with a banker. Your credibility is your most important asset. It may not be on the balance sheet you present to your banker, but it is on the balance sheet she keeps on you. Your relationship with this banker will continue even if you are not successful this time; she will be in the community in which you do business. You might resubmit your request six months later when your situation improves, and you want to start out with her on your side. Or you may submit your application to another bank, and in the process of due diligence that banker might call the first banker to check you out. You want her to be able to say that you and your management practice George Washington management— you never lie.

Finally, make sure that all the information you present to your banker is always accurate, timely, and relevant. If the particular employees or consultants you are relying on cannot produce the information to meet the high standards you've set (and your banker expects), change employees and consultants. As I will discuss in Chapter 10, you are judged by the company you keep.

Introduction to Part II

Business loans are scarce resources, and there will usually be an oversupply of potential borrowers vying for them. The successful would-be borrower will have to propose a project that not only meets the bank's financial criteria but also interests and excites the banker so that he or she falls in love with the deal.

The process of falling in love with a loan, as with a person, is a complex process. In the case of lovers, psychologists are in agreement that we fall in love with a person who appeals to us physically and who has personality and intellectual attributes and interests that we value highly. We tend to gravitate to people who like the things we like, value the things we value, and have skills and interests that tend to fill in the recognized voids in our own persona.

The banker is no different. He will only consider a deal that appears to meet the minimum financial criteria of his institution. If he falls in love with the deal, however, his evaluation of the five C's—all of which are subjective—will be affected positively by his enthusiasm to do the deal. In other words, his zeal for your company and your proposal will lead him to support your loan.

On numerous occasions a banker who was telling me about an applicant admitted, "I'd love to get into this company myself; it's exciting. I'm confident that with my financial and administrative skills I could make a real difference."

Those are the words of a banker who has fallen in love. So how do you get the banker to fall in love with your deal, assuming it makes economic sense? The fact is that the banker will fall in love with your deal if she sees in you the attributes she would bring to the company if she were in your place—in short, if she discovers in you and your management team many of the attributes she feels are essential to the success of the business.

There are six essential characteristics and skills that will help you win your banker's support. You can expect the banker will be looking for evidence of them during the loan approval and due diligence process. She will want you to be a person of unblemished and stellar character, be financially literate, be a prudent negotiator, a strategic thinker, have the ability to select and use advisors, and finally, be an effective and skillful leader.

All of these characteristics and skills are rarely found in the entrepreneurs who found and manage small and middle market companies. An analysis of one hundred companies from my client base revealed that 20 percent had one or more of these characteristics, and only 2 percent had all six. Is it any wonder it is so tough for a small or medium-size company to obtain financing?

In Part II, I will discuss each of these attributes in some detail. I will also provide you with some rudimentary tools to begin to develop these six very important characteristics and skills, so that you can effectively charm your banker.

6

A Question of Character

Character is much easier kept than recovered.
                              —*Thomas Paine*

The measure of a man's real character is what he would do if he knew he would never be found out.
                              —*Thomas Babinton Macaulay*

Throughout the ages a person's character has been accepted as the most fundamental measurement of a person's worth to herself, her family, her friends, and society. It is valued more highly than social position, wealth, physical appearance, intellect, or prowess for business achievements. When we choose a friend, hire an employee, elect a representative to the legislature, or vote for a president, there is an underlying assumption in our action that we've selected a person of good character. When subsequent actions by that person indicate our judgment was faulty, we cannot but help feel discouraged and betrayed.

I visited the issue of character in the discussion in Chapter 4. The character factor is so central to the lending process, however, that its assessment is the foundation of the banker's evaluation. If the banker discovers during the initial acquisition of information or the due diligence process that one of the principals of the prospective borrowing company has a questionable character, the loan evaluation process will be aborted. The manner in which you create, nurture, and project your character thus will have a major influence on your success in the loan acquisition process. A banker cannot afford to place the institution's funds in the hands of someone whose character may be blemished.

The issue of character, and what traits constitute a good character, have been explored and discussed since ancient times. Plato defined the cardinal virtues that were essential for good character as wisdom, courage, temperance, and justice. To Aristotle, a person of high character was above all a rational, temperate person who could keep nonrational desires under control and who was concerned about the welfare of others. Various thinkers and writers have added other traits and virtues. Plutarch, the Roman historian, added honesty and humility; Tacitus added energetic, tactful, incorruptible, and dignified; Christian thinkers added faithful and hopeful; and Einherd, a ninth-century Frankish historian, added being patient, loyal, studious, and articulate.

When the U.S. Constitution was being drafted, many Americans understood that the model for the chief executive was George Washington, the victorious commander of the Continental army and a person whose character was universally respected. Thomas Jefferson paid tribute to Washington's "perfect character," noting especially his integrity, prudence, dignity and sense of justice. Americans have always sought presidents possessing those character traits specified by Jefferson and universally agreed upon by philosophers as being prerequisites for a leader.

Bankers seek in borrowers the same character traits that voters seek in their presidents. They are as follows:

Integrity: Defined as soundness and firm adherence to a code of especially moral values, honesty, and uprightness.

Prudence: Defined as cautious practical wisdom, good judgment, discretion, and provident care in the management of resources.

Temperance: Defined as moderation or self-restraint in action and in statements, self-control, and rationality (having or exercising reason, sound judgment, or good sense).

Courage: Defined as that quality of mind or spirit that enables one to face difficulty, danger, pain, and the like with firmness and without fear.

Unfortunately for the banker, these traits are more easily defined than found in their prospective borrowers.

Golden Hen Enterprises: A Financial Fairy Tale

Everyone knows the tale of Jack and the beanstalk—the marvelous adventure in which he outwitted the giant and made off with a hen that laid eggs of pure gold. Our story begins where the fairy tale ends.

Once upon a time, there was a happy family that owned a very special hen. Regular as clockwork, with just a minimum of feeding and care, the hen would turn out twenty-four-karat solid gold eggs. Nobody else in all the land had a hen that laid just precisely this kind of golden egg, so the demand for the eggs was very high. All the family had to do was take care of the hen and wait for the customers to come and buy the eggs. Golden Hen Enterprises, as the family named their company, was very successful.

The growth of the business, with the resulting increase in inventory and receivables, created a new problem for Jack, the founder and CEO. He simply did not have enough cash to run the business. His customers typically were paying in sixty days; but the considerable number of family members on the payroll made it difficult to keep his checkbook in balance. In addition, Jack was concerned that the eggs that were in inventory were not sufficiently secure; he felt the business needed to have the equivalent of a bank vault on the premises to protect the eggs against thieves.

Reluctantly Jack paid a visit to Mr. Jones, the local banker, and requested a working capital loan and a capital improvement loan. Of course, everyone in the village knew the story of how Jack had outsmarted the giant and stolen the golden hen. Although there were some in the village that considered Jack a common thief and liar, the majority, including Mr. Jones, attributed Jack's indiscretion to the excesses of youth. And, to be frank, the giant never enjoyed much political support in the village. Jack was now a successful businessman who employed a large number of citizens and who accounted for a major percentage of the gross domestic product of the village.

Mr. Jones visited the facility where the hen was kept. He was suitably impressed by the modern equipment that measured the feed to the hen and cleaned up and disposed of the hen droppings in accordance with health department and EPA regulations. Jack was most proud of the R & D laboratory, where substantial investments were being made in an effort to discover how to create "GH II," a second golden hen. Jack introduced Mr. Jones to the manager of the R & D lab, a microbiologist with extensive experience in gene splicing.

After the tour Jack and Mr. Jones discussed the company's requirements, and Mr. Jones provided an outline of the loan proposal Jack would need to fill out. Mr. Jones indicated that the loan request appeared to be reasonable and was well within the range the bank could fund. He advised Jack that the bank would need a security interest in the receivables, the inventory of golden eggs, and of course the hen itself. The banker left, and Jack was elated. He was confident his cash flow problems were at an end.

A week later Jack submitted the loan proposal. Mr. Jones had the staff work rushed through on a high priority, because there were rumors that Jack had been seen having lunch with a rival banker. The staff reported that the numbers looked excellent; the cash flow and collateral showed Jack could handle twice the loan being requested.

The only problem the staff encountered was that they did not have any way to determine the equity in the business, because there was no way to appraise the hen. There certainly were no comparable sales, this being the only golden hen in existence. If they valued the hen on the basis of the discounted value of the eggs it produced (less the cost of producing the eggs), they had to make assumptions about the production rate in the out years, the longevity of the hen, and so on. Assuming the historical production rate and normal life span for the hen, however, the value of the hen was such that the loan would result in a debt to equity ratio for the business that was well below 1.

As Mr. Jones prepared his report for the loan committee, he smiled as he gave Golden Hen Enterprises the highest possible scores for capacity, collateral, capital, and conditions. His smile faded, though, when he attempted to formulate a score for character. He carefully reviewed the bank's file and summarized everything that was known about Jack's character. In order to organize the information he prepared the following chronology, along with his opinion as to what those events revealed about Jack's character.

Jack, the only son of a poor widow, is very disrespectful of his mother and has a reputation for being indolent, careless, and extravagant. He trades the family's only asset, a milk cow, for a handful of "magic beans." This stupid bargain earns him the scorn and ridicule of the villagers.

Despite his fear of heights Jack displays a certain bravery in climbing the beanstalk. Although Jack is befriended, fed, and protected by the giant's wife, he steals her husband's hen that lays the golden eggs. Jack starts Golden Hen Enterprises and is moderately successful. The family is brought out of poverty, and Jack creates jobs for all his relatives.

For reasons that Jack has never satisfactorily explained, he climbs the beanstalk again. Despite the fact that the giant's wife again befriends him, feeds him, and hides him from the giant, he steals her husband's bags of gold and silver. He explains his actions by saying that a fairy he met near the giant's house told him that all the giant's possessions had been stolen from Jack's father, and that it was OK for Jack to steal them back.

Three years later Jack climbs the beanstalk and deceives the giant's wife for a third time. When the giant is asleep, Jack steals the golden harp. When the Giant pursues Jack down the beanstalk, Jack cuts it down, knowing full well that the giant will fall to his death. Jack pleads self-defense and is acquitted. With the beanstalk destroyed, Jack turns his full attention to Golden Hen Enterprises and builds it into a profitable business and the village's largest employer.

Mr. Jones leaned back in his chair and thought long and hard about the information that was in front of him. It was clear that Jack had exhibited some serious character flaws on his way to achieving prosperity. He had lied, cheated, and stolen. He had, to be sure, exhibited extreme loyalty to his mother and bravery in repeatedly climbing the beanstalk. Since his business prospered, he gave generously to charity and was active in numerous community organizations. But there was no question that Jack's character was not perfect. Banker Jones swallowed hard and, using a scale of zero to ten, he gave Jack a seven rating on character.

The loan was approved, and the business grew. At the urging of his mother, Jack hired several more family members. Business was excellent, and it seemed that the growth would only be limited by production. But a small problem developed. Occasionally one of the family members would secretly take an egg from underneath the hen, sell it, and pocket the money. When one of Jack's loyal employees told him about it, Jack promised to look into the matter. Of course, the employee did not know that Jack was also taking eggs and selling them for cash as a way to avoid taxes; the other family members had started to take eggs surreptitiously only after they learned Jack was doing it. But business was good, and who'd miss an occasional egg, anyway?

As the number of family members involved in Golden Hen Enterprises grew, so did the number of eggs that were being taken. Every time members of the family saw someone else take an egg, they felt like they were entitled to another one, too. Before long, a lot of the eggs were going into the pockets of the family members, rather than being sold to the customers of Golden Hen Enterprises. But times were good, and there was a high demand for eggs. Jack, meanwhile, had established a very extravagant life-style that was difficult to maintain on the salary Mr. Jones had written into the loan agreement.

Golden Hen Enterprises had some employees who were not family members. They knew some of the eggs were disappearing out from under the hen, and they began to worry that if the company didn't have enough eggs to sell, they wouldn't have jobs. The nonfamily employees couldn't get at the golden eggs themselves—only family members could do that—but they could collect hen droppings and sift them for gold dust.

As the family took more and more eggs, the employees became more concerned with collecting hen droppings, and less concerned with doing a good job. Some days, the hen didn't even get fed; the employees took the food and sold it out the back door to give themselves a little additional income. The hen began to look just a little peaked, and occasionally it would lay a lead egg.

Jack was now newly married. He was no longer involved in the day-to-day operations and spent a good deal of time at his beach condo. So Jack was not fully engaged in the business when Golden Hen Enterprise began to decline. The deterioration was not immediately apparent to Mr. Jones, either, because the company was late in submitting their financial statements. The audit of receivables showed that sales had fallen off, but Jack explained the decline as a seasonal fluctuation. The audit of the inventory indicated that the egg collateral was still adequate.

Actually, the inventory had deteriorated substantially, because the hen was laying a considerable number of lead eggs. Jack, however, had ordered that all the lead eggs be painted gold and listed in the inventory so the company could maintain the collateral necessary to support the loan.

Golden Hen Enterprises was rolling along on momentum. A lot of Jack's and his relatives' time and attention was focused on the use of the pilfered eggs in pursuit of business activities outside of Golden Hen Enterprises. The problem wasn't helped by the fact that some of the younger family members coming into the business—who were having to do more and more of the work—were less adept than their parents at getting the hen to lay satisfactory eggs.

Golden Hen Enterprises continued to stumble along. With the hen being fed less, it was laying more lead eggs. The lead eggs were always painted gold and listed in the inventory to maintain the collateral position. Occasionally a lead egg would be shipped by mistake. If the customer discovered the lead egg and complained, Jack would personally call and apologize for the error, saying that a new employee had mistakenly shipped a "display" egg for a real egg.

It was difficult to meet the demands for golden eggs and still satisfy the family's need for golden eggs to fund their "off the books" endeavors. All the family members knew there was a problem. And they all knew that the other people knew, and that the employees knew.

Because of neglect, the hen began to lay a still higher percentage of lead eggs. To meet demand, Jack authorized that gold-painted lead eggs would, if necessary, be used to fill orders; he would "deal with the fallout." Finally, the hen died. Jack ordered the hen stuffed and set up on its nest. He found a vendor who would supply lead eggs, which were painted gold and shipped as "golden eggs."

One day Mr. Jones received a late-night call from a colleague who had heard rumors that Golden Hen Enterprise was shipping gold-painted lead eggs and representing them as authentic golden eggs. The next day, Mr. Jones and a team of bank auditors appeared at the Golden Hen Enterprises facility and performed a surprise audit. Shortly thereafter, Golden Hen Enterprises was shut down, and Jack was arrested.

When Mr. Jones was assembling his files on Golden Hen Enterprise in preparation for turning them over to the workout department, he came across the analysis he had performed in order to arrive at a character score for Jack. He distinctly recalled the anxiety he had felt when he wrote down the score of seven.

You could make the case that Mr. Jones had only himself to blame for making the loan to Jack. He had ample evidence that Jack had very little integrity. Jack had repeatedly deceived the giant's wife, burglarized the giant's home, and ultimately murdered the giant. His second and third forays up the beanstalk and back into the giant's house showed that he lacked prudence, temperance, and rationality. Returning to the scene of his first crime (stealing the golden hen) and placing himself in jeopardy made no sense; the golden hen was itself a source of more riches than Jack and his mother needed. Jack might be entitled to high marks for courage, but in the context of everything Mr. Jones knew about Jack's history, he should have concluded that Jack was foolhardy rather than courageous.

Mr. Jones made a bad loan, and he should have known it was going to be bad before he made it. It's hard to feel sorry for him; a more astute loan officer would have passed.

In the non-fairy tale world of banking, determining that a prospective borrower has a defective character is a good deal more difficult. Even the best of loan officers can make a loan to a borrower from hell.

Borrowers from Hell

The story of Golden Hen Enterprises might be a fairy tale, but in many respects it is no more bizarre than the tales of corporate greed and malfeasance that occur all the time. The following stories were all extensively covered in the financial press during the past several years. In each case a fraudulent financial scheme was planned and carried out by the managers of a highly regarded company in order to enrich themselves irrespective of the risk and loss they caused the other stakeholders in the company.

MiniScribe

In September 1988, MiniScribe, a highly touted Colorado disk drive manufacturer with annual sales of approximately $500 million, announced that its senior management had perpetrated a massive fraud on the company, its directors, and the investing public. The fraud had been ongoing for the previous three years and had required the active participation of many company personnel. The rampant dishonesty was apparently common knowledge within the company.

In their report the investigators stated that the company officials went to extraordinary lengths to create the illusion of unbounded growth in sales and earnings, ostensibly to manipulate stock prices and benefit from insider trading. Senior management actually did the following:

- Broke into locked trunks containing auditors' work papers during a year-end audit and changed inventory figures in order to inflate inventory values.
- Packaged bricks and shipped them to distributors as disk drives, recording sales and gross profits for such shipments. When the shipments were returned, MiniScribe inflated its inventory by the purported cost of the bricks.
- Wrote off accumulated scrap in one year, then included it as part of the inventory and valued it as usable merchandise the following year.
- Shipped large amounts of product to the company's remote warehouses, recording the shipments as sales and booking gross profits as if they had been shipped to a customer.
- Created a software program (designated "Cook Book") that inflated inventory figures.

Perhaps most surprising about the MiniScribe situation was that the chief executive of the firm was Q. T. Wiles, chairman of Hambrecht & Quist, a highly respected venture capital firm that in 1985 had injected $20 million into the company and placed Mr. Wiles at the helm. Mr. Wiles enjoyed a reputation as a turnaround manager who could resurrect ailing companies and was hailed in the press as "Dr. Fix-It."

When the dust finally settled, a bankrupt MiniScribe was sold to a competitor. Secured creditors lost approximately 50 percent of their investment. In March 1993 Q. T. Wiles was indicted on federal securities and wire fraud charges for his role in the collapse of MiniScribe.

Revere Armored Inc.

In February 1993 federal authorities, acting on evidence of apparent irregularities in the operation of Revere Armored Inc., raided the company's headquarters on Long Island (east of New York City) and uncovered a huge scandal: accounting records missing or destroyed, mounds of cash of undetermined ownership strewn about, and $38 million missing from the Revere vaults. Revere, one of the nation's ten largest armored car companies, served as a storage depot for coins and cash collected from merchants in the Northeast. Rather than let their own branches collect and count the cash and coins to be deposited by merchants, banks contracted out the pickup, counting, and delivery of money from the large retail outlets.

In May 1993 the owners of Revere—Robert Scaretta and his wife, Susanne—were indicted along with several of their employees and a former bank customer. The indictment alleged that approximately $38 million collected on behalf of bank customers was missing, and that the Scarettas and others took the cash for their own personal use for gambling, off-the-books salaries and bonuses for employees (to avoid taxes), and payments to construction workers for repairs and renovations on their residence.

The indictment further stated that to advance their scheme of fraud and deception they routinely faxed fraudulent "proof sheets" that overstated the amount of money being stored on behalf of six banks (including Citibank and the Bank of New York) in the Revere vault. When auditors of any one bank appeared to inspect the facility, company employees would take money belonging to another bank and put in the area of the bank performing the audit. The banks who trusted Revere Armored Inc. lost at least $13.5 million.

Leslie Fay

In March 1993 Leslie Fay, a manufacturer of women's apparel with sales of approximately $800 million, announced that it would report a loss of $13.7 million for 1992, rather than the $23 million profit it had previously announced. The company further stated that its previously reported 1991 earnings would be reduced by 40 percent. The company explained that the restatements of earnings were made necessary when the company's controller admitted during the year-end audit that he and other employees had made false financial entries, the effect of which was to inflate the company's earnings.

An audit report issued six months later revealed that the combined pretax losses for 1991 and 1992 would be in the range of $100 million. The report described how the company inflated its profits by overstating its inventory and understating the cost of making garments. The report also described how, as retail sales slowed because of the recession, the false entries grew more extensive.

As pressure from its banks and suppliers drastically reduced credit availability, Leslie Fay filed for Chapter 11 bankruptcy protection. Leslie Fay's bankers were somewhat more fortunate than Revere's and MiniScribe's; all they lost was their confidence in the management.

Fairy Tales Can Come True

Fraud, deceit, and company looting thus are not confined to the realm of fairy tales. They are everyday occurrences to which bankers must be highly attuned. Line lenders are trained and motivated to try and make a deal; therefore, some will discount what may appear to be character flaws or management weaknesses. For the majority of bankers, however, a character flaw on the part of their borrowers is the equivalent of a *force majeure* clause in a contract saying that if war or insurrection occur, all bets are off. If a borrower has a serious character deficiency, the consequences for the loan can be both unpredictable and disastrous and cannot fail to frustrate the management efforts of the most experienced banker.

As a result, you can expect that your banker will carefully review the record of your business dealings for any evidence of deceit, failure to live up to financial commitments, actions that have jeopardized public safety, sharp business practices, and outright illegal activity. If you have such skeletons in your closet, your best course of action is to prepare a detailed explanation and bring both the "skeleton" and the explanation to the attention of the banker early in your discussions. This way she can acclimate herself to the fact that you may have flaws and perhaps rationalize them (as Mr. Jones did when he reviewed Jack's background). The worst situation that can occur is that the derogatory information about you is discovered independently by the banker late in the loan review and due diligence process. In that event, you can expect your loan request will be buried—along the prospects of your ever doing business with that banker again.

7

Financial Literacy

Picture yourself in the plush Beverly Hills offices of your very successful lawyer. The sixteen-foot mahogany conference table is polished to a very high gloss that reflects the overhead lights. The leather high-back chairs match the hunter-green carpeting. The walls are adorned with English hunting scenes whose burgundy and green colors blend with and contrast with the carpeting. The ambiance definitely supports the billing rates of $250 an hour and above that the lawyers in the firm charge.

Sitting across the table from you, your attorney, and your chief financial officer are your banker and her assistant. Your banker has called for the meeting to present the bank's proposal to provide the financing that is critical to implementing your business plan. You're literally bursting with anticipation as your banker drones on about how optimistic she is about the relationship with the company. Finally, your banker's assistant hands copies of the proposal to your attorney, your CFO, and yourself. You stare blankly at the several pages of single-spaced type, none of which you can read. The banker, who doesn't know that you can't read, looks over to you with a quizzical smile. After your attorney finishes reading the document, he leans over to you and whispers that the document is in order and you may sign it. He places a check on the line where he wants you to sign. Your CFO nods in agreement.

You then reach into the breast pocket of your jacket, take out your $300 Mont Blanc pen, and carefully unscrew the top. You lick your dry lips, carefully place a large "X" on the line designated by your attorney, and hand the document across the table to your banker. As she looks at your "signature," you see from her expression that she is astonished to learn you are illiterate. She hands your signed document to her assistant, who doesn't attempt to conceal his amazement as he stares at the prominent "X" on the signature line. Suddenly you become nauseated by the thought that this new knowledge has dampened your banker's enthusiasm for the financing.

It certainly should be no surprise that a banker would not be excited about lending you money if you could not read or write. Do you think she would feel differently if you were financially illiterate? Well, she won't. Financial statements, projections, cash flows, and ratio analyses are the language of business in much the same way as English is the language of the government of the United States, Braille the language of the blind, and signing the language of the deaf. If you intend to be successful in business and in the acquisition of bank financing, you must be skilled in the language of business and finance. If you don't, your efforts to secure bank financing will be adversely affected in three ways:

- You will not be able to communicate in the language the banker understands. Remember, his skill is in finance, and he looks at all businesses in the context of numbers that are presented in specific formats.
- You will not be able to understand your banker's comments, since he will be using the language of finance to ask questions and express his concerns.
- You will be viewed as a Rodney Dangerfield—you won't "get no respect."

What do I mean by "financially literate"? Simply that you possess the key financial skills that are essential for you to be able to manage your business financially. At the minimum these skills are as follows:

1. The ability to read, interpret, and analyze the four types of financial statements: balance sheet, profit and loss statement, cash flow statement, and reconciliation of changes in working capital.
2. An understanding of the key business ratios and how they are used in financial statement analysis.
3. An understanding of break-even operations and the ability to calculate break-even sales under various conditions.
4. An understanding of how projections of financial statements are developed and used.
5. An understanding of the concept of working capital and how it relates to the viability of a business.
6. An understanding of how operating budgets are prepared and used.

Understanding Financial Statements

A very large percentage of business owners and managers do not believe that personally knowing these skills is critical to the success of their business. They think they can rely on their bookkeepers, accountants, CPAs, and chief financial officers to have these skills. I have personally sat through many a meeting where the dialogue went something like this:

Banker:(*to the CEO*) Fred, in reviewing your financials for the last three years, we notice that your inventory growth has exceeded your sales growth by a significant percentage and has resulted in a large amount of your working capital being invested in inventory. Why is that?

Fred: Well, umm ... I ...

Nancy: (*the chief financial officer*) It's because we've had to restructure our product line. Three years ago, widgets accounted for 60 percent of our sales; they generated twelve to fifteen inventory turns a year. Unfortunately, we lost half our market share to Deep

Pockets Inc., who developed a new process that cut the manufacturing cost—and therefore their price—by 15 percent. In order to maintain our sales growth level we developed the gidget, which replaced our widget sales but requires that we maintain higher inventory because of all the various models that we have to offer.

Banker: (*turning to Fred*) Do you agree?

Fred: Yeah, I think that explains it.

Banker: (*looking at Fred*) Well, then how do you explain the dramatic improvement in inventory turns that you are projecting next year?

Fred: Well, now let me see. (*shuffles some papers*) Nancy, can I borrow your copy of the projections? I seem to have misplaced mine. (*grabs at papers sliding away*) You say we're forecasting a dramatic improvement in inventory turns? (*stares at the documents for about two minutes*) Y'know, I don't really personally get into the details of the numbers. I pretty much let Nancy handle them. My motto is never to second-guess the bean counters.

Many business owners and CEOs operate under the assumption that because they are experts in either sales, marketing, production, or engineering, bankers don't expect them to have these financial skills. That may be true of some bankers. What business owners and CEOs often lose sight of, however, is that the business doesn't exist to generate sales, create customers, or make products. It exists to generate profits and cash; otherwise, it's a hobby. If you don't understand the rudiments and can't use the tools of financial management, why should your banker have confidence in your ability to manage a profit-making enterprise? As an analogy, how would you feel about booking passage to cross the ocean on a ship whose captain did not understand the rudiments or know how to use the tools of navigation? Would you be comfortable about entrusting your life and the lives of your family to an "illiterate" captain? Probably not. You can expect that a banker will be equally cautious about entrusting her money to a business owner or CEO who is financially illiterate.

In the balance of this chapter I will discuss a number of financial concepts and issues that invariably arise during the preparation of loan proposals and in the due diligence meetings with bankers.

These discussions presuppose a certain level of financial literacy on the part of the reader. In presenting these concepts, I have a dual purpose. For those who possess the appropriate level of financial literacy, I believe the concepts will prove helpful in their pursuit of financing. For those who are not familiar with the terms or cannot fathom the discussion, consider this chapter a wake-up call. You need to get busy and improve your financial literacy skills if you're serious about getting financing.

In the discussions that follow, I will use as my example the XYZ Company, a manufacturer of women's suits, skirts, sportswear, and coats. XYZ's balance sheets and profit and loss statements (P/Ls) for the four years 1990–1993 are shown in Tables 7–1 and 7–2.

TABLE 7–1

XYZ Company

Historical Balance Sheets (Figures in Thousands of Dollars)

	1990	1991	1992	1993
Assets				
Cash	288	294	280	340
Accounts receivable	1,524	1,356	1,336	1,420
Inventory	1,556	1,932	2,144	2,340
Prepaid expenses	256	272	280	300
Total current assets	3,624	3,854	4,040	4,400
Fixed assets	760	760	780	840
Notes receivable	264	324	352	400
Total noncurrent assets	1,024	1,084	1,132	1,240
Total assets	4,648	4,938	5,172	5,640
Liabilities				
Accounts payable	760	767	990	832
Notes payable	1,682	1,825	1,536	1,544
Accrued liabilities	150	160	170	180
Total current liabilities	2,592	2,752	2,696	2,556
Long-term debt	268	212	328	344
Total liabilities	2,860	2,964	3,024	2,900
Net worth	1,788	1,974	2,148	2,740

TABLE 7–2

XYZ Company
Historical Profit and Loss Statements
(Figures in Thousands of Dollars)

	1990	1991	1992	1993
Net sales	6,168	6,832	10,500	13,176
Cost of goods sold	4,504	5,136	7,768	9,832
	1,664	1,696	2,732	3,344
Expenses				
G & A	475	369	916	1,080
Selling	605	725	995	1,220
R & D	311	355	485	650
Total expenses	1,391	1,449	2,396	2,950
Operating profit	323	347	336	394
Interest	175	183	168	170
Other revenue (expenses)	52	48	48	60
Net profit pre-tax	200	212	216	284
Taxes	28	24	32	84
Net profit	172	188	184	200

Financial Analysis and the Use of Ratios

The financial analysis of a company is focused on answering the following questions: (1) What is its condition of solvency? (2) How has it performed during the recent past? (3) How does it compare to other firms of the same size in the same industry?

The basic tools of financial analysis are *ratios*, numerical values calculated by dividing one financial quantity by another. They can be expressed as numbers or percentages. The theory underlying the use of ratios is twofold. First, certain financial relationships in themselves are measures of soundness; just as body temperature is a measure of the physical health of an individual, some ratios are a measure of the financial health of the company. Second, businesses in the same industry and catering to the same markets will exhibit financial relationships (normalized for volume) that are compara-ble. As mentioned previously, Robert Morris Associates annually publishes financial ratios by Standard Industrial Code (SIC) and business size within the SIC. A page from the 1992 *Annual Statement Studies* for SIC 2337 (38), the industry within which XYZ falls, is shown in Table 7–3.

Balance sheets and profit and loss statements from businesses within the same SIC are grouped to derive the upper quartile, the median, and the lower quartile for each ratio within each SIC number grouping. The upper quartile is the value that is better than three-fourths and worse than one-fourth of the ratios of the companies in the industry. The median is the value that separates the stronger half of the ratios from the weaker half. The lower quartile is the value that is better than one-fourth and worse than three-fourths of the ratios.

The ratios that are most used in financial analysis and the aspects of the firm they measure are shown in Table 7–4. The significance of these ratios are as follows:

- *Liquidity*. The liquidity ratios measure how well a firm can meet its obligations as they come due. The quick ratio is a "tighter" ratio than the current ratio in that it does not include inventory. Both ratios assume that all delinquent accounts receivable and slow-moving inventory are not included in the calculation of the ratio. A quick ratio of 1 or greater is an indicator of a highly liquid company.
- *Solvency*. The debt-to-worth ratio shows what percentage of the assets belongs to outside creditors and what percentage belongs to the owners of the business. I discussed the significance of this ratio in some depth in a previous chapter.
- *Profitability*. The gross profit margin is a measure of the ability of the operating departments to generate revenue to accommodate all operating and debt service expenses and company profits. The profit margin measures the rate of return on sales; it is what is left of net sales after subtracting cost of goods sold, selling, administrative and general expenses prior to the payment of interest and income taxes. It is a measure of the overall efficiency of the business.
- *Investment Management*. The return on assets measures the effectiveness of management in employing the resources available to it. The return on investment (ROI) represents the financial return on the owner's investment in the business and is a measure

TABLE 7–3

Manufacturers—Women's Suits, Skirts, Sportswear and Coats
SIC# 2337(38)

Current Data Sorted by Assets						Type of Statement	Comparative Historical Data	
1	8	16	21	5	2	Unqualified	57	39
5	13	29	6			Reviewed	48	44
7	9	1				Compiled	18	15
						Tax Returns		
1	3	1	1			Other	19	15
	41(4/1-9/30/91)		88(10/1/91–3/31/92)				6/30/87–3/31/88	6/30/88–3/31/89
0-500M	500M-2MM	2-10MM	10-50MM	50-100MM	100-250MM		ALL	ALL
13	31	49	28	6	2	NUMBER OF STATEMENTS	142	113
%	%	%	%	%	%	ASSETS	%	%
14.0	4.4	3.9	4.1			Cash & Equivalents	8.7	7.4
26.7	34.2	32.4	24.5			Trade Receivables - (net)	28.3	32.5
30.0	42.4	40.7	49.2			Inventory	38.6	40.1
2.1	1.7	7.5	5.4			All Other Current	3.2	1.6
72.7	82.7	84.4	83.2			Total Current	78.9	81.5
18.3	10.3	8.9	11.2			Fixed Assets (net)	14.1	11.2
.9	.1	1.3	2.0			Intangibles (net)	.6	1.4
8.1	6.9	5.3	3.6			All Other Non-Current	6.4	5.9
100.0	100.0	100.0	100.0			Total	100.0	100.0
						LIABILITIES		
14.9	19.1	17.4	18.0			Notes Payable-Short Term	16.3	19.4
3.5	3.1	2.5	1.2			Cur. Mat.-L/T/D	2.8	1.7
14.5	20.3	27.3	16.7			Trade Payables	18.1	17.7
.8	.6	.4	.6			Income Taxes Payable	1.4	1.0
10.2	8.8	9.1	8.2			All Other Current	11.3	11.0
43.8	51.9	56.8	44.6			Total Current	49.9	50.9
12.0	8.7	7.7	6.1			Long Term Debt	8.6	10.4
.0	.8	.0	.1			Deferred Taxes	.2	.1
3.9	5.9	1.7	2.9			Net Worth	38.1	36.3
40.3	32.6	33.9	46.3			All Other Non-Current	3.2	2.2
100.0	100.0	100.0	100.0			Total Liabilities & Net Worth	100.0	100.0
						INCOME DATA		
100.0	100.0	100.0	100.0			Net Sales	100.0	100.0
28.1	26.5	26.5	26.5			Gross Profit	29.4	28.6
24.6	22.9	21.4	22.9			Operating Expenses	25.4	24.0
3.5	3.6	5.1	3.6			Operating Profit	4.1	4.7
.0	.7	3.1	1.7			All Other Expenses (net)	1.4	1.4
3.4	2.9	2.0	1.9			Profit Before Taxes	2.7	3.3
						RATIOS		
2.1	2.4	1.9	2.5				2.1	2.2
1.7	1.5	1.5	1.7			Current	1.6	1.6
1.0	1.3	1.3	1.5				1.3	1.3
1.3	1.2	1.0	.9				1.1	1.0
1.0	.8	.7	.7			Quick (140)	.8	.8
.5	.3	.3	.3				.5	.5
8 48.2	24 15.1	11 32.1	15 25.0				18 20.5	20 18.7
17 21.7	48 8.0	44 8.3	43 8.4			Sales/Receivables	38 9.5	44 8.3
45 8.1	58 6.3	59 6.2	61 6.0				60 6.1	64 5.7
4 99.5	36 10.1	51 7.1	79 4.6				43 8.5	49 7.5
33 10.9	87 4.2	62 5.9	101 3.6			Cost of Sales/Inventory	66 5.5	78 4.7
56 6.5	118 3.1	85 4.3	152 2.4				101 3.6	104 3.5

TABLE 7–3 (*continued*)

Current Data Sorted by Assets						Type of Statement	Comparative Historical Data	
1	8	16	21	5	2	Unqualified	57	39
5	13	29	6			Reviewed	48	44
7	9	1				Compiled	18	15
						Tax Returns		
	1	3	1	1		Other	19	15
	41(4/1-9/30/91)		88(10/1/91–3/31/92)				6/30/87–3/31/88	6/30/88–3/31/89
0-500M	500M-2MM	2-10MM	10-50MM	50-100MM	100-250MM		ALL	ALL
13	31	49	28	6	2	NUMBER OF STATEMENTS	142	113
2 197.0	16 23.4	23 15.8	26 13.8				17 21.5	17 21.4
17 21.7	31 11.9	45 8.1	35 10.5			Cost of Sales/Payables	27 13.3	29 12.7
27 13.3	48 7.6	57 6.4	40 9.2				47 7.8	42 8.7
9.5	5.5	7.8	5.0				6.2	5.6
18.0	10.4	12.9	6.6			Sales/Working Capital	10.0	8.9
UND	34.1	18.2	8.6				20.8	16.3
7.2	6.7	4.4	3.5				5.3	7.6
(10) 3.2	(24) 2.8	(38) 1.9	(25) 2.4			EBIT/Interest	(113) 2.7	(98) 2.9
1.5	1.3	1.3	1.4				1.4	1.4
	10.0	12.6	7.4			Net Profit + Depr.,	17.5	15.2
	(11) 2.2	(19) 1.6	(11) 5.1			Dep., Amort./Cur.	(59) 4.0	(47) 4.0
	.5	.5	1.8			Mat. L/T/D	1.6	.9
.1	.1	.1	.2				.1	.1
.3	.2	.1	.3			Fixed worth	.3	.2
.9	.5	.3	.4				.5	.5
.8	1.2	1.1	.8				1.0	1.1
1.4	2.2	2.5	1.4			Debt/Worth	1.7	1.8
4.5	5.1	3.9	2.3				3.7	4.0
88.9	37.8	36.6	21.0			% Profit Before	43.5	38.2
(12) 33.6	(30) 21.0	(48) 23.4	10.3			Taxes/Tangible	(136) 22.3	(108) 19.3
7.6	7.7	8.7	3.3			Net Worth	3.0	5.5
27.3	11.9	10.6	6.8			% Profit BeforeTaxes/	14.9	11.8
12.6	7.5	5.6	5.3			Total Assets	7.5	6.6
2.3	1.5	1.7	2.1				1.2	1.5
231.0	125.4	156.1	31.8				68.8	109.6
43.0	45.9	84.2	24.1			Sales/Net Fixed Assets	36.1	38.4
21.1	16.6	23.4	14.5				12.5	18.8
6.6	3.9	4.2	2.8				3.9	3.4
4.4	2.9	3.1	2.3			Sales/Total Assets	2.8	2.8
3.7	1.9	2.3	1.8				2.2	2.1
	.3	.2	.6			% Depr. Dep.,	.4	.3
	(26) .6	(39) .3	(25) .9			Amort. /Sales	(116) .7	(98) .8
	1.1	.8	1.4				1.3	1.5
	1.5	3.4				% Officers', Directors,'	2.2	2.0
	(16) 3.0	(20) 4.4				Owners' Comp.Sales	(59) 4.8	(50) 3.3
	8.1	7.9					8.0	7.6
14078M	120822M	831654M	1337526M	844279M	586693M	Net Sales ($)	2590984M	189195M
2515M	35134M	253399M	577640M	37073M	323666M	Total Assets ($)	967483M	75846M

TABLE 7-3 *(continued)*

Manufacturers—Women's Suits, Skirts, Sportswear and Coats
sic# 2337(38)

	Comparative Historical Data			Type of Statement	Current Data Sorted by Sales					
	43	31	53	Unqualified	1	2	5	5	9	31
	50	28	53	Reviewed	3	8	6	9	15	12
	27	26	17	Compiled	7	8			2	
				Tax Returns						
	10	10	6	Other			1	2	2	1
	6/30/89–	4/1/90–	4/1/91–							
	3/31/90	3/31/91	3/31/92		41(4/1-9/30/01)			88(10/1/91-3/31/92)		
	ALL	ALL	ALL		0-1MM	1-3MM	3-5MM	5-10MM	10-25MM	25MM & OVER
	130	93	129	NUMBER OF STATEMENTS	11	18	12	16	28	44
	%	%	%	**ASSETS**	%	%	%	%	%	%
	7.6	7.1	5.0	Cash & Equivalents	13.3	6.1	4.0	2.0	4.5	4.2
	27.5	32.0	30.1	Trade Receivables - (net)	28.1	27.9	26.8	41.3	37.3	23.9
	38.8	39.2	42.2	Inventory	28.4	45.0	40.3	36.3	40.3	48.4
	4.5	2.6	4.7	All Other Current	2.2	1.2	3.8	2.1	4.1	8.2
	78.5	80.8	82.0	Total Current	72.0	80.1	74.9	81.7	86.3	84.6
	13.4	13.4	11.0	Fixed Assets (net)	17.3	14.1	14.1	10.2	7.7	9.8
	1.7	1.1	1.4	Intangibles (net)	1.2	.1	.0	3.8	.2	2.4
	6.4	4.8	5.5	All Other Non-Current	9.5	5.7	11.0	4.3	5.9	3.2
	100.0	100.0	100.0	Total	100.0	100.0	100.0	100.0	100.0	100.0
				LIABILITIES						
	17.1	21.2	17.4	Notes Payable-Short Term	22.8	16.6	13.2	23.8	17.7	15.0
	2.8	2.2	2.5	Cur. Mat.-L/T/D	3.1	3.5	3.8	3.2	2.2	1.5
	17.3	17.0	21.3	Trade Payables	11.0	15.0	20.9	31.8	2.18	22.3
	.8	.4	.5	Income Taxes Payable	1.0	.2	1.1	.4	.9	.3
	10.6	9.5	8.9	All Other Current	12.3	7.3	9.2	7.7	10.1	8.4
	48.6	50.2	50.6	Total Current	50.1	42.5	48.3	67.0	52.7	47.5
	9.2	9.3	9.1	Long Term Debt	10.2	13.1	13.9	6.3	4.1	10.0
	.1	.1	.3	Deferred Taxes	.0	.6	1.3	.1	.0	.1
	3.1	2.2	3.4	All Other Non Current	1.7	10.5	1.4	1.9	1.4	3.2
	38.9	38.2	36.6	Net Worth	38.0	33.2	35.2	24.8	41.8	39.1
	100.0	100.0	100.0	Total Liabilities & Net Worth	100.0	100.0	100.0	100.0	100.0	100.0
				INCOME DATA						
	100.0	100.0	100.0	Net Sales	100.0	100.0	100.0	100.0	100.0	100.0
	28.6	24.3	26.7	Gross Profit	27.2	28.3	23.6	27.4	25.5	27.3
	24.4	20.6	22.2	Operating Expenses	24.6	23.7	21.1	25.5	22.1	20.2
	4.3	3.7	4.5	Operating Profit	2.5	4.5	2.5	1.9	3.4	7.1
	1.5	1.7	2.1	All Other Expenses (net)	–.2	1.3	–.7	1.2	1.1	4.8
	2.8	2.0	2.4	Profit Before Taxes	2.7	3.2	3.2	.7	2.3	2.3
				RATIOS						
	2.3	2.1	2.0		1.9	2.7	1.9	1.4	2.1	2.1
	1.5	1.5	1.6	Current	1.4	1.7	1.5	1.2	1.6	1.7
	1.2	1.3	1.3		1.0	1.5	1.2	1.0	1.3	1.5
	1.2	1.1	1.1		1.2	1.4	1.0	.9	1.3	.9
	.7	.8	.7	Quick	1.0	.8	.6	.7	.8	.6
	.4	.6	.3		.3	.5	.2	.3	.5	.2
	13 27.7	24 15.0	17 21.8		7 50.8	15 23.6	9 38.9	43 8.4	33 11.2	11 33.7
	36 10.2	47 7.8	42 8.7	Sales/Receivables	25 14.7	44 8.3	26 14.3	51 7.1	54 6.7	33 11.1
	64 5.7	64 5.7	58 6.3		49 7.5	61 6.0	49 7.4	60 6.1	68 5.4	56 6.5
	38 9.5	49 7.4	53 6.9		3 113.7	58 6.3	29 12.8	37 9.9	51 7.2	65 5.6
	70 5.2	72 5.1	74 4.9	Cost of Sales/Inventory	55 6.6	85 4.3	74 4.9	57 6.4	64 5.7	83 4.4
	114 3.2	104 3.5	104 3.5		87 4.2	140 2.6	99 3.7	89 4.1	101 3.6	118 3.1

TABLE 7-3 (continued)

Comparative Historical Data			Type of Statement	Current Data Sorted by Sales					
43	31	53	Unqualified	1	2	5	5	9	31
50	28	53	Reviewed	3	8	6	9	15	12
27	26	17	Compiled Tax Returns	7	8			2	
10	10	6	Other			1	2	2	1
6/30/89–3/31/90	4/1/90–3/31/91	4/1/91–3/31/92		41(4/1-9/30/01)			88(10/1/91-3/31/92)		
ALL	ALL	ALL		0-1MM	1-3MM	3-5MM	5-10MM	10-25MM	25MM & OVER
130	93	129	NUMBER OF STATEMENTS	11	18	12	16	28	44
16 23.2	17 21.5	21 17.6	Cost of Sales/Payables	1 341.0	15 24.5	20 18.1	39 9.4	19 19.4	25 14.5
25 14.7	28 13.0	35 10.4		18 20.4	20 18.2	36 10.2	56 6.5	35 10.3	35 10.5
44 8.3	43 8.5	49 7.4		33 11.0	46 7.9	51 7.2	65 5.6	51 7.2	45 8.1
6.1	6.0	6.1	Sales/Working Capital	7.7	4.6	6.4	14.3	6.5	5.6
11.0	8.9	9.3		15.2	8.3	12.1	26.3	9.1	7.8
20.4	17.1	17.5		UND	19.7	32.2	NM	13.3	12.4
5.0	4.2	4.8	EBIT/Interest		5.4		6.6	5.7	3.2
(105) 2.3	(82) 2.1	(105) 2.4			(17) 2.7		(13) 2.1	(20) 1.6	(40) 2.4
1.2	1.3	1.3			1.0		.8	.9	1.6
9.2	13.5	10.1	Net Profit + Depr. Dep.,					7.3	10.3
(61) 3.0	(41) 3.2	(50) 2.2	Amort. /Cur.					10 1.3	(20) 5.2
.9	.7	.7	Mat. L/T/D					.4	1.7
.1	.1	.1	Fixed/Worth	.2	.1	.1	.1	.1	.1
.3	.3	.2		.3	.2	.4	.3	.1	.3
.6	.6	.5		1.0	.6	.6	3.1	.3	.4
.9	1.0	1.1	Debt/Worth	.8	1.2	1.1	1.9	.8	1.2
2.0	1.8	1.9		1.9	2.0	1.7	4.1	1.4	1.9
3.6	3.6	3.4		6.0	3.4	4.1	10.3	2.8	3.1
36.9	27.9	34.6	% Profit Before Taxes/Tangible Net Worth	66.7	34.4	33.9	55.1	39.3	27.5
(122) 17.9	(90) 14.0	(124) 17.3		(10) 32.2	(17) 20.5	17.7	(15) 23.6	12.0	(42) 16.1
5.2	3.5	6.1		6.6	3.0	2.5	3.9	3.9	5.9
13.1	9.0	10.1	% Profit Before Taxes/ Total Assets	25.0	16.0	20.4	8.7	10.3	8.5
5.7	4.0	5.8		7.9	6.5	4.5	6.1	5.3	6.1
1.9	1.4	1.4		1.9	.3	.4	1.0	1.1	2.4
74.9	78.7	125.3	Sales/Net Fixed Assets	54.7	377.3	71.1	143.4	154.3	95.6
30.2	28.9	38.3		28.0	58.9	30.3	54.1	70.2	28.6
17.1	14.1	15.9		15.0	14.8	12.6	12.1	20.6	15.1
3.6	3.3	3.9	Sales/Total Assets	4.4	4.1	4.3	4.1	3.6	3.8
2.9	2.4	2.8		3.8	2.3	3.1	3.4	3.0	2.7
2.0	2.0	2.1		2.2	1.7	2.5	1.7	2.3	2.1
.3	.4	.3	% Depr., Dep., Amort. /Sales		.4	.3	.3	.2	.3
(115) .7	(85) .7	(106) .6			(14) .6	(11) .7	(13) .8	(22) .5	(39) .7
1.2	1.2	.13			1.1	1.8	1.9	.9	1.3
1.8	1.6	2.6	%Officers', Directors', Owners' Comp./Sales		1.5		3.3	2.6	2.6
(65) 3.9	(45) 3.7	(53) 3.7			(11) 2.6		(10) 4.1	(11) 4.5	(11) 4.1
6.9	6.4	7.8			4.2		8.6	8.2	8.4
2707505M	2535679M	3735052M	Net Sales ($)	6520M	37793M	46954M	123913M	444702M	3075170M
1288913M	1069158M	1563085M	Total Assets ($)	2793M	16594M	19450M	46597M	173369M	1304282M

© Robert Morris Associates 1992   M = $thousand   MM = $million

TABLE 7–4
Definitions of Financial Ratios

Liquidity

Current ratio $= \dfrac{\text{Current Assets}}{\text{Current Liabilities}}$

Quick ratio $= \dfrac{\text{Cash + Cash Equivalent + Accounts Receivable}}{\text{Current Liabilities}}$

Solvency
Debt-to-worth ratio $= \dfrac{\text{Total liabilities}}{\text{Taxable net worth}}$

Profitability
Gross profit ratio $= \dfrac{\text{Sales – Cost of sales}}{\text{Sales}}$

Return of sales $= \dfrac{\text{Net profit}}{\text{Sales}}$

Investment Management
Return on investment $= \dfrac{\text{Net profit}}{\text{Tangible net worth}}$

Return on assets $= \dfrac{\text{Net profit}}{\text{Total assets}}$

Activity
$\dfrac{\text{Sales}}{\text{Working capital}} = \dfrac{\text{Sales}}{\text{Current assets – Current liability}}$

Assets/Liabilities Management

Accounts receivable Turnover $= \dfrac{\text{Sales}}{\text{Accounts receivable}}$

Accounts receivable days (ARD) $= \dfrac{365}{\text{Accounts receivable turnover}}$

Inventory turnover $= \dfrac{\text{Cost of sales}}{\text{Inventory}}$

Inventory days (InvD) $= \dfrac{365}{\text{Inventory turnover}}$

Accounts payable turnover $= \dfrac{\text{Cost of sales}}{\text{Accounts payable}}$

Accounts payable days (APD) $= \dfrac{365}{\text{Accounts payable turnover}}$

of management's overall capability. The ROI allows the owner to compare the return she is achieving in this particular business with the return she could realize if she made alternative investments.

• *Activity.* The rate of working capital turnover measures whether the working capital used in the normal conduct of the business is adequate to support the scope of operations.

• *Asset/Liability Management.* These ratios measure the ability of operating management to manage effectively the company's primary current assets (accounts receivable and inventory) and its primary liabilities (accounts payable). High values of the turnover ratios indicate that the company is able to generate a high level of business activity for the size of its current assets and liabilities. The average age of the accounts receivable is measured by the accounts receivable days (ARD); the average time inventory is maintained in stock is measured by the inventory days (InvD); and the average time trade creditors allow the company to pay its accounts payable is measured by the accounts payable days (APD). Typically, operating management strives to keep ARD and InvD low and APD high in order to maximize the leverage of its investment in working capital.

In Table 7–5 I have shown the calculation of the fourteen ratios of the XYZ Company for the period ended 1993. I've also included in the figure the values from the 1992 *Annual Statement Studies* for firm sizes of $10 million to $25 million. The comparison of the values of the ratios for XYZ with the *Annual Statement Studies* values reveals a number of important facts. The liquidity, profitability, return on assets, and accounts payable turnover of XYZ follow closely the median of the *Annual Statement Studies* values. The company appears to do an outstanding job collecting its accounts receivable; however, it does a poor job turning its inventory, and its ROI is below the *Annual Statement Studies* median.

Ratios are also used in financial analysis to identify and understand how the company has operated in the past and to explore what corrective actions might reverse a negative trend. Table 7–6 shows the fourteen ratios for each of the four years of operating history of the XYZ Company. Between 1990 and 1993 the company improved in its ability to manage its current assets, substantially

TABLE 7–5
Financial Ratios of XYZ Company

			Ratios of XYZ Company	Ratios for Industry		
				Upper Quartile	Median Quartile	Lower Quartile
Liquidity						
Current ratio	=	$\frac{4,400}{2,556}$	= 1.72	2.1	1.6	1.3
Quick ratio	=	$\frac{340 + 1420}{2,556}$	= 0.69	1.3	0.8	0.5
Solvency						
Debt to worth	=	$\frac{2,900}{2,740}$	= 1.058	0.8	1.4	2.8
Profitability						
Gross profit	=	$\frac{3,344}{13,176}$	= 0.254	N/A	0.255	N/A
Return on sales	=	$\frac{284}{13,176}$	= 0.022	N/A	0.023	N/A
Investment Management						
Return on investment	=	$\frac{284}{2,740}$	= 10.4%	39.3%	12.0%	3.9%
Return on assets	=	$\frac{284}{5,640}$	= 5.0%	10.3%	5.3%	1.1%
Activity						
$\frac{\text{Sales}}{\text{Working capital}}$	=	$\frac{13,176}{4400 - 2556}$	= 7.145	6.5	9.1	13.3
Assets/Liabilities Management						
Accounts receivable turnover	=	$\frac{13,176}{1420}$	= 9.3	11.2	6.7	5.4
Accounts receivable days (ARD)	=	$\frac{365}{9.3}$	= 39.2	33	54	68
Inventory turnover	=	$\frac{9,832}{2340}$	= 4.2	7.2	5.7	3.6
Inventory days (InvD)	=	$\frac{365}{4.2}$	= 86.9	51	64	101
Accounts payable turnover	=	$\frac{9,832}{832}$	= 11.8	19.4	10.3	7.2
Accounts payable days (APD)	=	$\frac{365}{11.8}$	= 30.9	19	35	51

TABLE 7-6
Historical Ratios of XYZ Company, 1990–1993

	1990	1991	1992	1993
Current	1.40	1.40	1.49	1.72
Quick	0.70	0.60	0.60	0.69
Debt to Worth	1.60	1.50	1.41	1.51
Gross Profit	0.27	0.26	0.26	0.25
Return on sales	0.032	0.031	0.021	0.021
Return on investment	11.2	10.7	10.1	10.4
Return on assets	4.3	4.3	4.2	5.5
Sales to working capital	5.98	6.19	7.81	7.15
Accounts receivable turnover	4.05	5.04	7.90	9.30
Accounts receivable days (ARD)	90.0	72.4	46.2	39.3
Inventory turnover	2.9	2.7	3.6	4.2
Inventory days (InvD)	125	135	101	87
Accounts payable turnover	8.1	8.9	10.6	11.8
Accounts payable days (APD)	45.1	41.0	34.4	30.9

increasing the turnover of accounts receivable, inventory, and accounts payable. Unfortunately, although sales doubled over the four years, the return on sales decreased by one-third, which does not reflect favorably on management.

Break-even Analysis

If the economy turns sour and sales begin to fall off, you may determine that it is time to retrench. A critical piece of information you will need to know is at what sales volume (units or dollars) you will break even on a profit and loss basis, and at what volume you will cover all your scheduled principal payments.

In order to perform a break-even analysis, all your operating expenses need to be placed into the following three categories: fixed, variable, and mixed. *Fixed* expenses are those expenses that, for a broad range of sales volume, do not vary with sales. They include the rent on business facilities, property taxes, salaries and expenses of administrative personnel, and insurance premiums. *Variable* expenses increase and decrease linearly with volume and include manufacturing materials, direct labor, packaging materials, and shipping costs. *Mixed* costs have both fixed and variable elements and need to be studied further and broken down into their fixed and variable parts. Utilities (such as telephone expenses, heating/air conditioning, and water) usually have both fixed and variable elements. Similarly, manufacturing supervision costs will probably include administrative personnel (such as the plant manager and purchasing supervisor) whose costs are fixed, but will also include the cost of foremen and buyers, the numbers of whom vary directly with sales volume. Compensation for salespersons will usually consist of a base plus a commission that varies with sales. When the analysis of the mixed costs is complete, all of the costs of the business will have been divided into fixed and variable costs.

An analysis we performed on the XYZ Company showed that at a sales level of $13,176,000, fixed and variable costs were as follows:

Fixed costs (F):	$5,400,000
Variable costs (V):	7,676,000
Variable costs as a percentage of sales (v):	$\frac{\$7,676,000}{\$13,176,000} = .582$

The equation for the after-tax profit of the firm, P, at a sales volume of S and a tax rate of t, is

$$P = (S - V - F)(1 - t) \qquad (7.1)$$

Since $V = vS$, the equation for the firm becomes

$$P = \{S(1 - v) - F\}(1 - t)$$

Assuming that $P > D$, where D is the scheduled principal payments, the sales level at which the company will break even, defined as S' ("S prime") is

$$S' > D/(1 - v)(1 - t) + F/(1 - v) \qquad (7.2)$$

Assuming that XYZ is in the 34 percent tax bracket, and that it must repay $100,000 of principal during the next year,

$$S' > \$100,000 / (.418) (.66) + \$5,400,000 / (.418)$$
$$> \$362,476 + \$12,918,660 = \$13,281,136$$

If there are no principal payments scheduled for the next year, the sales level required to achieve break-even operation is:

$$S' > F / (1 - v) = \$12,918,660$$

The previous equation can be used to calculate the effect on the break-even sales value, S', of increasing or decreasing fixed and variable costs and changes in product pricing.

Where Did the Money Go? Understanding Sources and Uses

The simplest way to view cash flow is to define it as the difference in the cash balances of the company on two dates; however, this view does not provide any information as to how that difference occurred. For example, if the cash balance on December 31, 1992, was $1,000,000 and the cash balance on December 31, 1993, was $2,000,000, does that mean that management did an outstanding job and should be rewarded with large bonuses? Not necessarily. Perhaps the company experienced substantial losses during the year, but management sold assets, borrowed up to the limit of the credit line, and delayed payments on accounts payable to create a huge war chest—not the kind of performance that usually results in accolades from directors. This example makes clear the fact that it's not the cash balance that is important, but how it was created.

In order to address this problem, in 1971 the Financial Accounting Standards Board mandated that as part of the financial reporting of public companies, a statement of "sources and uses" (also known as a statement of changes in financial condition) of funds must be included. A source and use of funds statement follows the money trail. It tells where the money came from to increase working capital, where it was spent to decrease working capital, and what changes took place in the current assets and current liabilities which make up working capital.

Changes in working capital can only take place as a result of changes in noncurrent balance sheet items—namely, net worth, noncurrent assets, and noncurrent liabilities. The changes in these accounts are also reflected in the sources and uses statement under financing activities (noncurrent liabilities) and investment activities (noncurrent assets). The net result of these transactions is manifested in a change in the net worth of the firm.

Table 7–7 shows the manner in which a sources and uses financial is created for the XYZ Company for the period ending 1993.

Working Capital

I discussed the concept of working capital briefly in Chapter 4; however, the concept is so important and is so poorly understood that it is appropriate to revisit it in this chapter on financial literacy.

Working capital (WC) is defined as current assets minus current liabilities, which is equal to cash + cash equivalents + accounts receivable + inventory + prepaids - accounts payable - short-term debt.

In most operating companies, the accounts receivable (AR), inventory (Inv) and accounts payable (AP) dominate the working capital account, with the other components usually being small and fixed. Accounts receivable, inventory, and accounts payable all vary linearly with sales. Therefore, $WC \approx$ (is approximately) $AR + Inv - AP$, which can, using our ratios, be written as

$$WC \approx ARD\ (S)/360 + InvD\ (S)\ (1 - g)/360 - APD\ (S)\ (1 - g)/360$$

Where ARD, InvD, and APD are the day's accounts receivable, inventory, and accounts payable, respectively, g is the gross margin, and S is the sales volume. Dividing both sides of the equation by S, we obtain the following:

$$WC/S \approx ARD/360 + InvD(1 - g)/360 - APD\ (1 - g)/360 \qquad (7.3)$$

TABLE 7-7

XYZ Company Sources and Uses of Funds, Year Ended 1993 (in Thousands of Dollars)

Funds provided by operations		
	Net income	$240
plus	Depreciation	100
equals	Traditional cash flow	340
plus	Other expenses not affecting working capital (e.g., deferred taxes)	-0-
less	Other income not affecting working capital (e.g., equity earnings)	-0-
equals	Working capital provided by operations	$340
less	Increase in accounts receivable	(84)
less	Increase in inventories	(156)
less	Increase in prepaid assets	(20)
plus	Increase in accounts payable	(160)
plus	Increase in notes payable	8
plus	Increase in accrued liabilities	10
equals	Net cash generated (used) by operations	(62)
Funds provided by investment activities		
plus	Payments received on notes receivable	40
less	Funds received from sale on fixed assets	-0-
less	Purchase of fixed assets	(160)
less	Increase in notes receivable	(48)
equals	Net cash generated (used) by investment activities	(168)
Funds provided by financing activities		
	Proceeds from bank loan	36
plus	Proceeds from sale of stock	-0-
less	Principal payments on debt	-0-
equals	Net cash generated (used) by financing activities	36

Increase (decrease) in cash = (62) + (168) + 36 =   (194)

The ratio of sales to working capital (which is *S/WC*) was discussed in Chapter 4, and Table 4–1 shows the values of *S/WC* for several industries. The previous equation shows clearly why the sales-to-working-capital ratio is characteristic of an industry, since it is a function of payment terms, collection terms, inventory turnover, and gross profit margin, all of which can vary enormously from industry to industry.

By this point you should appreciate the fact that if your sales grow, your accounts receivable and inventory will grow at a greater rate than your vendors will support with accounts payable. This gap—between the need to finance accounts receivable and inventory and the credit that the trade can be expected to provide—must be filled by internally generated funds (after-tax profits or the sale of fixed assets) or capital from an external source. If sales growth is attempted without the corresponding expansion in working capital, the company will inevitably experience cash flow problems and bring the expansion to a halt. Seventy percent of the financially troubled firms I've worked with over the past fourteen years created their own serious problems by expanding beyond the capacity of their working capital. Many of these firms were managed by former salesmen, for whom it is axiomatic that increased sales are good and occupy the same hallowed position in American life as do baseball, motherhood, and apple pie. Since they are not financially literate, they simply cannot comprehend the fact that increased sales not accompanied by a corresponding increase in working capital can be bad.

The amount of external funds needed to support an expansion can be easily approximated by the following calculation. Assume that your business is operating comfortably at a ratio of sales to working capital of K, and you are generating an after-tax profit of p percent. You wish to expand the company's yearly sales from S to $S + \Delta S$ during the next year. You have determined that in order to increase the capacity of your plant, you will have to add C dollars in fixed assets.

Assuming you pay taxes at a rate of t, the funds required, M, are therefore calculated as follows:

$$M = C + \Delta S/K - \{pS + p\Delta S/2\}\,(1 - t) \qquad (7.4)$$

if $C = 0$ (no investment in capital equipment is required), $S = \$5,000,000$, $\Delta S = \$2,000,000$ (a 40 percent increase), $K = 8.0$, $p = .025$, and $t = .34$, then $M = \$253,000$. This calculation can only provide a ballpark estimate, since it does not take into account the fluctuations in sales and cash requirements that occur on a monthly basis.

Before we leave the subject of working capital, I want to point out another error of commission that is frequently made by financially illiterate CEOs: purchasing fixed assets with funds required for working capital. A former client who owned a oil processing facility could never understand why, when the company appeared to be doing so well and was profitable, his controller was fighting with trade creditors. The reason was that he continually raped his working capital to purchase equipment that his bank would not agree to finance. The equation derived above to determine how much funds are necessary to support a growth in sales can also help us calculate the decrease in sales that must occur to accommodate a loss in working capital.

In Equation 7.4, if $M = 0$ (that is, if no funds are available), then the equation can be solved for ΔS as follows:

$$\Delta S = -\frac{C - pS(1 - t)}{1/K - \frac{p(1 - t)}{2}} \qquad (7.5)$$

If $C/(1 - t)$, the pretax investment in capital equipment, is greater than pS (the profit the company will generate), ΔS will be negative. Sales thus will have to decrease to accommodate the loss in working capital.

Assume that a CEO cannot persuade a bank to finance either the equipment she wants or the increase in working capital, but she is determined to go ahead with his expansion plans and purchases the equipment for cash, depleting her working capital. What effect will that ultimately have on her sales volume? Since $C = \$100,000$, $S = \$5,000,000$, $K = 8$, $p = .025$, and $t = .34$, $\Delta S = -\$149,572$. Sales will ultimately have to decrease unless the CEO can persuade her trade creditors to provide improved terms. Keep this analysis in mind the next time you are tempted to purchase a car, truck, machine, computer system, or the like without the necessary long-term financing.

Projecting the Future

The projection you will provide to your banker to support the loan request will consist of a projected income statement, a projected balance sheet, a monthly cash forecast, and a set of assumptions on which all three projections are based. In order to discuss these forecasts intelligently with your banker—which will be a very critical element in his decision whether to fund your loan request—it is important that you know how they are prepared and how the underlying assumptions become reflected in the projections.

The Projected Income Statement

The projected income statement is the company's best estimate as to what sales and expenses will be for the future period under consideration. It is the foundation of the forecasts; both the cash projection and the balance sheet projection are derived from the income statement.

For most companies, the sales forecast is the most difficult aspect of the projection in that it depends exclusively on the behavior of entities over which the company has no control—namely, its customers. In some firms, such as those engaged in the distribution and manufacturing of industrial products, the sales forecast is created on the basis of the estimates prepared by individual sales representatives as to what they expect their customers' needs will be, the extent to which the latter will have funds to meet those needs, and the nature and extent of the competition. In industries that service the general consumer (such as retail trade), the sales forecasts are created on the basis of historical trends, the condition of the economy, and the company's merchandising plans. In the case of a new product or a new service introduction, sales projections are always highly speculative.

Once the sales forecast is in place, forecasting expenses is not difficult. Expenses fall into six primary categories: cost of goods sold, selling expenses, research and development (R & D) expenses, general and administrative (G & A) expenses, interest, and other income and expenses. Costs of goods sold and selling expenses will vary with sales in accordance with formulae that reflect both the company's historical ways of doing business and relevant policies the company will implement during the projection period. The R & D and G & A expenses are to a large extent under the control of the management and can be estimated quite accurately.

In order for the income forecast to be as accurate as possible, all categories of expenses must be reviewed in detail to determine those that will remain unchanged, those that will be modified as a result of the sales forecast, and the new types/categories of expenditures that need to be created. Unless the expense projections accurately reflect the company's planned changes in policies and the actions it plans to take (for example, additions or reductions in personnel, the opening or closing of facilities, the consolidation of departments, or the expansion or curtailment of advertising), the effort will not be productive.

The income statement projection for the XYZ Company for December 1994 is shown in Table 7–8, along with the estimated P/L

TABLE 7-8

XYZ Company Projected 1994 Profits and Losses (in Thousands of Dollars)

	1993	Percentage Increase	1994	Ratio	1994 Adjusted[a]
Net sales	13,176	15%	15,152	100	15,152
Cost of sales	9,832	15%	11,307	74.6	11,306
Gross profit	3,344	15%	3,846	25.4	3,846
Expenses					
G & A	1,080	5.8%	1,143	7.5	1,143
Selling	1,220	13%	1,379	9.1	1,379
R & D	650	5%	683	4.5	683
Total expenses	2,950		3,196	22.3	3,196
Operating profit	394		640	3.1	640
Interest	(170)		(170)		(212)
Other Revenue (Expenses)	60	0%	60		60
Net profit pretax	284		530	3.5	488
Taxes	(84)		(180)		(166)
Net Profit	200		350	2.3	322

[a]Adjusted statement reflects increased interest costs that result from borrowings related to cash projection of Figure 7–4.

for 1993. Management has projected a 15 percent increase in sales, no change in gross margin, an increase in selling expenses of 13 percent, an increase in R & D expenses of 5 percent, and an increase in G & A expenses of 5.8 percent. The projection indicates that XYZ's pretax and preinterest operating income will increase by 62 percent to $640,000, and the after-tax income will increase by 75 percent to $350,000. As I discussed in Chapter 4, projections can reflect an optimistic scenario, a pessimistic scenario, or a "realistic" or median scenario depending on how management views the future prospects of the company. To cover the gamut of possibilities, you would prepare nine P/L forecasts: three sales forecasts to reflect the three sales scenarios, and three levels of expenses within each sales scenario.

The Cash Forecast

No matter how small or how large your company is, the cash projection provides the critical information you need to operate. Why? Because in the short term, every company moves on cash. A profit is a number on a financial statement; you can't pay bills with it, and you can't pay employees with it. The fact that you did not earn a profit last month will not affect tomorrow's business, and the lack of a profit will not cause you to shut down your business—but a lack of cash will. Whether your company is high-tech or low-tech, in agriculture or in mining, or wholesale or retail, if you don't have enough cash to pay your obligations when they come due, you will go out of business.

I can't recall the numbers of times I've heard an executive complain; "If our company is so profitable, why don't we have any money to pay our bills?" The cash budget should supply answers to that question, as well as the following ones: How much money will I need from external sources to support operations? When will it be needed? How can I pay it back?

Preparation of a cash budget involves the following steps:

1. Break down the projected income statement into monthly revenues and expenses. This can usually be accomplished on the basis of a review of the previous year's monthly pattern of sales and expenses. For most businesses that exhibit seasonal fluctuations in sales, the percentage of the yearly sales that are achieved in any

month is fairly consistent from one year to another. In other businesses, however, monthly sales can fluctuate all over the map, and all that management can do is to make its best guess as to how the monthly sales will be distributed over the year.

2. Analyze the collection pattern of the accounts receivable. Customers develop bill-paying patterns that need to be reflected in your cash budget. If the terms you offer are net thirty days, a certain percentage of your customers will pay within thirty days of shipment, another percentage will pay within sixty days of shipment, yet another percentage will pay within ninety days of shipment, and a small portion will pay after ninety days or not pay at all. Once you determine this pattern for your customer base, you can develop a formula that relates the timing of your sales to your collections.

3. Determine the requirement for the replenishment and/or the acquisition of inventory to meet the sales projection. The additional processing that must be performed on purchased inventory before it is available for sale will depend on the nature of the process and the operating methods of the company. Since the time that elapses between the acquisition of the inventory and its sale will have a significant effect on the company's cash budget, it is critical that the inventory forecast be realistic. In addition, you will need to estimate the composition of your cost of sales and determine the percentage contributions of direct labor, direct material, cash operating expenses and such noncash items as amortization and depreciation.

4. Analyze the company's payment pattern for trade payables and expenses. Your employees, suppliers, and lessors establish the terms according to which they will be paid. Payment for payroll lags your expense by ten to twenty days, depending on whether your payroll is paid on a weekly or bimonthly basis. Leases for property and equipment are typically paid at the beginning of each month. Accounts payable terms can vary from ten days to sixty days, depending upon the arrangements you have made with your suppliers. You will need to analyze your historical payment patterns to determine when a certain type of expense incurred in a particular month translates into a cash requirement on the company's checkbook. Cash budgets typically project all payroll, recurring expenses, and G & A expenses as being paid in the month incurred,

and they project accounts payable expenses on the basis of historical patterns.

5. Forecast unusual or nonrecurring receipts and expenditures, such as the acquisition of equipment, the receipt of funds for the financing of equipment, the payoff of a delinquent note, or interest payments on notes receivable.

6. Using the forecasts developed in the previous paragraphs record changes in the cash position of the company using a format similar to that shown in Figure 7–1. The cash changes are recorded on a monthly basis using this formula: Ending cash balance = beginning cash balance + cash received during the month - cash paid out during the month. The ending balance in the first month then becomes the beginning balance in the next month until all twelve months are completed. If during any month the cash balance is negative, this shows that the company probably does not have adequate funds to support its sales plan and will require borrowing in order to remain liquid. A proposed financing plan can be added to the cash budget (as shown in Figure 7–2) under the assumption that a financing plan that will meet the company's needs is in place.

Figures 7–4 and 7–5 show the cash budget and required financing for the XYZ Company. The accounts receivable and accounts payable histories, monthly sales plan, inventory plan, and accounts payable plan are shown in Figure 7–3, along with the additional assumptions on which Figure 7–4 and 7–5 are based. (Note: The carrying of numbers to the $1,000 level should not be construed to mean that the forecast warrants this level of precision. The primary purpose is to enable you as a reader to track the numbers.)

An analysis of Figures 7–4 and 7–5 reveals that the seasonal nature of XYZ's business will require interim borrowing up to $922,000 to finance inventory and receivables during the year. The company, however, should end the year with a lower note payable balance than its 1993 balance. The interest payments for the interim financing were not included in the original projection of the earnings statement in Table 7–8; I have therefore adjusted the 1994 income projection to reflect the additional $42,000 in interest. If the additional interest is incorporated into the cash projection of Figure 7–4, it will increase the cash demand by $42,000 and increase the borrowing requirement. You can see that the revising of

Cash Flow Forecast—Monthly

		JAN	FEB	MAR	APR	MAY	JUN	JUL	AUG	SEP	OCT	NOV	DEC	TOT
1	SALES PROJECTION													
	CASH IN													
	ACCOUNTS REC. COLL.													
2	– % FIRST MONTH													
3	– % SECOND MONTH													
4	– % THIRD MONTH													
5	– % BEYOND													
6	TOTAL AR COLLECTED													
7	NOTES RECEIVABLE													
8	OTHER RECEIVABLES													
9	TOTAL CASH IN													
10	CASH OUT NOV DEC INV. PROJ.													
11	PAYROLL & OVERHEAD													
12	ACCOUNTS PAYABLE 1ST MO													
13	ACCOUNTS PAYABLE 2ND MO													
14	G&A, R&D, SELLING													
15	OTHER EXPENSES													
16	TAXES													
17	FIXED ASSET PURCHASES													
18	INTEREST PAYMENTS													
19	PRINCIPAL PAYMENTS													
20	TOTAL CASH OUT													
21	BEGINNING BALANCE													
22	ENDING BALANCE													

Figure 7–1

Financing Plan—Monthly

		JAN	FEB	MAR	APR	MAY	JUN	JUL	AUG	SEP	OCT	NOV	DEC	JAN
1	CASH BAL BEGINNING													
2	CASH BAL ENDING													
3	REQ'D MIN CASH BAL													
4	REQ'D BORROWING													
5	ADDITIONAL BORROW (REPAY)													

Figure 7–2

XYZ Company
1994 Cash Budget Projection Assumptions

ACCOUNTS RECEIVABLE HISTORY
  20% Collected in 0–30 days
  30% Collected in 31–60 days
  30% Collected in 61–90 days
  19.5% Collected in 31–60 days
  .5% Not Collected

ACCOUNTS PAYABLE HISTORY
50% Paid in mo. following mo. in which merchandise is purchased
50% Paid in 2 mos. following mo. in which merchandise is purchased

MONTHLY SALES PLAN (in thousands of dollars)

	J	F	M	A	M	J	J	A	S	O	N	D
%	5	5	10	15	10	5	5	10	15	10	7	3
$	757	757	1515	2272	1515	757	757	1515	2272	1515	1060	455

MONTHLY INVENTORY PLAN (in thousands of dollars)

	1993		1994											
	N	D	J	F	M	A	M	J	J	A	S	O	N	D
$	819	603	603	1130	1696	1130	603	603	1130	1696	1130	791	339	603

Note: Inventory consists of the following:
    30% is Labor & Overhead
    70%+ is Purchased Material
Other revenue & expense consists of 120K non-cash revenue and 60K cash expenses

Figure 7–3

the income and the cash projections is an iterative process; however, it should converge by the second or third iteration.

The Projected Balance Sheet

The projected balance sheet is an estimate of what the company is going to look like at a given time in the future. It will be a function of the starting balance sheet, the projected income statement, and the projected cash budget. The construction of XYZ's 1994 projected balance sheet is shown in Figure 7–6.

Note a in Figure 7–6 requires some further explanation. On the basis of the projections of the income statement and the cash budget, we can forecast all of the 1994 balance sheet accounts with the exception of prepaid assets, accrued liabilities, and notes payable to the bank. The cash forecast of Figure 7–4 is deficient in that I did

XYZ Company 1994 Cash Flow Forecast—Monthly (Before Financing—Figures in Thousands of Dollars)

		JAN	FEB	MAR	APR	MAY	JUN	JUL	AUG	SEP	OCT	NOV	DEC	TOT
1	SALES PROJECTION	757	757	1515	2272	1515	757	757	1515	2272	1515	1060	455	1512
	CASH IN													
	ACCOUNTS REC. COLL.													
2	20% FIRST MONTH	151	151	302	456	302	151	151	302	453	302	212	91	
3	30% SECOND MONTH	116[1]	227	227	456	681	456	227	227	453	681	453	318	
4	30% THIRD MONTH	270[1]	130[1]	227	227	453	681	456	227	227	456	681	453	
5	195% BEYOND	487[1]	414[1]	214[1]	148	148	296	443	295	148	148	295	443	
6	TOTAL AR COLLECTED	1024	922	970	1287	1584	1584	1277	1051	1281	1587	1641	1305	15513
7	NOTES RECEIVABLE	3.3	3.3	3.3	3.3	3.3	3.3	3.3	3.3	3.3	3.3	3.3	3.3	40
8	OTHER RECEIVABLES	50				100								
9	TOTAL CASH IN	1077	925	973	1290	1687	1587	1280	1054	1284	1590	1644	1308	15703
	CASH OUT NOV 819 DEC 603													
10	INV. PROJ	603	1130	1696	1130	603	603	1130	1696	1130	791	339	603	11454
11	PAYROLL & OVERHEAD	181	339	509	339	181	181	339	509	339	237	102	181	
12	ACCOUNTS PAYABLE 1ST MO	211	211	396	594	396	211	211	396	594	396	277	119	4012
13	ACCOUNTS PAYABLE 2ND MO	285	211	211	396	594	396	211	211	396	594	396	277	4178
14	G&A, R&D, SELLING	267	267	267	267	267	267	267	267	267	267	267	267	
15	OTHER EXPENSES 60/12	5	5	5	5	5	5	5	5	5	5	5	5	60
16	TAXES				84									84
17	FIXED ASSET PURCHASES	50				100								150
18	INTEREST PAYMENTS	14.2	14.2	14.2	14.2	14.2	14.2	14.2	14.2	14.2	14.2	14.2	14.2	170
19	PRINCIPAL PAYMENTS	4	4	4	4	4	4	4	4	4	4	4	4	48
20	TOTAL CASH OUT	1017	1051	1406	1703	1561	1078	1051	1406	1619	1517	1065	867	
21	BEGINNING BALANCE	340	400	274	<159>	<572>	<446>	63	292	<60>	<395>	<322>	257	
22	ENDING BALANCE	400	274	<159>	<572>	<446>	63	292	<60>	<395>	<322>	257	698	

[1] Collection from 1993 Accounts Receivable

Figure 7-4

XYZ Company 1994 Financing Plan (Figures in Thousands of Dollars)

		JAN	FEB	MAR	APR	MAY	JUN	JUL	AUG	SEP	OCT	NOV	DEC	JAN
1	CASH BAL BEGINNING	340	400	274	<159>	<572>	<446>	63	292	<60>	<395>	<322>	257	
2	CASH BAL ENDING	400	274	<159>	<572>	<446>	63	292	<60>	<395>	<322>	257	698	
3	REQ'D MIN CASH BAL	350	350	350	350	350	350	350	350	350	350	350	350	
4	REQ'D BORROWING	-0-	76	509	922	796	287	58	410	745	672	93	-0-	
5	ADDITIONAL BORROW (REPAY)	-0-	76	433	413	<126>	<509>	<229>	352	335	<73>	<579>	<93>	

Figure 7–5

XYZ Company 1994 Projected Balance Sheet
(Figures in Thousands of Dollars)

	Assumption & Calculation	Projected Value
ASSETS		
CASH	From Cash Projection	$ 350
ACCOUNTS RECEIVABLE	From Cash Projection AR (1994) + Sales 1993 − Coll (1993) = $1420 + $15,152 − $15,513 =	1,059
INVENTORY	From 1993 Balance Sheet, 1994 Income Proj. and 1994 Inventory Forecast INV (1994) = INV (1993) + ΔINV (1994) − COS (1994) = $2,340 + $11,454 − $11,306 =	2,488
PREPAID	Turnover same as 1993 PP = $\frac{1994 \text{ Sales}}{1993 \text{ TO}} = \frac{\$15,152}{43.9} =$	345
	TOTAL CURRENT ASSETS	$4,242
FIXED ASSETS	Purchase of 150K equip, Dep. = $100 FA = $850K + $150K − $100K =	900
NOTE RECEIVABLE	No principal payments, Interest only	400
	TOTAL NONCURRENT ASSETS	$1,300
TOTAL ASSETS		$5,542
LIABILITIES		
ACCOUNTS PAYABLE	From 1993 Balance Sheet and 1994 Cash Flow AP (1994) = AP (1993) + ΔAP (1994) − Cash Payments (1994) = $832 + $8,071 − $8,192 =	$ 711
NOTES PAYABLE	Determine so that Balance Sheet is in balance [a]	1,116
ACCRUED LIAB	Turnover same as 1993 ACL = $\frac{1994 \text{ Sales}}{1993 \text{ TO}} = \frac{\$15,152}{73.2} =$	207
	TOTAL CURRENT LIAB	$2,034
LONG TERM DEBT	Assume 1993 Note principal reduced by 14%; and increased by 150K to finance new equipment LTD (1994) = LTD (1993) × .86 + $150 =	446
TOTAL LIABILITIES		$2,480
NET WORTH	From 1993 Balance Sheet and 1994 Income Proj. NW(1994) = NW(1993) + 1994 Net Income = $2,740 + $322 =	$3,062

[a]Note Payable = Total Assets − Net Worth − All Other Projected Liabilities

Figure 7–6

not designate separately those particular expenditures that arise as a result of having either to replenish the prepaid accounts during the year or to pay the accrued liabilities. This can and certainly should be done, especially if these accounts are significant. In this particular case, the prepaid assets constitute 5.3 percent of the total assets, and the accrued liabilities make up 6.2 percent of the liabilities; hence, their effect on the balance sheet is not likely to be significant.

The 1994 prepaid and accrued liability balances can be estimated by assuming that the 1993 turnover ratios will apply to the 1994 balances. The implicit assumption is that since financial ratios reflect the way management operates the company, it can be assumed—at least with respect to the manner in which prepaid expenses relate to sales and accrued liabilities relate to sales—that these ratios will be maintained in the projected balance sheet. Hence, 1994 prepaids = 1994 projected sales/1993 prepaid turns, and 1994 accrued liabilities = 1994 projected sales/1993 accrued liabilities turns. The 1994 notes payable balance is then calculated so that 1994 assets = 1994 liabilities + 1994 net worth.

A comparison of the 1994 balance sheet in Figure 7–6 with the 1993 balance sheet (Table 7–1) shows that total bank debt is projected to decrease by 17 percent from $1,888K ($1,544K+$344K) in 1993 to $1,562K ($1,116K+446K) in 1994. Moreover, the company's debt-to-worth ratio is projected to improve from 1.06 to 0.81, a trend that would bring a smile to every banker's face.

These represent the three projections you will need to discuss the future intelligently with your banker: the projected income statement, the projected balance sheet, and the monthly cash flow forecast. The process is complex and requires serious thought to be meaningful. Even then, despite all good-faith attempts to be accurate in your models, you have to remind yourself continuously that you are attempting to estimate the future—which in some circles is called fortune telling. Most of the things a CEO is required to do are a good deal more difficult than this exercise. That's why it is amazing to me that so many are content to bask in ignorance and leave this most important function to their "bean counters and numbers crunchers."

There are many computer programs and software packages that

automate the preparation of projections; assuming you have an adequate understanding of the process, there is every reason to use them. But remember, you will still have to be in a position to explain and justify the assumptions and rationalize the projections that are spit out by the printer.

Budgets

How does a budget differ from a forecast or projection?

As you have just seen, a forecast is a prediction of what you expect to happen in the future. A budget, in contrast, involves a commitment to make an agreed outcome happen. Budgets come in all sorts of variations: there are cash budgets, capital expenditure budgets, advertising budgets, and head count budgets. But wherever the term is used, it refers to a schedule of an organization's detailed expense accounts (and revenue accounts where applicable), grouped by operating unit or product line so that there's clear accountability. The department manager or product line manager is accountable for making sure that expenditures and revenue conform to the budget.

The budget is the vehicle that ensures that the individuals who are responsible for the day-to-day operation of the enterprise carry out their charter in an appropriate manner. As they pursue their independent agendas, the budget guarantees that the results of those efforts will be consistent with the company's forecast and its overall operational plan. The budget, in short, is the glue that makes the different parts of the organization fit together.

There are a number of issues that need to be addressed in implementing a budgeting procedure, including how tightly it should track the company's overall plan, the frequency with which it is revised, whether it should be fixed or periodically updated to incorporate actual performance, and whether it should be rolled forward as each calendar quarter expires. The key is that a company have a budgeting system that ties its forecasts to the specific action plans of the departments. This is the only way to guarantee that every executive, manager, and supervisor in the company is reading from the same page of the company's hymnbook.

You now understand what you need to know to be financially literate and to communicate with the banker in the language he or she understands. If you master the concepts that I have discussed and develop your financial skills so that they become an integral part of your methodology of management, you will place yourself at the forefront of those individuals with whom the banker wants to do business. If you've done any travelling in a foreign country, you know that it's pretty difficult to charm someone with whom you cannot communicate.

8

Diplomacy

The worst kind of diplomatists are missionaries, fanatics and lawyers; the best kind are the reasonable and human skeptics. Thus it is not religion which has been the main formative influence in diplomatic theory; it is common sense.

—Harold Nicholson, English diplomat, author, and critic

I hate your pen and ink men; a fleet of British ships of war are the finest negotiators in Europe.

—Admiral Horatio Nelson

Two major activities and responsibilities of every business manager or CEO are making deals and resolving disputes. These two activities are closely related in that they both require the CEO or manager to have diplomatic skills. He or she must be able to resolve differences between the company and its various stakeholders (customers, suppliers, bankers, employees, shareholders, or government agencies) without resorting to the use of such third-party methods as litigation, arbitration, and mediation.

The ability to negotiate effectively is a very valuable skill. Studies have shown that a typical senior manager in an American business spends at least 20 percent of her time negotiating. In all situations that affect the birth, survival, and growth of the business, the CEO is the ultimate dealmaker for the corporation. If she lacks the skill to conclude these critical deals in a satisfactory manner, she will invariably fail in leading her business to achieve its full potential.

Bankers are keenly aware of the importance of a business leader being a skilled diplomat because they know how valuable these skills can be, especially if a company finds itself in financial difficulty and must negotiate new agreements with its various stakeholders to survive. Therefore you can expect them to take every opportunity during the loan approval and due diligence process to learn everything they can about your diplomatic skills or lack thereof. In addition, if and when they make a proposal, it will be necessary for you to negotiate the terms and conditions of the proposed loan agreement; you can expect bankers to scrutinize your behavior very carefully during that process.

Bankers value and take great pride in their own negotiating skills and therefore want to see that their borrowers possess a modicum of diplomatic capability. They know that in the course of the relationship problems will arise that will require negotiations to resolve. They want to lend money to someone they feel they can deal with in a professional manner. In this chapter I will explain the essential elements that constitute negotiating skills, how these skills can be used to your advantage in the negotiations with your banker, and what you can do to improve your skills.

Because we begin to negotiate as a child, we do so largely without conscious awareness of the process. When we approached our mother with "If I eat my vegetables, can I watch TV?" and our mother responded with "Only if you clean up your toys first," we were negotiating. Adding to our lack of awareness is the fact that business negotiations tend to be accomplished in the context of an unwritten etiquette that masks the essence of the negotiating process by substituting form for substance. Since most businesspersons have never been exposed to any formal training in negotiation, much of their behavior is intuitive, reflecting their experiences in both business and nonbusiness contexts. Research has demonstrated that an understanding of the negotiating process will itself improve your negotiating skills.

Parties negotiate to resolve their differences and disputes because they believe they can achieve a better economic result through a cooperative effort with their present opponent. The possibility of gain through a cooperative effort with an adversary, friendly or hostile, is the key element that drives everyone to the negotiating table.

The huge cost and uncertainty associated with using the legal system to resolve disputes is another major reason so many disputes are settled through negotiation. The frustrations that are inherent in our legal system couldn't be better expressed than they were by Charles Dickens in *Bleak House*: "It's being ground to bits in a slow mill; it's being roasted on a slow fire; it's being stung to death by single bees; it's being drained by drops; it's going mad by grains."

A typical situation that will require you employ your negotiating skills is as follows: The bank has presented you with a loan proposal. The proposal offers to provide funds of $500,000, consisting of a revolving line of credit to a maximum of $300,000 (collateralized by 75 percent of eligible receivables and 40 percent of usable inventory) and a $200,000 term loan that will be repaid over five years in equal monthly principal payments. The loan will carry an interest rate of 3.0 percent over prime. The bank will require a security agreement for all the assets of the company, and it insists that you sign a continuing personal guarantee for the loan and agree not to further encumber your family's residence.

After extensive review of the bank's proposal with your staff and your family, you decide there are three aspects of the bank's proposal that are unacceptable. The revolving credit line is $100,000 less than the company requires; the payback period of five years will place too great a burden on the company's cash flow; and you and your wife cannot promise not to further encumber your house because you plan to use the equity in the house to provide funds for your children's college education. Your problem becomes how to resolve the differences with the bank in such a way that you get the loan and achieve your most important objectives.

The Negotiation Process

The negotiation process can be divided into nine major stages:

1. Identify all the issues in the negotiation that are likely to be important to you or your adversaries. If you are considering an offer, identify all the aspects of it that are unsatisfactory (for example, the amount of time the bank will give you to pay back the loan).
2. Establish realistic objectives for each issue. Also, determine your adversary's position on each of the issues (for example, you want a seven-year payoff of the loan, and the bank wants a five-year payoff).

3. Think about your alternatives in the event the current negotiation ends in a stalemate. This is called calculating your BATNA—your best alternative to a negotiated agreement.

4. Determine your negotiating leverage vis-à-vis that of your adversary, and the extent to which you are willing to use your leverage to achieve your objective.

5. Having determined your negotiating leverage and decided the extent to which you're willing to use it, formulate your overall negotiating strategy.

6. Try to persuade your adversary to move closer to your position, and resist his efforts (to the extent possible) to get you to move closer to his position.

7. Settle on mutually agreeable positions with respect to each negotiating issue.

8. Document the various agreements achieved in step 7.

9. Implement the agreement achieved in step 8.

Now let's look at each of these stages to determine what you need to know to gain mastery of the negotiation process.

The Issues That Divide

If we all agreed about everything there would be no reason to negotiate. The things about which we do not agree are the issues that give rise to the negotiation. For example, assume that after shopping some time for a car, you decide on a make, a model, and a dealer you'd like to do business with.

You approach the salesperson, tell her the various features you want along with the color, ask for delivery in three days, and make an offer to purchase at a specific price. If the salesperson accepts your offer, you have an agreement in principal, and all that remains to complete the transaction is to document the deal and exchange the car for the money. If the salesperson responds that she can provide the car as specified and meet your delivery requirement but cannot accept your price, however, you have an issue to negotiate. If she isn't able to provide your preferred color within the delivery time specified, you have a two-issue negotiation—price and color.

In the earlier example of the bank loan, three issues were identified: amount of funds to be provided, payback period, and the amount of personal assets that will serve as secondary collateral to secure the loan.

Positions: Wants, Expectations, and Needs

The positions that a party has on an issue can be specified by defining three quantities: what they want (their aspiration), what they expect to get (their expectation), and what they will settle for (their resistance point). The aspiration value (A) is defined as the maximum realistic objective of a party in an economic transaction. It is the price at which you will list your house—assuming you don't want to drive away potential buyers—or the price you will advertise a used car for in the paper. It is the price you hope to receive (or to pay) in those situations in which you are dealing with a very unsophisticated buyer (seller) or where you have some leverage advantage.

The expectation value (E) is defined as the likely market value of the item you are selling (or buying) as measured by independent market data such as the selling prices of comparable houses, the blue-book value of cars, or the salaries of athletes with similar statistics. The resistance value (R) is defined as that price below which the seller will not sell, and/or above which the buyer will not buy. The difference between the aspiration and the resistance establishes the negotiating ranges for both the buyer and the seller; their expectations usually fall within their respective ranges.

The top half of Figure 8–1 shows the relative positions of a seller (receiver of cash) and a buyer (payer of cash) for a single-issue monetary negotiation. In the case shown, the resistance points of the parties overlap; the maximum the buyer is willing to pay is more than the minimum the seller is willing to accept. Of course neither the buyer nor seller know each other's position, but since the resistance points overlap, the negotiation process should be successful, with the buyer getting the car and the seller getting the money. What happens during the negotiation process will determine the manner in which the funds represented by the overlap in the resistance points are divided between the buyer and the seller—namely, how much less than his or her resistance point the buyer

Example of Buyer and Seller Negotiating Positions When Overlap Exists

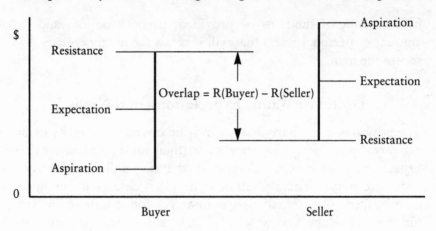

**Example of Buyer and Seller Negotiating Positions
When No Overlap Exists**

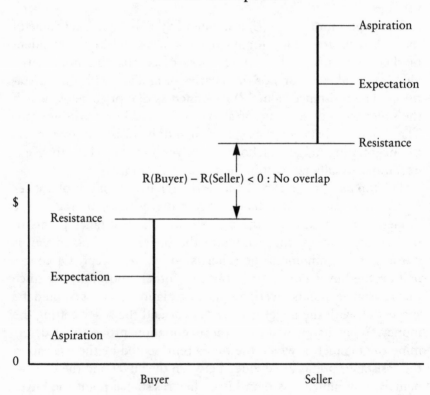

Figure 8–1

pays, and how much more than his or her resistance point the seller receives.

The bottom half of Figure 8.1 shows a different case for a buyer and a seller. In this situation, there is no overlap of resistance points; therefore the negotiation will not be concluded successfully unless one or both parties modify their resistance values during the negotiation process. A major aspect of the negotiation process, as I will discuss below, is the effort of both parties to modify their opponent's aspiration, expectation, and resistance values and resist modifying their own values.

When you are formulating a chart similar to Figure 8.1, recognize that you know what your A, E, and R are, and you can assume that the bank's offer is their A. You can perhaps estimate their E by talking with other banks, colleagues, and financial consultants to determine market data from the bank's prospective. Unless you have a source inside the bank on whom you can rely, however, you will have to guess at their R.

It is important to remember that an issue doesn't have to translate into a position with an A, E, and R value that each of the opponents define. Occasionally an issue can be reframed and, when viewed in a new perspective, can create new avenues for reaching agreement. A classic example occurred during the negotiations to achieve a peace treaty between Egypt and Israel during the 1979 Camp David meetings. A major sticking point in the negotiations was the control of the Sinai peninsula, which Israel had captured during the 1967 war. Each party demanded control of the Sinai, and efforts to compromise by dividing the territory in various ways failed. The outline of an agreement emerged when the parties achieved a better understanding of their interests: for Egypt, it was ownership of the land; for Israel, it was the security the land provided. The Camp David accord traded off these principal issues— Israel returned the Sinai to Egypt, and Egypt agreed to a demilitarized zone and new Israeli air bases.

What's Your (and Your Opponent's) Alternative?

Your BATNA is the alternative way you will fulfill your need in the event the current negotiation fails. The cost to you of failing to reach agreement is the difference between the cost of the deal that is presently available to you and the cost of your BATNA. For example, assume you're negotiating the purchase of a home that is in "move in" condition. The seller is firm at a price of $160,000, and there are other buyers competing with you for the purchase. There is another house you find acceptable that you can purchase for $145,000, but this house requires a minimum of $25,000 in repairs. Your BATNA cost is $145,000 + $25,000 = $170,000; therefore, the cost to you of not coming to an agreement is $170,000 - $160,000 = $10,000.

If you are negotiating rationally, your resistance point (the value of the transaction at which you are indifferent) must be closely related to the cost of your BATNA. If it's not, there is an error in your thinking process, because it simply doesn't make sense to give up an agreement that is economically better than your BATNA. Similarly, it makes no sense to conclude an agreement that gives you an economic result that is worse than BATNA. The goal of negotiating is not just to reach agreement, but to reach an agreement that is better for you than what you would achieve without negotiating.

Negotiation researchers have discovered that executives rarely think seriously about their alternatives to a negotiation; it is even rarer for them to think about their opponent's alternatives. Considering the other party's circumstances and their alternatives in the event no agreement is reached, however, will allow you to empathize with their situation and possibly derive some insight into their objectives.

To return to the earlier example, suppose you and the bank came to an impasse over the issue of your personal guarantee and the pledge that you wouldn't use the family residence as collateral to finance your child's college education. What is your best alternative to the offer that the bank has made? Is there another bank or finance company that wants your business? If so, you can calculate the cost of a loan from that source, compare it with your present offer, and determine the cost to you of your unwillingness to sign the personal guarantee and the negative pledge. Perhaps you don't have any financing alternative to the bank's offer. This is a very unhappy position to be in, because it means you don't have any leverage.

Leverage

Probably the most important concept in the science and art of negotiation and diplomacy is that of leverage—the advantage enjoyed by a party as a result of the environmental and situational aspects of the negotiation. The term derives from *lever*, the word for a tool that achieves mechanical advantage by converting a force applied at one point to a greater force at another point. Archimedes's comment "Give me where to stand, and I will move the earth" shows that the ancient Greeks understood the power that can be achieved with the lever. The concept of leverage in negotiation has nothing to do with the merits of the issues being negotiated, the claims being made by the parties, the fairness of one party's position with respect to the other's, or the skill of the negotiators. It is only dependent on the environment in which the negotiation takes place and the relative situations of the parties.

There are five important types of leverage in a negotiation:

- The *power* (P) one party has to control the behavior of another party. Al Capone's famous maxim comes to mind: "You can get more done with a kind word and a gun than with a kind word."
- The *rewards* (R) one party can offer to another (which can consist of money, promotions, perks, property, or introductions).
- The unique and valuable *information* (I) one party has that can help or hurt the other party, either directly or indirectly.
- The number of *alternatives* (A) the party has available for meeting his or her needs that do not depend on a successful conclusion to the negotiation.
- The amount of *time* (T) the party has available for reaching and consummating an agreement.

I have found it to be very helpful in assessing a complex negotiation to create a simple model to calculate the relative leverages of each of the parties. In many negotiations, relative leverage determines the outcome; the parties never get to use their sophisticated bargaining ploys to influence the other side.

Figure 8.2 shows what is referred to in mechanics as a Class I lever, also known as a seesaw. Let's assume you are Party One, whose situation will be represented on the left side of the lever in capital letters. The situation of your opponent, Party Two, is on the

Class I Lever

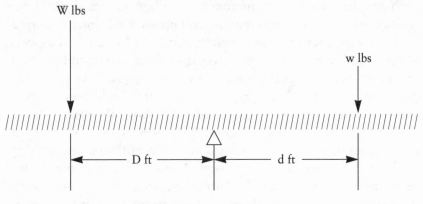

Figure 8–2

right and is represented by lower case letters. The weight you exert on your side of the lever is W, and the weight your opponent exerts is w. Similarly, your distance from the fulcrum is D, and your opponent's distance from the fulcrum is d. Your leverage on the seesaw is proportional to W multiplied by D—written here as (W) (D)—and your opponent's leverage is (w) (d). According to the laws of mechanics, if (W) (D) = (w) (d) the leverages are equal, the system is in balance, and the seesaw will not tip to either side. If (W) (D) is greater than (w) (d), however, the seesaw will rotate counterclockwise, indicating that your leverage is greater than that of your opponent. If (W) (D) is less than (w) (d), the seesaw will rotate clockwise, indicating that your opponent's leverage is greater than yours.

We all know from our experiences as children that the way to balance the seesaw is to add or subtract weight on one side (add or subtract your sister, for example) and/or move closer to or further away from the fulcrum. The analogy to a negotiation situation should be apparent. The total of your power (P, your ability to control your opponent's behavior), rewards (R, your ability to provide your opponent incentives for behaving as you would like) and your information (I, knowledge could help or hurt your opponent directly or indirectly) constitutes the "weight" component of your leverage. The more P + R + I you have, the more potential leverage you have in comparison to your opponent.

Negotiation Model

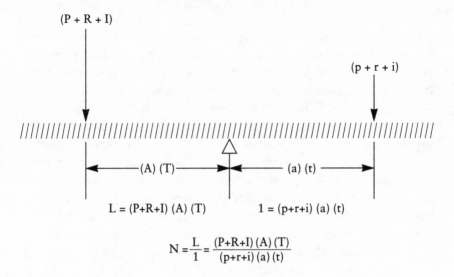

$$N = \frac{L}{1} = \frac{(P+R+I)\,(A)\,(T)}{(p+r+i)\,(a)\,(t)}$$

Figure 8–3

Similarly, the combination of *A* (the number of alternatives you have for filling your needs if you cannot strike a deal with this particular opponent) and *T* (the amount of time you have for making and consummating a deal), which we will write as the product (A) (T), is equivalent to your distance from the fulcrum, *D*. The greater (A) (T) is, the higher the length component of leverage; the smaller (A) (T) is the lower the length component. Your negotiation leverage (*N*) over your adversary is simply the ratio of your leverages: *N* = *L/l*. Figure 8–3 shows the seesaw with the negotiation variables identified and the equations for calculating the leverage of the two parties.

Ratios that are greater than 1 indicate that you have a leverage advantage over your opponent. Ratios that are less than 1 indicate that he or she has a leverage advantage over you. Having a negotiating leverage advantage places you in a position to motivate your adversary to conclude the negotiation on terms that are favorable to you—that is, to obtain a result closer to your aspiration than to your resistance.

Using the Leverage Model to Understand Different Negotiation Situations

The following examples will give you some insight into how to use the model introduced above to determine your relative leverage. For the purpose of these examples, I will use the following arbitrary values to quantify certain of the variables: none = 0, very low = 1, moderate = 5, large = 10, very large (or infinity) = ∞.

You are a buyer negotiating the purchase of a car that is in short supply (that is, there are very few models of this particular automobile available in your geographic area). You cannot force the dealer to do anything ($P = 0$); you can pay for the car ($R = 1$); you have no information that can help or hurt the dealer ($I = 0$); you have found two other dealers who have the model you desire ($A = 2$); and this is a second car and you are under no time pressure ($T = \infty$).

As to the dealer's situation, he cannot force you to do anything ($p = 0$); he can provide the model you want ($r = 1$); he has no information that can help or hurt you ($i = 0$); he has at least five other customers who are interested in this model ($a = 5$); and it is close to the end of the month and he would prefer to get the sale in this month's results ($t = 5$).

Your leverage is $(0 + 1 + 0) (2) (\infty) = \infty$. The dealer's leverage is $(0 + 1 + 0) (5) (5) = 25$. Your negotiating leverage is $N = \infty/25 = \infty$. You thus have an infinite negotiating advantage over the dealer, assuming that he is anxious to complete the sale in this financial month and you are on the premises with your checkbook open. If the dealer is indifferent about getting the sale in this month's figures, his leverage would be calculated as $(0 + 1 + 0)$ $(5) (\infty)$, and your negotiating advantage over the dealer would be $2\infty/5\infty = \infty/\infty$, which is indeterminate. Neither party has negotiating leverage.

But suppose the car you want to purchase is a one-of-a-kind handmade model you desperately need for your collection of classic cars. You only recently learned about the car being available, and you're concerned that other collectors will soon drive up the price. Your leverage would be calculated as follows: $(0 + 1 + 1) (0)$ $(1) = 0$. $A = 0$ because there are no alternatives to this car, and $T = 1$ because you want to complete the purchase before your competitors can make a bid. The dealer's negotiating leverage is $(0 + 10 +$

0) (5) (∞) = ∞. $r = 10$ because the car is unique and very valuable and is coveted by you; $a = 5$ because the dealer knows there are at least five collectors worldwide who would be interested and have the resources to purchase the car; and $t = ∞$ because the dealer has absolutely no time pressure to sell. Your negotiating leverage in this situation is $N = 0/∞ = 0$. You have no leverage, which means that if you want that classic car badly enough, you will pay the dealer's aspiration.

Let's now look at your negotiation with the bank. Your leverage will be calculated as follows: you have no power over the bank ($P = 0$); you can pay the loan fees and interest if they should award you the loan ($R = 1$); you have no information that can help or hurt the bank ($I = 0$); only one other bank has expressed interest in your company ($A = 1$); and your need for funds is immediate ($T = 1$). Therefore, your leverage is $(0 + 1 + 0) (1) (1) = 1$.

The bank's leverage is as follows: The bank has no power over you ($p = 0$); they have the ability to provide the funds you desperately need ($r = 10$); they probably have information about you that can help or hurt you, but using it would breach the agreement to maintain the confidence of all information on present and prospective borrowers, ($i = 0$); they have at least three other applicants for the funds they have available for your industry ($a = 3$); and they are only under modest time pressure to get the funds placed and start earning interest ($t = 5$). Therefore, the bank's leverage is $(0 + 10 + 0) (3) (5) = 150$. Your negotiating leverage vis-à-vis the bank is therefore $1/150 = .0067$, which means your negotiations with the bank are likely to wind up closer to their aspiration value than yours.

The leverage situation would be entirely different if you were a borrower and had a substantial loan that was in default. The bank has the option of foreclosing and liquidating the underlying collateral which gives them power ($p > 0$); it also has the ability to waive the default, which would constitute a reward ($r > 0$). If the loan was substantially undercollateralized (so that liquidation would not recapture the principal) and you were judgment proof (so that your personal guarantee was not worth anything), the bank would need your continued effort, cooperation, and expertise to help them recover their loan; that situation puts you in the position to reward the bank ($R > 0$). If you have a wealthy associate who believes in you and is willing to invest additional funds in the business provided that the bank cooperates, you're also in a position to provide a reward.

If you learn through your contacts that another firm with a weaker financial situation has negotiated a better deal than has been offered to you, the information would be helpful in your negotiations with the bank ($I > 0$). If the bank discovers that you've just inherited a large sum and are no longer judgment proof, that information would give the bank increased leverage ($i > 0$). Banks always have many alternatives for investing new money; they can lend it to consumers or other business borrowers, invest in real estate mortgages, or purchase securities. Therefore, when negotiating with a bank on a new loan $a \gg 0$; once their money is invested and their problem becomes how to get you pay it back, however, their alternatives diminish ($a > 0$). But unless yours is a very successful company and has several prospective lenders fighting with each other for the opportunity to deal with you, you will usually have very limited alternatives, whether you're a borrower or a prospective borrower.

As bureaucracies, banks are rarely under time pressure. This situation can change if they become aware of the fact that their collateral is at risk and in jeopardy of being impaired; under these circumstances, they can and do act very quickly. In contrast, you as the entrepreneur are always under serious time constraints. You needed the money last week, and your principal competitor will certainly beat you to the market if you can't get your new development program funded immediately. The bank will always have a time advantage over you—which, all things being equal, will always give them negotiating leverage.

Once you understand the model and are comfortable with the concept, you will quickly be able to understand your relative leverage in various negotiating situations, which cannot but help make you a much more realistic negotiator. There are three important points, detailed below, that you must understand in order to take full advantage of this concept.

1.   Negotiating leverage is not a static quantity; during the course of a negotiation it will probably change. In fact, you will want to change the situation to increase your leverage advantage,

and you need to recognize that your opponent will be doing the same thing. For example, you may negotiate a contract with a supplier who is the only source for a particular component which means your leverage with that supplier is zero. If you can locate another qualified source during the course of the contract negotiation, however, you will change your negotiating leverage significantly. The same is true of all the other variables that enter into the calculation of your leverage. You want to do everything in your power to increase the values of your variables and recognize that your opponent will probably being doing the same thing.

2.   Having negotiating leverage over an opponent allows you, as I will discuss below, to use so-called hard tactics to motivate your opponent to settle on terms favorable to yourself. The by-product of hard tactics, however, is usually a deterioration in the relationship between the adversaries, a consequence that may have other implications outside the particular negotiation. Therefore, having a great deal of leverage may be of little or no use when your desire to preserve a relationship is greater than your desire to succeed in a particular negotiation.

3.   No negotiator should ever believe that a position of overwhelming leverage will guarantee her success. If you resort to hard tactics that enrage your opponent, the opponent may terminate negotiations or seek some other form of retribution even though such actions may not be in her economic interest. The rule to remember for leverage is this: get as much as you can, but use it sparingly.

The Five Strategies

There are five distinct negotiation strategies available. Which one you select will be a function of the situation, your objectives and your negotiating leverage.

* *Ignore/avoid.* You refuse to enter into negotiations. Your reasons may be that you don't think the other party is legitimate (as in the Israeli/PLO relationship that existed until 1993); you don't have sufficient leverage and are awaiting developments that will create leverage advantage; or you want to avoid interacting with

your opponent for fear that he or she will discover information during the negotiation that can hurt your position.

- *Accommodate.* In this strategy you merely comply with the opponent's demands. This may be because the matter is inconsequential and isn't worth the time or energy to achieve a better deal; you are loathe to do anything that could damage a very tenuous relationship; or your opponent has an enormous negotiation leverage, and you feel an attempt to improve terms could be dangerous (as in the case where a robber holds a gun to your head and demands your money) or futile (as in the case where a bank holding a loan on which you defaulted presents you with their terms for a workout).

- *Competitive* (also called *distributive*) *strategy.* In this strategy the so-called pie is fixed and you want to achieve as large a slice as possible, leaving your opponent the piece that is left over. You would employ the competitive strategy in negotiating with a car dealer, a home seller, or your opponent in a lawsuit.

- *Cooperative* (also called *integrative*) *strategy.* Here the assets that will be available for distribution between yourself and your opponent are not fixed but are a function of events that will occur after an agreement is initiated. In this strategy you and your opponent are baking the pie together, and you want to create as large a pie as possible and then cut yourself a substantial piece. You would employ this strategy in negotiating a contract with an independent sales organizations, a royalty agreement with a licensee, or a joint venture land development deal.

- *Termination.* You would use the strategy of terminating negotiations if you conclude that your objectives will not be achieved through continued negotiation and you have other alternatives available to meet your needs.

A cooperative strategy is optimum when dealing with a bank, since you're hopefully entering into a long-term relationship that will create value for both organizations. If you don't perform on your loan agreement and the bank determines it would prefer not having you as a long-term customer, however, you can expect that you'll begin using competitive and accommodating strategies as you work your way out of the relationship.

The Interaction Phase

Until this stage of the process virtually all the activity has been focused on the planning and strategic aspects of the negotiation—namely, to understand the issues, objectives, and leverage of the parties and to select a negotiating strategy that is appropriate for the situation. Now is the time to enter the arena.

Your goal in the interaction phase is to achieve your objectives on the various issues. Your adversary has the identical goal. You will both pursue your objectives using the following maneuvers:

1. *Bargaining* (also referred to as haggling, dickering, or "handling"). You will formulate offers and deliver them verbally or in writing to your adversary, and he or she will do likewise.
2. *Persuasion and counterpersuasion.* You will influence your adversary to accept your perception of the negotiation situation and your proposal and withstand his or her efforts to influence you with counterproposals.
3. *Problem solving.* You will discuss and resolve impediments to achieving a mutually acceptable agreement.
4. *Exchanging information.* You will share information about interests, positions, and circumstances that relate to the issues being negotiated.
5. *Attitude structuring.* You will attempt to improve the relationship between the parties to facilitate communication and create an atmosphere for compromise.
6. *Leveraging.* You will improve your leverage or make your leverage advantage evident to your adversary.

Which maneuvers are used in a negotiation is a function of the situation and the negotiation strategy. For example, if you're negotiating with a merchant in the grand bazaar in Istanbul over the purchase of a leather jacket, you employ a competitive strategy. Undoubtedly, you will bargain (the tour director has told you the asking price is always at least 50 percent higher than what they expect to get), persuade (you saw the same jacket down the street at half the price), exchange information (he will tell you that he personally knew the sheep that were slaughtered to provide the hides), and solve problems (he doesn't take American Express, your Visa card is over the limit, and you left your traveler's cheques on the ship). It will probably not be necessary—nor will you have the time—to structure his attitude, and there's very little possibility that (if you forswear the use of firearms) you will be able to leverage the merchant.

If you're attempting to negotiate a resolution to a lawsuit, you will most likely again be using a competitive strategy, and all six maneuvers will see action. If you have selected the strategy of accommodation in your negotiations with a major customer whose business you desperately need, you would definitely not want to risk leveraging because of the potential negative consequences on the customer's attitude.

In the case of the example of negotiating the terms of the loan agreement with a bank, you will want to select a cooperative strategy. Since you don't have a leverage advantage going into the negotiations, it's not likely you will be able to use leverage unless you suddenly find that you don't need the financing or another funding source appears. By the time you're negotiating over the terms of the loan agreement, you will have provided the bank with all the information that could possibly have any bearing on the issues. Therefore, in your negotiations with the bank over the loan agreement, you will have to rely on bargaining, persuasion, problem solving, and attitude structuring to influence the bank to move closer to your objective.

Tactics

Tactics in negotiation have a purpose similar to those employed in war or in sports; they are devices for implementing a strategy. An example of a bargaining tactic employed by a seller is to make a very high initial demand that will be valid for a very brief period. Tactics that are used in negotiation can be placed on a spectrum ranging from "soft" to "hard." Soft tactics are not likely to cause the relationship between the parties (either the negotiators or their principals) to deteriorate; hard tactics, in contrast, have a high probability of causing the relationship between the parties to worsen. The following are some frequently used soft and hard negotiating tactics that are employed to further the several maneuvers.

Bargaining

Soft: Making a reasonable offer that is supported by relevant facts; responding to a concession with an equally valuable concession; offering the opponent something that is of considerable value to them, but of little value to you, without insisting upon a quid pro quo

Hard: Making an extreme demand that appears arbitrary and not offering any justification; refusing to make a concession after the opponent has made a significant concession; withdrawing an offer

Persuasion

Soft: Making promises; being casual about timing of meetings
Hard: Making threats; imposing strict deadlines

Problem Solving

Soft: Enthusiastically helping the opponent to formulate arguments to sell a proposed settlement to the opponent's constituents
Hard: Refusing to participate in problem solving

Information Exchange

Soft: Providing information requested promptly and in an organized fashion; asking questions in order to understand your opponent's position
Hard: Providing information reluctantly, in increments, and in an unreadable form; refusing to provide direct answers to questions; stonewalling

Attitude Structuring

Soft: Being open, friendly, and offering to meet offsite to discuss issues informally; expressing empathy
Hard: "Good cop–bad cop" negotiating (as used in the movie

The French Connection); remaining aloof and unfriendly; showing disdain for your opponent

Leveraging

Soft: Referring to your leverage advantage only obliquely and indirectly

Hard: Taking a surprise action (a *fait accompli*) that directly affects your opponent's situation and improves your negotiating leverage

There are several books devoted to the classification and analysis of negotiation tactics, along with anecdotal material on how they have been used. The important thing to realize is that every time you implement a tactic you incur a risk. If you confine yourself only to soft tactics, your opponent may perceive this as a sign of weakness and implement hard tactics in an effort to crush you. If you employ hard tactics, though, you run the serious risk of the relationship deteriorating and possibly causing your opponent's behavior to become irrational and unpredictable.

Reaching Agreement

The culmination of what Howard Raffia, the Harvard negotiation scholar, has called "the negotiation dance" will occur in one of three ways: the parties will break off their negotiations and go their separate ways; they will commence litigation; or they will reach agreement. Once the parties have agreed to negotiate, certain economic and psychological mechanisms will become operative, and the negotiation will take on a life of its own. The negotiators in the ring will experience pressure not only from their opponent but from their own constituents, who may have only reluctantly agreed to negotiations. Each negotiator must reconcile four sets of objectives: the opponent's, those of the opponent's constituents, those of his or her constituents, and his or her own. As the negotiation process unfolds, it's likely that all these objectives will change.

The economic mechanisms that drive the parties toward agreement are as follows:

1.   The costs incurred as a result of the parties not coming to agreement motivate one or the other or both parties toward a resolution. For example, a tenant who is paying above market rent on a lease that will soon end is willing to sign a long-term lease at market rates. The landlord needs the tenant's long-term lease to refinance her building at a lower interest rate. The continued costs being incurred by both tenant and landlord motivate them toward agreement.

2.   In many situations the parties have a symbiotic relationship; they need each other to survive, and as a consequence they cannot disengage from each other. In these situations the relationship of the parties drives the negotiation to eventual agreement. The negotiation between a city and its police force, and that between an aerospace company and the Department of Defense, are examples of such a relationship.

3.   Events that occur during the course of the negotiation result in one of the parties' BATNA changing (for example, the supplier whose price was only 3 percent greater than the supplier you're negotiating with just filed bankruptcy, and the next qualified supplier is 20 percent higher).

The psychological mechanisms that drive the parties toward agreement are as follows:

1.   The maneuvers that occur during negotiation (especially information exchange, problem solving, and attitude structuring) provide an opportunity for the opponents to get to know each other's issues and discover areas of mutual interest and expand the so-called common ground between their positions. Consequently, they will embrace a cooperative strategy when possible and tend to employ soft tactics.

2.   The negotiators feel they have invested so much time, effort, energy, and prestige in the process that they cannot afford not to agree. For example, you've been chasing a contract for a year and have invested thousands of dollars and hundreds of hours of effort; you know that if you don't accept the lousy offer that's on the table, your competitor will, and you can't afford to go home empty-handed.

3.   Time allows individuals to get used to an initially unpleasant reality and discover redeeming features. For example, the CEO

who has been reluctantly negotiating a merger with a larger company receives an offer that he knows his board will accept, resulting in his termination. After a period of reflection and viewing his situation in a different framework, though, he realizes the merger will make him wealthy, release all of the collateral he had been obligated to pledge to the bank, and give him the opportunity to pursue other interests.

4. The term *cognitive dissonance*, coined by Leon Festinger, describes the psychological stress induced when an individual holds conflicting ideas simultaneously. The stress persists until the conflict is resolved. For example, assume a negotiator is being pressured to employ hard tactics in order to achieve unrealistic objectives. The negotiator realizes she is at a leverage disadvantage, and the company's BATNA is significantly less than the deal on the table. She will experience stress from cognitive dissonance because of the two simultaneous thoughts:

- the deal on the table is quite acceptable and we should take it; and
- our negotiating tactics are likely to lose the deal on the table.

The negotiator will not be fully effective as long as the dissonance persists.

Similarly, we feel cognitive dissonance when there is a conflict between our attitude toward another person and the beliefs and opinions of that person. If dissonance develops in that relationship, we will either begin to accept our opponent's belief or opinion, discount the importance of the matter, or become less positive to the other person. During the course of a negotiation, if we tend to develop an affinity to the other negotiator, we may find his or her positions less offensive.

5. As a result of events that occur within or outside the negotiating arena, one party may achieve a sudden leverage advantage over the opponent, motivating the opponent to settle on the first party's terms. For example, during the maneuver of information exchange, assume that a company inadvertently delivers a highly sensitive and privileged memorandum to its union that would reflect adversely on the company if it became public. The union threatens to release the memorandum to the press. The company settles close to the union's offer in order to retrieve the memorandum.

6.   There may be differences in *utility*, which is defined as the subjective value of an item for a particular individual. For example, the objective value of a dollar is exactly the same in the hands of a beggar or a millionaire; however, the subjective value of the dollar will be far greater to the beggar than to the millionaire. That single dollar may be what saves the beggar from starvation, and he values it subjectively as he values his life. To the millionaire, the dollar is pocket change, a possible tip for the doorman. One person's worn-out furniture is another's antique. A house that simply doesn't work for one family becomes another family's dream house. During the course of the negotiation process, the negotiators may discover certain items that are valued differently by the parties and can be traded to reach agreement; thus, giving one party something they value highly (high utility) that is regarded as having low utility by the party giving it up.

If the parties manage to reach agreement, the mutual understandings of the negotiators with respect to all the issues that were in contention are usually documented in an "agreement in principal." This document then serves as the framework for drafting the final agreements, contracts, legal documents, releases, and so forth required to implement the overall agreement. It is understood and usually clearly spelled out in the agreement in principal that the deal is not final and binding until all the documents necessary to fully implement it are signed by the responsible parties on each side.

Documenting the Deal

The tough work is over; the champagne cork is popped. Senior managers and office staff gather around to congratulate you on your great accomplishment. You smile, acknowledge the accolades, and don't let on that you're still anxious. As a skilled diplomat you know that, in the words of Yogi Berra, "it ain't over till it's over," and it won't be over until all the papers are signed. Whereas the drafting and wordsmithing will be done by the lawyers, the principals should (and most will) read and understand every word as if they were reading a love letter. A skilled diplomat will never approve or sign a document she does not fully comprehend or completely agree with.

The time, energy, and money that are consumed during this phase of the negotiation process will be a function of the attitudes and motivation of the principals. Some parties are so delighted with the agreement, and so anxious to consummate it, that they will be very accommodating to their opponent in resolving language issues that arise. A typical case is a company negotiating an agreement with an investor for the infusion of capital. The CEO, knowing how desperately the company needs the funds, instructs the attorneys to "get this damn thing done. If we don't get the funds into our bank soon, it will all be academic because we'll be out of business." You can expect the attorneys to remind the CEO of these instructions when the deal collapses soon after it is implemented.

In other situations, at least one party views the documentation phase as another opportunity to improve the deal. Each paragraph is subjected to careful scrutiny to see if there is any way to rewrite it to be more favorable. Documents are marked up and passed back and forth between attorneys, along with detailed analyses of the reasons why the language posed by the opponent is unacceptable. Meetings drone on into the early morning hours. The bills for attorney time, copying, messengers, and telephone and fax expenses mount. Progress occurs at an imperceptible rate. Both parties continuously reassess their positions and interests to determine whether a deal is still in their best interest, and they frequently threaten to terminate negotiations and "blow the whole deal." Here is where a capable transaction lawyer will earn her fees and your eternal appreciation. It's her tenacity and focus that will finally bring about the close.

Implementing the Deal

The easiest type of agreement to implement is one in which neither party has any obligation to the other once the transaction closes. The purchase of a house through an escrow is such a transaction. The seller receives his funds, the buyers receives their house, the escrow company makes sure all transaction fees are paid, and neither buyer nor seller has any continuing obligation to the other. The settlement of a lawsuit between hostile parties is usually settled in a closing where all issues that may have given rise to the disputes—

from "the beginning of time" to the moment of closing—are addressed, and there is no further need for the parties ever to interact with each other.

Agreements arrived at through a cooperative strategy are the next easiest to effect, because both parties have a stake in the future results. At least initially, both are motivated to perform and maintain a cooperative relationship. Cooperative agreements fail for many reasons: assumptions about future events don't prove out, the parties to the agreement don't have the resources or capabilities to implement the agreement, or one party decides that it been much too generous to the other party and wants to claim more value. If any of these situations develop, you can expect the agreement will begin to crumble as one or both of the parties look for ways to restructure or terminate the agreement.

The most difficult agreement to implement is one that is arrived at through a competitive strategy and in which only one of the participants has an obligation to perform, as in the case of a delinquent and insolvent debtor agreeing to make periodic payments to induce a trade creditor/supplier not to sue. The trade creditor in this instance has no continuing leverage over the delinquent debtor. Should the debtor stop paying, the only alternative available to the trade creditor is to sue and perhaps force the debtor into bankruptcy, neither of which results in payment.

Fairness, Emotion, and Rationality

When deals that make economic sense to both parties fail to close, it is usually because those deal breakers *Fairness* and *Emotion* are mucking up the works. Ben Franklin wrote about this problem: "Trades would not take place unless it were advantageous to the parties concerned. Of course, it is better to strike as good a bargain as one's bargaining position permits. The worst outcome is when, by overreaching greed, no bargain is struck, and a trade that could have been advantageous to both parties does not come off at all."

Potentially successful negotiations are often aborted because one party perceives the offers being made by the other as "unfair" and not made in "good faith," or decides that the other party was too abusive and obnoxious to deal with. The culprits Fairness and Emotion are present at every negotiation, always looking for their opportunity to do mischief. All negotiators need to be aware of their existence and to protect themselves from their machinations.

FAIRNESS.

Fairness (or unfairness) is not an objective state, and it is difficult to predict exactly what one person would consider fair or unfair. But nonprofessional negotiators have a mental fairness calibrator against which they will judge their adversary's negotiating position; if this calculation registers "unfair," it is possible that they will react emotionally, make decisions that are not in their economic interest, or both. One possible decision might be to terminate negotiations and pursue an alternative way to satisfy their needs, even if the BATNA has a higher cost. Hard tactics and the naked use of leverage are usually regarded as evidence that a party is unfair.

EMOTION.

Professional negotiators do not become emotional except to make a point. They've learned to stay in control in all types of situations and to use emotion as another tactic to achieve their objective. Nonprofessional negotiators often get caught up in the proceeding and become emotional as a result of the process. Unfortunately, when they are emotional they are not able to make good decisions, and they invariably achieve outcomes that are lower than what they could have achieved had they stayed in control.

Conversely, skilled negotiators know how to pander to the emotional needs of their adversaries. They look for their opponent's "hot button"—and when they find it, they can literally play their opponent like a violin. I once represented a client who was attempting to sell his business in order to pay off a delinquent bank loan. Several groups were competing for the company. All but one had made it clear that my client, the CEO/owner, would not be the CEO of the company after the acquisition, a fact that caused my client great discomfort. The one buyer recognized my client's anxiety and in a series of meetings—from which I was barred for being "noncooperative"—persuaded my client he would remain CEO if the buyer was successful in purchasing the company. My client conducted secret negotiations over a period of months, without benefit of either my counsel or that of his attorney. By the time I realized what had happened, in order to remain as CEO my client had accepted a deal that was substantially worse economically than what was available from another bidder. In frustration I advised my client he was "literally crazy" and that he would not last a year after the acquisition. I was wrong; he lasted a year and seven days.

RATIONALITY.

Professor Max Bazerman of Northwestern University conducted a number of studies which demonstrated that rational negotiators—those that understand the process and don't get caught up in issues of fairness and good faith or become emotional—tend to achieve higher outcomes than irrational negotiators. One of the best ways to ensure that you negotiate rationally is to be well prepared before you start. Think the process through and discuss the issues that are likely to come up with your colleagues and professionals so you are prepared when these issues arise. Many mistakes are made in negotiations when one is caught unprepared and is confronted with a critical issue that one has never given adequate consideration.

The Effective Negotiator

There's an aphorism that states "a little knowledge is a dangerous thing." This aphorism has particular relevance to diplomatic and negotiating skills. You can thoroughly absorb everything in this chapter, and read every book on negotiation on my two-yard-wide shelf, and still not be a very competent negotiator. The reason is that diplomatic and negotiating skills cannot be learned from a book any more than can debating or selling skills. These skills derive from and rely to a large part upon personality, psychology, and behavioral traits.

Despite the plethora of books and tapes on the negotiation process and the deluge of three- and five-day courses promising to transform you into a Henry Kissinger or James Baker III, the average businessperson simply has no appreciation for the amount of training and experience it takes to become a good negotiator, or for the vast chasm that exists between the abilities of the average businessman and a top-flight negotiator. Negotiation skills are developed after years of experience, study, and practice; they cannot be learned by reading a book, listening to a tape, and/or taking a three-day seminar.

To develop proficiency and ultimately mastery in negotiating requires practice, with feedback on your performance in terms of both the results you achieve in any given situation and the specific competencies you exhibit. Learning how to be an effective negotiator has a lot in common with learning a foreign language. It's not too difficult to learn enough words to find your way around town, locate a good restaurant, and ask where the restrooms are—but you wouldn't want to use that newly acquired skill to structure an important business deal.

What are the characteristics of an effective negotiator? James Freund, an attorney who specializes in negotiating complex business agreements, identifies four basic skills:

1. An appreciation for the leverage that exists in each situation, plus the ability to apply it when you're at an advantage and to cope when you're at a disadvantage.
2. The knack of ferreting out and evaluating information about the other side and protecting information about your side that you would prefer not to reveal.
3. The credibility to persuade your opponent that when you state facts you're speaking truthfully, and that when you state opinions and take positions you mean what you say.
4. The judgment to strike a balance between gaining advantage and reaching compromises, both in the substance of the issues being negotiated and in your negotiating style.

Research has shown that experience alone will not usually improve negotiation skills as measured by negotiation outcome. This is because feedback about successful strategies is often unclear, delayed, and not available in a meaningful way. Experience supplemented by training, however, can definitely improve negotiating performance. If you're serious about expanding and improving your negotiation skills, I suggest you pursue the following regimen:

• Read several of the books listed in the bibliography to gain some insight into how various experts have approached the subject and the discoveries they've made as a result of their various research efforts.
• Enroll in a negotiating training course that stresses mock negotiations and individual counseling and criticism. Several business

schools now include such courses in their curriculums, most notably the Massachusetts Institute of Technology, Stanford University and Harvard Business School.

- Each time you become engaged in a negotiation, discipline yourself to follow the nine stages I have outlined in this book, and use these actual negotiations as learning experiences by conducting critical postnegotiation reviews with members of your staff. Try to learn something from each negotiation experience so that you will be a better negotiator when the next opportunity arises.
- Finally, never think that your "superior" diplomatic skills will ever bring you an easy win, even over the most incompetent negotiator. They won't!

You now have a framework to negotiate successfully. If you display this ability to your banker, you cannot help but earn his respect, which will enhance your prospects of obtaining a loan. If he entrusts his money to you, he'll know that you are be able to negotiate agreements that benefit your firm and that if your business encounters serious problems, you have the ability to negotiate accommodations with your creditors. He will be attracted to you because he'll believe that you can protect the interests of your company and, consequently, the quality of his loan.

9

Strategy

For one who has no objective, nothing is relevant.
—Confucius

Each day hundreds of thousands of CEOs go to work and do the daily business of running their companies. They call on customers, meet with subordinates, check on the status of production and development programs, resolve personnel problems, lunch with prospective employees, review and approve drafts of correspondence, and complete their day by returning telephone calls. The next day is likely to consist of more of the same, as will the next day, and the next . . . ad infinitum until the business fails, the CEO retires or dies, or the business is sold.

Save the Tiger, a novel by Steve Shagan that is on my list of must-reads for the thoughtful businessperson, is the story of Harry Stoner, a Los Angeles–based manufacturer of women's dresses. Harry, a World War II veteran, started the business with his accountant and partner, Phil. The story focuses on Harry's efforts to manufacture a new line of dresses and the daily problems he has to deal with as he works to achieve this goal. These include conflicts among his employees, getting financing without having adequate collateral, and an upcoming IRS audit for which he is ill prepared.

After fifteen years of business problems and the resulting stress, Harry has drifted over the line and become a sociopath. He influences department store buyers by providing prostitutes. Since he doesn't have adequate collateral to borrow from legitimate lenders, he plans to finance the new dress line by arranging to have a small but well-insured warehouse torched; he hopes the fire will not

171

cause too much damage to the shirt factory located under the warehouse. He and Phil have "cooked the books" for many years and must continue to cook them in order to avoid the tentacles of the IRS. The stress he's experiencing leads him to daydream about his wartime experiences and the buddies of his that were killed. He often deals with his stress and anxiety by engaging in furtive sexual encounters with hookers he picks up on Sunset Boulevard.

In a key scene Harry meets with Meyer, a Jewish cutter who escaped from a Nazi concentration camp. Meyer has had one of his very frequent arguments with Rico, a homosexual designer, and Harry is trying to patch matters up.

> The old man leaned over the pattern table. He sucked his tea through a cube of sugar in his left hand. In his right he held the stub of a pencil and made small notations on the paper patterns. A Camel burned in the red ashtray.
>
> Meyer looked up as Harry entered. "Hello, boss."
>
> Harry sat on a high stool opposite Meyer. "Don't call me boss."
>
> Meyer put the pencil down and picked up his cigarette. "But you are the boss. You built the business."
>
> "Don't call me 'boss.'" Harry inclined his head toward the patterns. "How does it look?"
>
> "You'll need money."
>
> "We'll get money."
>
> Meyer dropped the Camel onto the wooden floor and crushed it carefully. "I don't want to talk about the line."
>
> Harry sighed. "I need you. I need Rico. What do you want? What do you want me to say?"
>
> Meyer sucked some more tea. "I'm old. I can't be in a playpen with fairies. Even talented fairies. You can't give me dignity from the fairy. I understand that. A cutter you can always get. A designer is something else. Tell me what to do?"
>
> "You have a job here. Till we go out of business or till you die."
>
> Meyer dipped the sugar cube. "You need Rico. Tell me to get out. Go on Harry, tell me."
>
> Harry loosened his tie and unbuttoned his top button. "I don't want you out."
>
> The old man moved around the table. "What do you want, Harry?

Come on, tell me. I'm an old stone. I don't talk. Tell me. What is it you want?"

Harry leaned over and picked up a small square of black faille. He thought about the old man's question, looked up at the neon tubing and said, "More."

"You mean money?"

"No . . ."

"What?"

"Another season."

The old man smiled. "And that's everything? Another season?"

"That's right. It is. The average life in this business is seven months. We've survived for fifteen years—that's something. Godammit, it's everything."[1]

Harry Stoner is the archetype of the post–World War II business-man, determined to keep his company alive at all costs, driven to succeed, harassed, and learning to dance on the head of a pin. In my work as a turnaround consultant I've gotten to know many Harry Stoners. Their energies are consumed by the operational aspects of their business, and their vision of the future is rarely longer than the next season, the next product, or the next deal. Unfortunately for them, their intense focus on operations and the perpetual trauma of juggling finances to survive doesn't guarantee their business will be successful and that they'll be able to sell it one day and retire to Hawaii. Exhaustive hours of hard work, perseverance, and positive thinking will not in themselves guarantee that a business will be suc-cessful in the long term. What the Harry Stoners need, and rarely have, is a coherent business plan to guide their decisions and invest-ments and to ensure that the hard work has a purpose.

Why does your banker want you to be a strategist? Because she knows that absent a long-term guiding strategy that forces the busi-ness to plan how it will adapt to changing circumstances, the forces of economic Darwinism will cause the business to be selected out of existence. A business that doesn't have an effective strategic plan-ning function is no more able to deal with long-term threats to its existence than were animal species that are now extinct. Animals are only able to respond to immediate stimuli. They don't have the ability to anticipate what a future environment is likely to be, or to determine whether their natural response to a stimulus is in the long-term interest of their species. The consequence for animals, as discovered by Charles Darwin 140 years ago, is that they surrender their destiny to the forces of natural selection. Only those that can adapt to a changing environment will survive.

A business operating without a strategic plan, but with a product or service that is well accepted and a cost structure that is profitable, may survive for a period of time. But eventually technological, market, or regulatory factors that it has neither anticipated nor planned will conspire to select the business out of existence. The customers it has served will be absorbed by those firms that are more prepared for the changing market.

The banker intuitively understands this process because she has seen so many of her "excellent customers" fall upon hard times and fail. She knows that the probability is very high that many of her present customers will encounter difficulty during the term of her banking career, and she wants to take every precaution to ensure that this doesn't happen while they are her customer. The banker knows that if you're not a strategic thinker, you won't be a long-term player, regardless of the magnitude of your current success.

Having a strategic planning function doesn't guarantee prosperity; one only has to review the recent histories of IBM and General Motors to prove this point. The strategic plan has to be consistent with the reality of the current business, the competitive environment, the existing and emerging trends, and the resources that can be acquired and allocated to implement the plan. If the assumptions of the plan are unrealistic when they are made, or if the future does not cooperate with the realistic assumptions, you can easily wind up with a debacle like that of IBM. Not having a strategic plan, however, is tantamount to trying to disprove the theory of natural selection and the survival of the fittest—something no mature businessperson would ever want to do.

Operations Versus Strategy: Balancing Today's Beans Against Tomorrow's Wealth

The daily activities that company employees perform to provide the goods and services to their customers are subsumed under the term *operations*. The operational activities of a business have momentum and will move the business in some direction. That direction will be determined by the customers that are solicited, the orders accepted, the price lists published, the merchandise purchased, the employees hired, the government regulations accommodated, and the capital investments made. If these operational decisions aren't made in the context of an overall strategy by management, the direction of the business will develop in a haphazard manner, its direction determined either by the others inside or outside the organization or by events not under management's control.

A businessperson who allows the business to develop in accordance with such a modus operandi is like Alice in Lewis Carroll's *Alice in Wonderland*. Alice comes to a fork in the road and, seeing the Cheshire Cat, asks, "Would you tell me, please, which way I ought to go from here?" "That depends a good deal on where you want to get to," says the Cat. "I don't much care where … ," replies Alice. "Then it doesn't matter which way you go!" says the Cat.[2] If you don't have a strategy to guide your operational decisions, you often have no basis for making these decisions.

Strategy is the framework guiding the choices that determine the nature and direction of the business and are critical to its achieving its long-term objective. These choices predominantly relate to the scope of the business's products and services, the markets it services, the key capabilities it develops, the growth and return it strives for, and how it allocates its resources. The strategy is the organization's blueprint for ensuring it will be one of the "fittest" and thus survive.

Businesses that don't operate with a strategy strive to adapt by continually improving operational effectiveness, employing such tactics as restructuring staff, tinkering with the price list, reducing overheads, cutting out free coffee and bottled water, or curtailing medical benefits. But as management consultant and writer Ben Tregoe aptly states:

> The operations palliative, if taken alone, is dangerous medicine for treating a crisis or change which could threaten the survival of the business. If an organization is headed in the wrong direction, the last thing it needs is to get there more efficiently. And if an organization is headed in the right direction, it surely does not need to have that direction unwittingly changed by operation action taken in a strategic void.[3]

Operations Versus Strategy

Operations	Strategy	
	Effective	Ineffective
Effective	I High probability that business will survive and create wealth	II Probability that business will survive and be profitable in the short term
Ineffective	III Business will survive only until competition selects it out of existence	IV Business will not survive; high probability of failure in the short term

Table 9–1 illustrates the relationship between operations and strategy and their effect on the survival, growth, and success of the business. I have, as you might expect, had clients that fall within each of the quadrants shown in the figure, and I can attest that the predictions are repeatedly borne out by experience. Below are a few examples.

Quadrant I: Effective Strategy and Effective Operations

A physician with a specialty in dermatology decided to found a clinic that would specialize in solutions to male pattern baldness. His decision was prompted by two events that occurred in the late 1970s: the removal of restrictions on physician advertising, and the development of new medical techniques for hair transplants. His strategy was to appeal to the unmet needs of prematurely bald men to be attractive and desirable to women, and he promoted this benefit in his advertising and slick brochures. His vision was to locate clinics in major metropolitan areas so that he could deliver his services conveniently throughout the United States.

When I reviewed his business, his financial controls were excellent. He hired an operations manager/controller who had been very successful in his own business and had already made a nest egg that he did not want to risk. The operations were tightly controlled, and the staff was continuously queried for inputs that would improve quality, service, and profitability. The combination of a realistic strategy and good operational controls propelled the firm to achieve continuous profitable growth.

Quadrant II: Ineffective Strategy, Effective Operations

A distributor of beauty supply products began to see the revenue from its customer base of large retail chains and beauty supply stores drop off. The rate of decline was such that the controller was predicting the firm, which had been profitable over most of its fifty-year history, would soon be operating at a loss. In order to replace the revenue, the company decided to purchase another firm in the beauty supply business that primarily serviced individual beauty shops. The concept was that the acquisition would utilize the same warehouse, computer and billing systems, and operations management as the acquiring company. The only assets that needed to be absorbed were the inventory, the customer list, and the field sales force that called on the beauty shop.

The merger didn't go smoothly, for reasons that should have been apparent. The size of an order to a beauty shop was approximately one-tenth the size of an order to a retail store; the beauty shop owners were weak financially, and many orders needed to be shipped C.O.D. and were returned when there were no funds to pay for them; and the size of the inventory exploded because of the much lower turnover achieved through distributing to beauty shops and the larger number of products that needed to be stocked. Finally, the level of service that needed to be provided to both the newly absorbed sales force and their customers overloaded the support system. This ill-conceived strategy resulted in huge losses for the first time in the company's history; in order to preserve the parent company, it was necessary to liquidate the newly acquired one.

Quadrant III: Effective Strategy, Ineffective Operations

A former client had created a chain of proprietary postsecondary schools, the purpose of which was to teach secretarial, computer, electronics, and welding skills that would qualify the graduates for various entry-level positions in industry. The working capital of the school was provided by the fees paid by students, who in turn were funded by the federal government through grants and loans.

The schools operated for several years. But although enrollments and revenue should have produced substantial profits, the lack of financial and operational controls, inappropriate nepotism, high employee turnover, and overexpansion of the business beyond the capabilities of both its management and working capital created an atmosphere of perpetual crisis. When enrollments began to drop off as a result of increased competition from other schools and the decline of the economy, and government regulations required more stringent operational controls, the client was no longer able to make a profit and decided to shut down the business.

Quadrant IV: Ineffective Strategy, Ineffective Operations

An executive with a background in the entertainment business decided to invest in a company that was manufacturing data modems for personal computers. He soon was devoting all of his energies and his resources to the business. The product his firm offered, like most products in the PC industry, met with stiff price competition. Since all the competitive products were manufactured from the same groups of chips and all employed virtually the same electronics, the differences in features between my client's product and those of his competitors were primarily cosmetic. Unfortunately, our product was assembled in the United States, whereas the competitors' were manufactured offshore, providing them with a substantial additional margin. The client readily admitted he would have to develop additional products to maintain the business, but he was too consumed with operational matters to devote much energy to this matter.

Since he had never previously been in business, and certainly had never managed a manufacturing business, operations were abysmal. The company was substantially undercapitalized and was experiencing creditor pressures. They were financing their receivables at an interest rate of 40 percent per year; there was no inventory control; and financial reports, such as they were, were several months late. Employee morale was low, and there was extensive dissension among the managers, many of whom were focused on trying to preserve their fiefdoms in view of an impending layoff.

In short, there was no reason for this firm to continue to exist. After a relatively short time, it did not.

Competitive Advantage and Generic Strategies

A competitive advantage is something a customer can obtain by buying your product or service that is not available from a competitor. This advantage can be based on distinctive competencies or valuable resources that you possess. It can be manifested in a lower price for the same performance, unique features, reliable performance over extended periods of time, ease of maintenance, shorter delivery times, or unique trade-up or trade-in plans. Examples of distinctive competencies are Disney's maintenance of its theme parks, McDonald's meal consistency, Frito-Lay's route servicing, and Nordstrom's sales training. A valuable resource is something the company owns that gives it a competitive advantage, such as a patent, a license, a mineral lease, an office building in a good location, or a brand name.

Sustainable competitive advantage implies that the competitive advantage cannot easily be duplicated or undermined as a result of changes in the environment or the actions of competitors and new entrants to the marketplace. Simply stated, a sustainable competitive advantage is designed to cause a customer to purchase at your store rather than that of your competitor. Such advantages are invariably based on one of the four generic strategies that derive from the company's deciding where it wants to operate on the product cost–product features spectrum and the broad market–target market spectrum. As Michael Porter points out:

> Achieving competitive advantage requires a firm to make a choice. If a firm is to attain a competitive advantage it must make a choice about the type of competitive advantage it seems to attain and the scope within which it will attain it. Being "all things to all people" is a recipe for strategic mediocrity and below-average performance, because it often means that a firm has no competitive advantage at all.[4]

The four generic strategies are illustrated in Table 9–2. Examples of the four generic strategies are illustrated below.

LOW COST (BROAD MARKET, LOW COST).

The majority of companies that pursue a low-cost strategy remove all frills and extras from the product or service. The archetype of the low-cost product designed to appeal to a broad market was the

TABLE 9-2
Generic Strategies

	COST	FEATURES
BROAD MARKET	LOW COST MODEL T, COSTCO, KIWI	DIFFERENTIATION TANDEM, CATERPILLAR
NARROW MARKET	FOCUSED COST CHARLES SCHWAB	FOCUSED DIFFERENTIATION NORDSTROM

Model T Ford. It was offered in a single color (black) with no options. Retail discounters such as Costco and Price Club, no-frills airlines such as Kiwi Airlines, and ARCO service stations (which don't take credit cards) build a competitive advantage by striving to offer the consumer the lowest-cost alternative.

DIFFERENTIATION (BROAD MARKET, PRODUCT FEATURES).

Companies that base their strategy on differentiation offer the customer a trade-off—a higher price, but the product the way they want it. Tandem Computers (which offers computer systems that can operate in tandem so that the failure of any one will not cause an interruption in service) and Caterpillar tractor (which offers twenty-four hour parts service anywhere in the world) are examples of companies whose sustainable competitive advantages are derived by differentiating the product from those offered by competitors.

FOCUSED COST (NARROW MARKET, LOW COST).

Focused cost strategies derive a competitive advantage by appealing to a subset of the normal customer base for the product or service. Discount brokerage companies are an example of a focused strategy. Whereas the large full-service brokerage houses (such as Merrill Lynch) market to the entire population of investors, discount brokers (such as Charles Schwab) primarily target investors who want to make their own investment decisions and don't want to pay for the advisory services offered by the full-service firms. Another example of a focused cost strategy would be firms that perform private-label manufacturing for large distributors.

FOCUSED DIFFERENTIATION (NARROW MARKET, PRODUCT FEATURES).

Competitive advantages in this case are achieved by offering product features to a narrow market. For example, Nordstrom has been very successful in luring more affluent customers away from Broadway, Macy's, and May Company by offering services that are simply not provided by these traditional department stores. These extras include a "shopping service" where a salesperson will stick with a particular customer as he or she moves from one department to another, or will go into various departments and choose items for the customer to try. In addition, the no-questions-asked return policy gives customers security when they purchase expensive merchandise, since they know they can return it if they decide in the comfort of their home that they're not happy with it.

The Strategic Plan

The strategic plan is the road map for the operational and financial management of the firm in the near term to ensure that you move the company in the direction of your vision and achieve your objectives in the long term. The issues a business owner must address with respect to the business plan are as follows: What does it consist of? How do I create one? How do I know whether it's any good? How do I make sure that I keep it current? I will examine each of these issues in the balance of the chapter.

The following is a typical structure for a strategic plan.

1. INTRODUCTION

A brief statement describing the business, history, products, and services of the firm, the industry in which it competes and its current position in the market.

2. MISSION STATEMENT

A brief statement of the mission of the firm and the vision of the CEO. The statement will include a description of the broad business area in which the company will compete, the products and services it will offer, the competitive advantages it has or will develop, and how it plans to grow and maintain its viability.

3. KEY SUCCESS FACTORS

The identification of those factors—especially those related to capability, resources, and finance—that are critical to the success of the firm in the market in which it is competing or plans to compete. A key success factor is a competitive skill or asset that is particularly relevant to the industry. To be successful in the industry, a company will usually need to have a substantial level of skill or asset quality in each of the industry's key success factors. For example, the key factors for the success of a land developer are (1) the ability to raise equity and debt capital; (2) a skill at locating and optioning desirable properties; and (3) the ability to recruit architects, engineers, designers, and consultants who will contribute to the development of a concept in the hope of being retained if the project should fund.

4. STRATEGIC ASSUMPTIONS

Those assumptions about the present and the future on which the strategic plan is based. Assumptions will encompass anticipated demographics of the customer base, the projected purchasing power of the various segments of the customer base, the inflation rate, the availability and cost of critical resources, and the company's labor costs. Since the assumptions are the very foundation of the plan, each needs to be supported by facts, expert opinions, and analysis, all of which are clearly referenced.

5. OBJECTIVES

The quantified goals on which the strategic plan is focused (such as sales, ROI, profitability, market share, resources, and capabilities), along with the date at which each goal will be achieved.

6. SITUATION ANALYSIS

A detailed discussion of the current condition of the firm, the industry in which it operates, and the companies against which it competes. This section will consist of the following subsections:

• Analysis of the internal strengths of the firm. A strength is a resource or capacity the organization can use effectively to achieve its objectives (for example, the ownership of a patent on an invention with a large potential market).

- Analysis of the internal weaknesses of the firm. A weakness is a limitation, fault, or defect in the organization that will keep it from achieving its objectives (for example, a leaderless and demotivated sales organization).
- Analysis of the internal strengths of each of the firm's major competitors.
- Analysis of the internal weaknesses of each of the firm's major competitors.
- Analysis of what is known about the plans, investment programs, and long-range strategies of each of the competitors.
- A discussion and analysis of each identified opportunity that, if exploited, could move the firm in the direction of its vision. An opportunity is a trend or event that could lead to a significant rise in sales or profits given an appropriate management response (for example, if a major competitor withdraws from the market, allowing your firm to expand its market share and earnings).
- A discussion and analysis of each identified threat that, if not neutralized, could seriously hinder the company's progress toward its vision. A threat is a trend or event that could result in a deterioration of present sales or profit patterns, requiring a management response to either mitigate or eliminate its effect (for example, a potential strike by a union organization that would disrupt operations).

7. STRATEGIC OBJECTIVES

A discussion of those opportunities and threats that will or will not be addressed by the action plans, along with the rationale on which these decisions are made. For opportunities and threats that will be addressed, identify the departments/individuals within the company who will be responsible for implementing the action plans associated with each opportunity or threat.

8. ACTION PLANS

Detailed action plans for each operating department or task force that has responsibility for implementing any part of the strategic plan. The action plans spell out the who, what, where, how, and when of specific tasks.

9. FORECAST

A multiyear financial forecast of the firm based on all the assumptions and plans set forth in the previous sections.

10. APPENDICES

Any industry studies, market research reports, or newspaper and magazine articles that were relied on in preparing the strategic plan, plus any other information that would assist the reader in understanding the plan (for example, detail schedules and analysis).

The Strategic Planning Process: How You Do It

The strategic planning process is concerned with answering three questions: (1) Where are we? (2) Where do we wish to arrive and by when? (3) How do we get from here to there? The result of this process is the strategic plan that I described above.

The creation of a strategic plan is a creative and demanding activity that, if it is to be meaningful, must be a priority activity for the CEO, the management team, and the necessary support staff over the duration of the planning process. To create a strategic plan for an ongoing business, you need the following elements:

1. A decision by the CEO to commit the necessary resources to the planning process. This will include a large block of the CEO's time and that of the senior managers, as well as funds for consultants, data gathering, and offsite meetings.
2. A planning team consisting of the CEO, senior management, and key department managers. The planning team should consist of between six to twelve participants and will function as a committee in which the participants leave their rank and titles at the door.
3. The services of a management consultant, who will act as the facilitator, educator, and coach and provide structure, motivation, focus, and direction.
4. Support staff as required to accumulate the data, perform research, and prepare reports as required by the planning team.
5. A series of meetings of the planning team, some of which will be offsite retreats to review progress, discuss issues, review and

criticize reports, and reach consensus on the elements of the strategic plan.

The planning process for a manufacturing organization was accomplished in the following manner. At the commencement of the planning process, the consultant conducted a daylong offsite introductory meeting with the members of the planning team to explain the planning process, the tasks that were to be accomplished, and the schedule for accomplishing the various tasks. The consultant distributed survey forms that were designed to elicit ideas and opinions of the team members, then conducted a free-form discussion among the participants during which they shared their ideas and goals for the planning process.

Over a period of two weeks, the consultant interviewed each member of the planning team to ensure that the survey material being collected was complete and actually reflected each member's individual thinking. The consultant used these interviews to identify potential problem areas in which data were either not available or highly suspect.

Approximately one month after the initial meeting, the consultant distributed the compilation of all the survey material and conducted a daylong offsite preplanning meeting to review the compiled survey material and solicit thoughts and opinions about the material from the team members. Two weeks later, a two-day strategic planning session was held offsite.

Several weeks after the strategic planning session, the consultant delivered a draft plan to the members of the team and met with them shortly afterward in a daylong meeting to review, discuss, and modify the plan. The consultant incorporated the modifications into the final draft of the plan and distributed it. At various times during the planning process, employees in the operating departments prepared schedules and forecasts and compiled data as required by the facilitator.

A productive strategic planning activity will provide many benefits to the organization. It creates a collegial atmosphere in which the key personnel can focus on the long-term survival and growth of the business. It makes salient many issues that get ignored in the day-to-day bustle of servicing customers. It also builds team spirit because the members of the team feel they are all participating in creating the future rather than just responding to their boss's orders. Moreover, it allows the CEO and the senior managers to articulate and share their values, beliefs, and aspirations with each other so that differences in perception can be identified and reconciled.

There are many roadblocks and hurdles that can (and often do) derail the planning process. If the company isn't prepared to neutralize their effect, the strategic planning process will prove to be an exercise in futility. Some of the obstacles are as follows:

1. *Lack of commitment on the part of the CEO.* This is the kiss of death for the planning process. The CEO cannot merely pay lip service to the process, but must be an active participant. He or she must show dedication both in word and deed.

2. *Lack of time, attention, and focus on the part of senior managers.* These members can be so involved in resolving day-to-day crises within their organizations that they find it very difficult to shift gears and start thinking about long-term issues. In many planning meetings, certain senior managers are only present physically; mentally, they're down on the production floor, hovering over a late shipment to an irate customer.

3. *Cost.* Strategic planning can be expensive. Even if you ignore the cost of diverting executives from their daily responsibilities, the out-of-pocket expenses are not trivial. At the least, the latter will include the cost of the consultant, the offsite facilities, and the cost of research, data accumulation, and report preparation. It is not uncommon for certain senior managers who don't see the need for strategic planning to grouse, "How can we justify spending this money when I can't get a purchase order approved for [whatever]?"

4. *The unknowable future.* Executives who are unfamiliar with strategic planning may throw up their hands in desperation over creating scenarios for three or five years in the future. The point is that even though we cannot predict the future, we must use all the information we know to make our best guess, since we are better off confronting the future with a plan than with no plan.

5. *Informational weakness.* Much of the information that is need-

ed by the planning team may not be readily available in a usable form. The consultant will often make the judgment as to the particular information that must be dug out, even if it delays completion of the plan.

6. *The action-oriented mind-set.* People who work in operations are action-oriented, and they're usually uncomfortable with the gestalt of strategic planning. Sitting around a conference table for hours talking about what the market and technology will look like in the future, or arguing about the wording of a mission statement, is not the way most manufacturing managers or sales managers would like to spend their time. It will take dedicated effort by the CEO and the consultant to persuade potential rebels continuously about the importance of the planning process.

7. *The pain of discussing weaknesses and threats.* That part of the planning process in which strengths and opportunities are discussed invariably generates a high degree of energy and enthusiasm. It provides the department managers that are responsible for the strengths to expound on why "we're the greatest," to denigrate the competitors, and to speculate on the various opportunities that the strengths would allow the company to exploit. The identification and discussion of weaknesses, however, may lead to defensive reactions on the part of the executives (including the CEO) who are deemed to be "accountable" for them. Other executives may react negatively to what they see as finger pointing: or the CEO may take umbrage over the identification of a particular weakness, especially if he has been closely associated with the capability or resource that's considered weak. This is an area in which a good consultant can save a planning activity. As the one participant who is absolutely unbiased and can be objective, he or she will have to move the process beyond the defensive behavior.

Evaluating Corporate Strategy

The dissection and analysis of every failed strategy uncovers reasons why any clear-thinking person would have seen that the strategy was flawed from the outset. In the comfort of their riskless environment, Monday-morning quarterbacks are often brilliant. While there is certainly no clear test to determine the viability of a strategy up front, a series of questions can be posed for any strategic plan that should at least identify the areas in which the plan is most vulnerable and/or offers the highest risk:

1. Is the strategy based on a competitive advantage that is sustainable? If we introduce the product or service to the market, how will we maintain our competitive advantage when our major competitor introduces their "knockout" product or service? Do we have—and are we willing to commit—the resources to fight them in the marketplace, and do we have the staying power to remain in the game?

2. Is the strategy internally consistent? Do the policies, organizational structure, and financial plan all move the company in the direction of the strategic objectives? A company that expects to fund an expansion plan with outside investment would have to ensure that its financial and accounting department was professionally managed.

3. Is the strategy consistent with the current environment? The future is unpredictable, but the present cannot be denied. The strategy must at the very least deal with the weaknesses of the company and its vulnerability to immediate threats. Otherwise, there may be no future with which to be concerned.

4. Is the strategy appropriate in view of the resources that are likely to be available? The resources that are usually critical to the successful implementation of a strategic plan are money, competence, and physical facilities. Many plans fail because one or more of the critical resources was not acquired in sufficient amount. For example, the late Malcolm Forbes explained that his magazine *Nation's Heritage* failed in 1949 because he failed to match his strategy to his resources: "It was a fiscal flop. . . . After one year we discontinued it. I think the timing was right but we didn't allow for [the cost of] the selling process."

5. Does the strategy involve an acceptable degree of risk? The strategy and the resources being committed determine the degree of risk the company is undertaking. Has the risk been quantified? If the strategy doesn't work, can the business sur-

vive? If not, the management is implementing a "bet the company" strategy.

6. Is the time frame for implementing the strategy appropriate in light of the way the market is developing? Timing is often crucial in the pursuit of a new market opportunity. Those participants who gain market share early enjoy high margins and often define the framework for the competitive battles that will occur in the future. If the time frame for your strategy is such that you will be trailing the market, you may have to invest more resources to cover the cost of taking away market share from the early entrants.

7. How are we doing? Are we meeting the milestones as set forth in the various action plans? If not, why not? Does our failure to meet the milestones indicate a lack of commitment to the plan on the part of management, or a lack of resources? Should we rethink the strategy and perhaps modify the plan?

A strategic plan will remain current and vital if it is continuously subjected to the scrutiny implied by the above questions. A strategic plan that is carefully placed in a three-ring binder and filed until next year's planning meeting represents a substantial waste of resources. The strategic plan is a working document—but you have to work it.

You now have a clear understanding of what a strategy is, as well as how it guides and gives purpose to your operational decisions and your capital investments. If you apply that knowledge to formulate and implement a strategic plan for your company, you will distinguish yourself from the majority of executives who apply for loans. The clarity and coherence of your descriptions and explanations of your actions will convince your banker that, at the very least, you understand what it takes for a business to survive and grow. That knowledge cannot help but make him feel better as he considers your loan application.

10

The Company You Keep

No man is so foolish but he may sometimes give another good counsel, and no man so wise that he may not easily err if he takes no other counsel than his own. He that is taught only by himself has a fool for a master.

—Ben Johnson

Arthur Miller's play *All My Sons* focuses on Joe Keller, a businessman who owns a manufacturing plant. During World War II Joe had been in a partnership with the father of Ann, the fiancée of his son, Larry. Larry, a pilot, has been missing in action for several years. Joe's other son, Chris, has fallen in love with Ann and wants to marry her.

During the war Joe's business had a contract with the government to manufacture cylinder heads for aircraft engines. Many of the heads were defective; however, the heads were shipped past the government inspectors and accepted. The cylinder heads were eventually installed and several planes crashed, killing the pilots. In the resulting investigation, Joe was exonerated, but his partner (Ann's father) was convicted and sent to prison. There remains a suspicion among the neighbors that Joe was also guilty but has somehow "beaten the rap." Throughout the investigation and its aftermath, Chris remained unshaken in the belief that his father was innocent. Subsequently, though, Chris discovers information indicating that Joe may actually have been guilty. In a key scene in the play, Chris confronts his father.

CHRIS: (*quietly, incredibly*) How could you do that? How?

KELLER: What's the matter with you!

CHRIS: Dad . . . Dad, you killed twenty-one men!

KELLER: What, killed?

CHRIS: You killed them, you murdered them.

KELLER: (*as though throwing his whole nature open before Chris*) How could I kill anybody?

CHRIS: Dad! Dad!

KELLER: (*trying to hush him*) I didn't kill anybody!

CHRIS: Then explain it to me. What did you do? Explain it to me or I'll tear you to pieces!

KELLER: (*horrified at this overwhelming fury*) Don't, Chris, don't . . .

CHRIS: I want to know what you did, now what did you do? You had a hundred and twenty cracked engine-heads, now what did you do?

KELLER: If you're going to hang me, then I . . .

CHRIS: I'm listening. God Almighty, I'm listening!

KELLER: (*their movements now are those of subtle pursuit and escape. Keller keeps a step out of Chris's range as he talks.*) You're a boy, what could I do! I'm in business, a man is in his business; a hundred and twenty cracked, you're out of business; you got a process, the process don't work, you're out of business; you don't know how to operate, your stuff is no good; they close you up, they tear up your contracts, what the hell's it to them? You lay forty years into a business and they knock you out in five minutes, what could I do, let them take forty years, let them take my life away? (*his voice cracking*) I never thought they'd install them. I swear to God. I thought they'd stop 'em before anybody took off.

CHRIS: Then why'd you ship them out?

KELLER: By the time they could spot them I thought I'd have the process going again, and I could show them they needed me and they'd let it go by. But weeks passed and I got no kick-back, so I was going to tell them.

CHRIS: Then why didn't you tell them?

KELLER: It was too late. The paper, it was all over the front page, twenty-one went down, it was too late. They came with handcuffs into the shop, what could I do? (*He sits on the bench.*) Chris . . . Chris, I did it for you, it was a chance and I took it for you. I'm sixty-one years old, when would I have another chance to make something for you? Sixty-one years old you don't get another chance, do ya?

CHRIS: You even knew they wouldn't hold up in the air.

KELLER: I didn't say that . . .

CHRIS: But you were going to warn them not to use them . . .

KELLER: But that don't mean . . .

CHRIS: It means that you knew they'd crash.

KELLER: I don't mean that.

CHRIS: Then you *thought* they'd crash.

KELLER: I was afraid maybe . . .

CHRIS: You were afraid maybe! God in heaven, what kind of man are you? Kids were hanging in the air by those heads. You knew that!

KELLER: For you, a business for you![1]

The play underscores a problem that causes bankers a great deal of anxiety: the lack of accountability that exists in owner-operated businesses. Joe Keller, like so many of his real-life small business colleagues, made a unilateral decision to slip defective cylinder heads past government inspectors; to do otherwise would result in the failure of his company. In deciding on the illegal course of action, he expected that the defective heads would not be installed in aircraft, so there would be no serious consequences. When he learned that his worst fears were realized and that twenty-one pilots died as a result, he covered up his culpability and allowed the blame to fall on his partner.

Joe Keller never discussed his plan with anyone–not his partner, his wife, or his son. No doubt he concluded that they would all have pointed out his plan was not only illegal but immoral and could produce the dire consequences that ultimately came to pass. Joe acted on his own and attempted to avoid being accountable for a thoroughly despicable act.

Business owners are confronted with moral dilemmas on a daily basis, and in many of the decisions they are forced to make their company's existence hangs in the balance. Some sell inventory for cash to avoid paying taxes, pledge falsified invoices as security for loans, issue false financial statements to their bankers to maintain their lines of credit, provide prostitutes to important buyers, or burn plants to collect insurance. In those instances where their illegal actions have been discovered, they explain that they acted the way they did to "preserve the business." In their calculus, the goal of preserving the business can justify virtually any illegal act short of murder.

The problem for small businessmen is exacerbated by the fact that they are not accountable to anyone for their actions, and they usually lack the professional support system with which to discuss and think through difficult and morally challenging decisions. Although autonomous business executives standing alone, making independent judgments that affect their lives, their businesses, and society are the stuff of romantic novels (Ayn Rand's *Howard Roark* comes to mind), bankers don't find them particularly attractive as borrowers because of their fierce independence and autonomy.

A Biblical proverb tells us that "plans fail for lack of counsel, but with many advisors they succeed." Everyone in business needs advisors on whose judgment and criticism they can rely. This is particularly true in family-owned businesses where there is no board of directors (the institution typically charged with the responsibility of holding the CEO accountable). Absent a board, there is literally no one to whom the CEO must explain and account for his or her actions.

That is what makes bankers nervous. They have seen many instances where an owner/CEO has been successful in obtaining a loan from a bank on the basis of what appears to be a prudent business plan. Once the funds are received and safely deposited in his or her checking account, though, the CEO embarks on a course of action unrelated to the business plan and engages in behaviors that could be judged counterproductive at best, and self-destructive and illegal at worst. Every experienced banker can tell stories about how a borrower used his newly acquired liquidity to purchase luxury cars, yachts, airplanes, speculative real estate, place his girlfriend on the payroll, take expensive vacations, use working capital to finance capital improvements, or finance an addition to his residence. Bankers understand that if independent-minded and seasoned professionals are involved in the business, helping the CEO oversee operations and plan strategy, the likelihood of the CEO resorting to illegal and immoral acts is greatly reduced.

Many entrepreneurs and CEOs have very limited business experience. They have spent the better part of their careers in a single industry and in many cases a single company, performing a specific management function such as managing a sales organization or a manufacturing plant. Their understanding of and experience with the fundamental business skills is, as a result, very often primitive. For the most part they are not financially literate, diplomatic, strategic thinkers, nor do they have particularly good leadership skills. But the good news is that they can make up for their personal shortcomings if they appreciate the value of and surround themselves with skilled and talented people who will compensate for their deficiencies.

Ideally, the CEO's team will be made up of the following entities/professionals:

- An accountability entity (either a board of directors or an advisory board), the members of which are experienced, independent businesspersons.
- A management staff composed of seasoned, competent, and independent executives who are eminently employable at other firms.
- A corporate attorney who will ensure that the firm operates in accordance with applicable laws and, to the extent possible, avoids litigation.
- A CPA who will ensure that the financials issued by the firm are timely, accurate, relevant, and appropriate.
- Consultants who at the very least will keep the firm in touch with current reality and future trends with respect to its operations, technology, and markets.

Boards of Directors

The board of directors is the governing body of a corporation. Its members are nominated and elected by the shareholders, and they manage the corporation subject to the by-laws and the corporation code of the state of incorporation. The members of most small to medium-sized corporations are selected from the following groups: the founder and the founder's family; senior managers; major investors and their representatives; professionals who have been selected because of their experience, skills, and stature in the industry; or retired executives. In a public company the CEO is hired by the board, which monitors his performance; the directors are subject to claims from the shareholders if they fail to discharge their responsibilities competently.

These responsibilities focus on the following areas:

- Recruitment, monitoring, appraisal, and compensation of top management
- Formulation of long-range corporate objectives
- Planning corporate strategies for meeting objectives
- Allocation of major resources
- Major financial decisions, including changes in capitalization
- Mergers, acquisitions, and divestitures

Being overseen by the board forces the CEO to prepare her plans carefully and defend them against the crucial analysis of board members, as well as to be accountable for the results achieved. The board members theoretically bring wisdom and judgment to the CEO to help her in her decision making. A substantial aspect of their value is that they can take a broad view of the business in that they are not involved in the hand-to-hand combat of daily operations.

In most closely held companies that don't have a board with some outside members, CEOs tolerate or foster sloppy operational procedures, inadequate record keeping and accounting, and little or no planning. Business graveyards contain the tombstones of many once-promising enterprises that, after an initial period of high growth, fizzled and collapsed. Outside board members bring in a dimension of experience, objectivity, and candor that will not be present among the family members and other insiders on the board.

The attitude of most CEOs of closely held companies is something like this: "I created this company, I control the majority (or all) of the stock, and I make all of the important decisions. Why do I want to subject myself to the criticism and/or control of an outsider?" Research studies have shown that although only 18 percent of closely held firms had one or more outside board members, 88 percent ranked their boards in the range of "useful" to "valuable."

The CEO of a closely held firm is certainly not obliged to accept the advice and counsel of the board; however, if the outside members of the board are serious about their fiduciary obligation to the company, they can always resign if they believe the CEO is using them only as window dressing.

In those situations where boards are not of value, either the board members do not invest the time and energy to be fully informed as to the business of the enterprise, making their advice irrelevant or shallow, or they are so closely aligned with the person or the interests of the CEO that they invariably rubber-stamp his plans and actions and rationalize his blunders and failures. Many outside board members get so used to their retainer and meeting attendance fees that they are reluctant to take any action that might jeopardize them, especially if there are no minority shareholders that could pose a threat. Fees for directors range from $2500 to $10,000 per year, depending on the size of the business and the number of meetings.

Advisory boards were created to provide a helping vehicle to CEOs without having the members subject to the legal liability being a board member entails. The advisory board operates independent of the legal board and has no authority for corporate governance. The members of the board are typically independent businesspeople, academics, and professionals who have been selected by the CEO for their experience, wisdom, skills, and creativity. They are usually paid a fee that is related to their time and effort.

The Management Staff

Robert E. Kelley, a management consultant and author of *The Power of Followership*, has done extensive research on the subject of effective leadership. He defines *followership* as that quality in people that allows them to take actions to bring about the reality of a leader's vision. As such, it is the flip side of leadership. According to Kelley, followership and leadership are a dialectic: just as the word *right* makes no sense without *left*, they depend upon each other for existence and meaning. Kelley points out that without the followership of his armies, Napoleon was just a man with grandiose ambitions; without the followership of three hundred sailors, Columbus would never have reached the New World. Organizations stand or fall on the basis of not only how well they are led, but also how well followers follow.[2]

Several research studies have examined the relative contribution to the success of an enterprise made by leadership and followership. The conclusion is that the leader's effect on organizational success is only 10 to 20 percent. Followership is the real "people" factor accounting for the other 80 to 90 percent that brings about the success the leader glories in. It is the senior managers responsible for the major functions of the business (such as sales, manufacturing, finance, and research and development) who must be the excellent followers.

Just as not all bosses are necessarily good leaders, not all subordinates are effective followers. In order for a business to achieve its maximum potential, it needs good leaders and effective followers. Kelley has identified these essential qualities of effective followers:

1. They manage themselves well. They have the ability to think for themselves, to work independently without close supervision. They freely accept responsibility that is delegated to them and feel a sense of ownership in each task they undertake.
2. They are committed to the organization and to a purpose, principle, or person outside of themselves. They are willing to subordinate and defer the satisfaction of their own needs in order to achieve the greater goals of the organization or movement. The "freedom riders" and marchers that pressed their cause under the leadership of Martin Luther King exemplify this quality. Their commitment is contagious, and their high morale acts as a magnet to attract other potential followers.
3. They build their competence and focus their efforts for maximum impact. They invest their own time to master skills that will be useful to their organizations and generally achieve higher performance standards than the particular job requires.

They understand the organizational mission and are constantly searching for overlooked problems that can interfere with the mission.

4. They are courageous, honest, and credible. They establish themselves as independent, critical thinkers whose knowledge and judgment can be trusted. They are generous in their praise of peers and subordinates, are quick to admit their own mistakes, and scrupulously avoid placing blame when projects fail. They have high ethical standards and aren't bashful about speaking up if they detect behavior that's inconsistent with those standards. They have the courage to openly disagree with leadership and aren't intimidated by the hierarchy and organizational structure.

The banker understands that a management staff composed of effective followers will act as a check and balance on the grandiose plans of an overly optimistic and ambitious CEO.

Attorneys: Knights in Not-So-Shining Armor

Every business owner needs a lawyer to help navigate the ever-expanding labyrinth of laws that affect businesses. Since the 1970s there has been an explosion of laws and regulations that directly or indirectly affect virtually every business in the United States. They include laws for the protection of the environment, endangered species, the nation's wetlands, the rights of minorities, women, the disabled, the health of the populace, the safety of employees, and on and on. Violations of these laws can result, in the worst cases, in criminal indictment and serious impairment of the business and the reputation of the principals; even in the best cases, they may result in lawsuits and fines.

I am familiar with the cases of several businesspersons who have seen the net worth of a business lifetime evaporate as the result of a complaint by a government agency. Having as part of your professional team an attorney who is familiar with your business and is knowledgeable about the various laws and regulations that are relevant to your operations will greatly minimize the probability of your being exposed to serious potential liability.

The presence of an attorney on your team will not be much of an asset, however, unless he or she is also interested in you and your business; is mature, intelligent, and creative; and has the negotiating and people skills that are invariably required to resolve complex corporate problems. Finding such an attorney is a daunting task.

In 1986 the United States had 3 lawyers per 1,000 residents, and the law schools were pouring out 30,000 new lawyers each year. The United States has more lawyers than Iceland has people, twenty times as many lawyers per capita as Japan, and three times as many lawyers per capita as England. Two-thirds of the world's lawyers practice in the United States, which has 6 percent of the world's population, thereby giving us an eleven-to-one "advantage" over the rest of the world in average per capita representation. On the basis of these statistics, one might think that it's a relatively simple matter to find a good lawyer. Wrong!

My own experiences exemplify the difficulty. I once hired an attorney who appeared to be mature, technically knowledgeable, and very experienced, but his negotiating skills were so poor that the opposition became enraged over his conduct and what should have been a minor scrimmage escalated into nuclear war. Another attorney, after working on a matter for several years, abruptly withdrew from the case because of marital and financial problems, forcing me to start over with a new firm. I hired an attorney who did an excellent job during the discovery and pretrial aspects of a complex litigation but fell apart during the trial and was crushed by the opposition. And finally, I was represented in several matters over a period of years by a prominent attorney who was given the opportunity to represent a party adverse to me in a major litigation and promptly accepted, in total breach of the canon of ethics to which lawyers subscribe.

Of the hundred-plus attorneys who have represented me or my opponents during my business career, I would consider rehiring approximately ten. My experience isn't surprising considering former Supreme Court chief justice Warren Burger's statement: "Up to one half of the nation's trial lawyers are unfit to appear in [any] court."

How do you go about identifying, hiring, and developing confidence in an attorney? The process I suggest—which is also applicable to the recruitment of the other types of professionals for your team (such as CPAs, consultants, and board members) discussed in this chapter—is as follows:

1. Develop a list of candidates by getting referrals from colleagues and professionals whose opinion you value. Be specific and ask them who they would hire if they had the same problem you do. If they were facing bankruptcy, what bankruptcy attorney would they select? If they had a securities problem, which attorney would they consider to be a securities expert? If they had a serious business problem that would likely end up in litigation, which trial attorney would they select? Tell the referrer that you're looking for the very best talent, and that cost is no object. You'll find that there will be considerable overlap in the names provided by different sources; you should be able to develop a list of perhaps five to ten candidates.

2. Interview each of the respective candidates in depth. Discuss your business plans, objectives, and needs. Be candid about your style and what you expect from your attorney. Probe the attorneys' background, education, and legal experience. Ask about their various clients and the types of work done for them. As the interview progresses, continue to ask yourself whether you feel comfortable placing control of your success and solvency in this person's hands.

3. At the conclusion of the interview process you will find that you feel an intellectual and emotional rapport with some of the attorneys; they will constitute your "short list." They are the ones you want to work for you.

4. As situations and projects develop that call for the services of an attorney, retain one from the group that you've recruited. Use each assignment as an experiment to measure how well the attorney meets your needs. Is he or she responsive? Can you see flaws in the quantity or quality of the work performed? Are you satisfied with the results? Does he or she perform well in court? Are the billings reasonable? Do you still trust this person?

5. Over a period of a few years, you will find that you feel better and work better with two or three of the attorneys on your short list, and you will use them more frequently. They will

have become, by evolution, the "good lawyers" on whom you can rely.

Certified Public Accountants: Scorekeepers Extraordinaire

A CPA firm performs two vital functions for the business. First, they will certify that the financials have been prepared in accordance with generally accepted accounting principles and that they are accurate, timely, relevant, consistent, and appropriate. Therefore both you and your banker will have a basis for evaluating the financial condition of the business and its progress against a financial plan. Second, they will help you plan your business and financial operations and prepare your tax returns to minimize the portion of your wealth that will be transferred to the ubiquitous taxing authorities.

In recent years, in an effort to increase revenues, major CPA firms have branched out into other areas that were traditionally the province of management consultants, including systems analysis, data processing, financial restructuring, and litigation support; however, preparing tax returns and certifying financials continue to be the core businesses of most CPA firms. CPAs differ radically in their philosophy with regard to planning for and paying taxes. They range from the very conservative, who recommend caution in the interpretation of the tax code (which results in your paying the maximum tax), to the very aggressive "catch me if you can" philosophy and the payment of minimum tax. Independent of where your CPA falls on this spectrum, it is the business owner who is ultimately responsible for the fines, penalties, and interest in the event the taxing agency is successful in challenging the returns.

Generally, it is a good deal easier to hire a competent CPA than a competent attorney, largely because the tasks of a CPA are more structured and administrative. Incompetence exists, however, and it can have very serious consequences for your business. For example, a client in the construction business didn't distinguish between bookings (orders in hand but not yet completed or billed) and accounts receivable (invoices outstanding for work completed but not yet paid). The client had been keeping his books in this manner for a period of two years, and financial statements were prepared monthly by a well-respected CPA firm. Two banks had reviewed these financials without comment, and both had provided lines of credit. It was apparent to me the banks hadn't realized that bookings were being included in the accounts receivable, since no distinction was made on the documents specifying the collateral for the loans. The effect of this error was that earnings, accounts receivable, net worth, the bank's collateral, and the tax obligations were all overstated.

Sometimes the CPA firm and the client conspire to create an accounting system that will confuse the taxing authorities in order to minimize the federal and state income taxes the company pays. As an example, one of my clients distributed his business transactions over five separate companies, each with a different fiscal year end. Although his business consisted of distinct strategic business units, he would run the transactions for a single unit through several of his corporations. Whether these machinations actually resulted in his paying less taxes is conjecture; what was certain was that neither he nor his CPA firm nor his banker ever really knew the real score.

I've seen instances where neither the business owner nor the CPA fully understands the scope and operation of the business. As a consequence, they are unable to construct an accounting system that will reflect accurately what happens in the business and the information the business executives must have to be able to monitor and control operations. The mountains of schedules and spreadsheets that are produced by the system therefore ignore critical aspects of the performance of the business operations. I recall an instance where a CPA firm was providing an oil-drilling contractor with a monthly financial statement that was approximately a half-inch thick. The statement contained a detailed analysis of the operation of every single rig and auxiliary item of equipment, including the costs of fuel, maintenance and depreciation. What the CPA did not provide, however, was a consolidated financial statement for the several core businesses. If he had, the consolidated statement would have shown that although the oil-drilling business appeared to be profitable, it was financing a losing construction company. The loans, while classified as assets on the balance sheet, would never be collected.

Occasionally, as the hundreds of millions of dollars in malpractice judgments against CPA firms will attest, the CPA firm and the company engage in the process of "creative accounting" to show the best face to the company's banks, trade creditors, bondholders, and stockholders. One example of such shenanigans came to my attention recently. A client had a large "current receivable" on his balance sheet that had been inactive for years. The receivable was owed by an insolvent partnership, one of whose partners was the CEO of the client company. In order to avoid writing off the receivable—which would've been appropriate considering its collection history—the CPA asked for a representation letter from the CEO setting forth the latter's opinion that the debt was fully collectable because all of the partners were willing and able to pay it. The CPA firm issued its opinion that the debt was fully collectable without ever contacting the other partners. Had they done so, they would've learned that only the CEO considered the debt valid; the other partners disavowed it.

Your banker knows that a CPA's certification of a financial statement is only a starting point for the bank's evaluation. You want that financial to be as close to reality as feasible when you present it to your banker. Your credibility depends on it.

Consultants

Consultants offer a business the opportunity to enhance its skills without materially increasing its ongoing costs of operation. The unique capabilities they bring to the business to solve a particular problem, perform a difficult task, or provide advice and counsel would not be available or affordable if those needs had to be satisfied by hiring full-time employees. Consultants can keep a business owner in touch with the realities of the marketplace by helping her determine how her business, products, technology, and personnel measure up against those of her competitors.

Many business owners are reluctant to retain consultants even when they are confronted with a vexing problem. A survey conducted by Krentzman and Samaras of seven hundred managers of small companies located across the country probed their apprehensions about hiring consultants and inquired about their experiences in using consultants. The survey revealed that the reluctance to hire consultants was due to concerns about fees, disclosure of confidential information, and the risk of hiring someone who would prove to be ineffective. Eighty percent of the managers who had used consultants reported they were very satisfied with the results that were achieved.

The principle reasons for hiring consultants fall into five broad categories:

1. *Reduce uncertainty.* Often the CEO is confronted with making a decision that is dependent on a large number of assumptions and variables that are difficult to quantify. A consultant can help the CEO think through the various assumptions and help quantify the variables in order to reduce the uncertainties associated with the decision.
2. *Provide independent and unbiased judgment.* The CEO is frequently faced with making a decision in a matter where all of the manager-advocates for a particular alternative have a vested interest in the outcome of the decision. Consequently, the CEO has no source of unbiased advice. A consultant, who has no relationship with any of the participants and no ownership of any of the alternative plans being offered, can make an independent assessment of the situation and provide a frank, unbiased recommendation to the CEO.
3. *Provide creative ideas and fresh approaches to a problem.* The experience of most business executives is limited to a very few businesses in a single industry, and their personal encyclopedia of business solutions is obviously limited by their own restricted experience. In contrast, as management consultants pass through many organizations in different industries and different locations they learn how to use experience from previous assignments to help their clients deal with new situations. As a result of being exposed to varying circumstances, they learn how to integrate their specific experiences into general trends and common causes of problems. They keep abreast of the current literature and the developments in their particular field. As a consequence of this broad exposure, consultants are an ideal source of creative ideas and solutions that are beyond the ken of the CEO and his management staff.
4. *Facilitating the process of diagnosing and solving problems.* Situations in which consultants are retained to facilitate problem solving are those where the size and scope of the problem can-

not be defined, when the problem is unique and does not fall within the experience of the company or the consultant, or when the company and the problem involve as-yet-unidentified unknowns. In such situations the organization needs a change agent to act as a business therapist, making the organization aware of its problems and soliciting ideas for dealing with these problems. In this role the consultant will attempt to raise consciousness, stimulate thinking, and create commitment and consensus among the personnel charged with the responsibility for dealing with the problem. The consultant refrains from promoting or imposing her own solutions. She is more concerned with passing on her approach, methods, and values so that the client organization has a substantial participation in the diagnosis and remedy of its problems.

5. *Act as a resource for information and performs tasks that are beyond the skills of permanent employees.* In this role the consultant assumes specific responsibility for performing a specific project under the direction of the CEO or a member of his staff.

Unfortunately, many executives either fail to recognize needs that consultants can satisfy or choose to meet those needs using either company employees or professionals with whom the CEO normally deals (such as a CPA or attorney). If the CEO fails to avail herself of the very best talent, she will unintentionally undermine her efforts to meet the goals of her business plan.

Quality Control

In Chapter 5 I described an actual meeting between bankers and a company that occurred as part of the due diligence investigation by the bankers. You may recall that the bankers' group consisted of a number of skilled professionals. Although the bankers were very impressed with the management staff and the consultants who represented the company, that meeting did not yield a positive outcome for the company, largely because the owner/CEO effectively undermined his team's presentation and alienated various members of the banker's contingent.

Suppose the company's representation was the mirror image of that which I described. For example, suppose the owner/CEO was the paragon of dignity and statesmanship and comported himself in a very professional manner. Conversely, assume that in place of the professional consultant and turnaround manager, the owner/CEO had engaged a cousin whose sole business experience was as a real estate salesman for a large developer. Instead of a chief financial officer with a CPA certificate, assume that the source of all financial information was a loyal bookkeeper with no formal education or substantial experience outside of the company. Assume that the financial projections were prepared by a local accounting firm who had been engaged exclusively for that purpose, and assume that the vice presidents of marketing and R & D were long-term employees who'd been rewarded with these titles because of their unswerving loyalty and unflinching compliance to the demands of the owner/CEO. Would the loan have been granted?

Probably not. While the owner/CEO might have appeared to be competent on the surface and favorably impressed the bankers on a personal basis, the weakness of the supporting members of his team would have severely undercut the image of leadership he was trying to project and neutralized every positive impression he might otherwise have made. In short, you will be evaluated and judged not only by your own resumé, the impression you make, and what your references and the bank's sources say about you personally, but also by the company you keep—the composition and quality of your management staff and professional advisors. If their stature isn't up to the level you've espoused and attempted to project, the picture the bankers see will definitely dampen their enthusiasm for a deal.

The Issue of Cost

Professional help is expensive, and competent professional help is very expensive. You can pay $20,000 for a Buick, $30,000 for a Cadillac, and $40,000 for a Lexus. All will have four wheels, brakes, a steering wheel, and lights; all will transport you from point A to point B in relative comfort. The automobiles may differ in amenities, reliability, and comfort, but not even the Lexus dealer would tell you were taking a huge risk if you bought the Buick rather than the Lexus in order to save $20,000. That's the major difference between buying products and hiring professionals.

When you buy a product you expect that you can rely on a specification, available to you before you make the purchase, that clearly describes what you will get for the money you invest. Differences in specifications usually are manifested by differences in price, supporting the old adage that "you get what you pay for."

When you hire a professional there is no specification available, so you rely on reputation, references, and the opinions of other professionals whom you trust. Without the availability of a clear specification, you may find it difficult to justify hiring a lawyer for $250 an hour when another lawyer who charges $125 an hour is willing and able to take on the assignment. Both lawyers are capable of doing research, preparing motions, appearing in court, and arguing the merits of your case before a judge and/or jury. The competence exhibited by the various attorneys and the results achieved, however, can vary by orders of magnitude. In the case of professional help, the results achieved are not linearly related to the fees paid, nor is there any guarantee that by paying a high hourly fee you will obtain much better results.

The only strategy that makes sense is to hire the professional you feel can accomplish the task at hand, then live with his or her fees. The professionals you will need as part of your team have expended years developing their skills, and they expect to be paid for their expertise. Many CEOs are understandably "turned off" by what they view as stratospheric hourly rates and are outraged when such rates are quoted. Recently, a CEO of a failing wood-products firm was referred to me by his banker to see if I could help him find replacement financing. In a lengthy telephone conversation he described the multiple horrors that had brought his thirty-year-old company to extremes. I outlined what I believed his current options to be and how I might help him refinance and revitalize his company.

When I quoted my fee, which at that time was based on a billing rate of $250 per hour, he expressed shock and stated he couldn't possibly justify paying fees of that magnitude; they were appreciably higher, he said, than those to which he was accustomed. Since I knew that the fees I quoted were comparable to those of other experienced turnaround consultants in California, I asked him what his alternatives were. He stated that he planned to rely on the advice and help of some friends, one of whom was an ex-banker. He felt the advice he would receive would be "just as good" as that which I could offer, and it would be provided gratis! Such an attitude is tantamount to thinking you can give yourself a heart bypass operation in order to avoid the surgeon's fee.

I do empathize with the CEO who is trying to buy professional help on the cheap. I fell into that trap when I was the owner/CEO of an electronics firm in the 1960s and 1970s. Because I didn't want to pay much, I hired professionals who were willing to work at the low end of the fee structure precisely because their services weren't in that great a demand. I suffered the consequences of my parsimony—unpleasant surprises and disappointing results. It was only after I started working as a consultant, receiver, and trustee (which necessitated that I become a sophisticated consumer of professional services) that I found it in my best interests to hire at the top of the professional pay spectrum, and—surprise, surprise—I reaped the rewards of my superior strategy: no adverse surprises, and gratifying results. While there is no guarantee of success simply on the basis of cost of compensation, in the case of hiring a professional you can safely bet that "you get what you pay for."

A banker will feel substantially more comfortable lending to a closely held or family business if the CEO's team includes respected attorneys, CPAs, consultants, a board of directors, and independent-minded managers. Why? Because the banker knows that reputable professionals will not jeopardize their reputation for a few pieces of silver from a corrupt business owner, nor do they want to be associated with a failing business. The banker knows he can rely on the fact that the professionals will do everything in their power to keep the business owner honest, legal, and focused. If several of these key players are missing from your team's roster, however, you can expect your banker to be nervous.

11

Leadership

"Human beings are controlled through their imaginations; that is what distinguishes them from animals. A soldier does not face death in order to earn a few pence a day, or to win some paltry order of merit. None but the man who touches his heart can stir his enthusiasm."

—Napoleon Bonaparte

Why does your banker care whether you're a skilled leader? Because both she and you know that you don't do all the work of the business by yourself. Your business employs people to carry out the various sales, production, engineering, and administrative work. They need to be managed, and they need to be led. The banker will be able to determine from the financial and operational information you provide and from her due diligence investigation whether your business is being properly managed. What will not be readily apparent is whether you are an effective leader—a much rarer commodity than an effective manager—and that cannot help but cause her some anxiety. A CEO who is an effective manager will help sell the banker on making the loan; a CEO who is an effective leader will vastly increase the probability of that loan remaining a valuable asset in the bank's portfolio.

Every experienced banker has a favorite story about some previous customer who was confronted with immense problems that threatened to sink the company and the banker's investment along with it. The charismatic leader, though, determined a creative course of action; promoted his vision; galvanized the employees, creditors, bondholders, and government agencies into a creative force to achieve the vision; built a successful company, and saved the banker's loan. As Manfred F. R. Kets de Vries, a business consultant and educator, observed:

> A good leader can inspire subordinates to do things beyond their normally accepted capabilities, can foster their enthusiasm for challenging new ventures, and can give them confidence to make them succeed. Exceptional leaders seem to have a mysterious power over their subordinates; they somehow seem to woo their followers into deep loyalty and almost unquestioning compliance with their wishes.[1]

More Than a Manager

Many businesspersons don't understand the difference between management and leadership. They use the terms interchangeably and assume that if someone is regarded as an effective manager, she is automatically considered a good leader, and vice versa. On the contrary, leadership and management are two distinctive and complementary systems of action for achieving the objectives of an organization, be it business, military, or social. Each has its own function and characteristic activities, and both are necessary for the success of the enterprise; however, not everyone is good at both leading and managing. A business needs a leader if it is to grow and be successful.

In his *Harvard Business Review* article "What Leaders Really Do," John Kotter[2] clearly discusses the differences between management and leadership. Management is about coping with complexity and relies on practices, policies, procedures, systems, organizations charts, job descriptions, action lists, schedules, hierarchies, and the like to create order and consistency in an enterprise. Without management a business becomes chaotic, since there's no structure to establish standards of performance or clear assignments of authority and responsibility.

Leadership, by contrast, is about coping with change. As the business world has become more competitive and volatile and product life cycles have shrunk, businesses must continually redefine their operations, technology, products, and markets in order to survive and remain competitive. Leadership is required to be able to effect these kinds of changes; the more rapid the changes are, the more effective the leadership must be.

One of my clients operates a mine that produces agricultural gypsum, a soil amendment that is often effective in increasing crop yields and maintaining soil quality. This mine has been operating for fifty years, serving essentially the same customer base. No major changes have occurred in the product, the mode of distribution, or the competitive environment. The company continues year in and year out, effectively converting gypsum into money—or, to be more poetic, dirt into gold.

The company should continue to be successful in the future until one or both of the following occurs: the mine runs out, or a more effective/less expensive product is introduced. This type of business does not require a great leader at the helm, but it does require a good manager to maintain quality and profitability. In contrast, businesses in the electronics and computer fields—where continuously changing technology, rapid product obsolescence, short product life cycles, frequent predatory pricing by competitors, and frequent changes in customers and suppliers are the norm—demand superior leadership to survive.

The differences between management and leadership can be best understood by comparing what managers and leaders do in carrying out their respective responsibilities. Each system of action involves deciding what needs to be done, creating agendas and networks of people that can accomplish an agenda, and then acting to make sure that people actually do the job. Each accomplishes these three tasks a different way and, most importantly, requires very different skills.

Managers decide what needs to be done by dissecting historical performance on various levels (product, division, department, or process), determine areas in which improvement (in revenue, cost, quality, and delivery) is required or possible, identify the increases or decreases in costs and resources that will effectuate these improvements, and prepare forecasts of revenue and costs for a variety of scenarios. This process is referred to as planning and budgeting, and it is the method by which managers communicate to their superiors and subordinates what is to be done in the future.

Leaders are charged with the responsibility of producing change and setting a direction for that change. They perform a broad analysis of how their business compares with others in the industry; they examine their strengths and weaknesses compared to their competitors; they gather and examine extensive data on trends that will affect their products and services in the future; and they try to identify opportunities to exploit and threats to defend against. They attempt to understand where future business will come from and how to develop competitive advantages to achieve their unfair share.

The result of this activity will be a vision of what the business should look like at some future time, plus a broad strategy for achieving that vision. In addition, for the vision to be credible, it must be consistent with reality and serve the interests of the leader's constituents. The vision and the strategy may only be casually related to the current business operations of the company; that is why leadership is so difficult. To be effective, the leader must somehow rise above the grubby mundane activities of her marketplace and engage in what Disney refers to as "imagineering." She must be able to see the future and have a good idea as to how she will achieve it. Examples are the vision Henry Ford had of the potential of the automobile and the vision Thomas J. Watson, Jr. (of IBM), had of the future of the computer industry.

Managers create the networks of people and relationships needed to do the business of the company by creating an organizational chart and job descriptions for each position; formulating policies, procedures, reporting requirements, and control systems that specify how each person interacts with every other person in the organization; recruiting individuals to fill the positions and training them appropriately; and then monitoring the performance of the various departments and individuals to identify and correct problems.

The job of organizing and staffing, while complex and challenging, is quite structured. Kotter likens it to making architectural decisions once you've conceptualized the plan and elevation of a building. Leaders create their networks and relationships by communicating their vision using every communication medium and rhetorical and symbolic device available. The manager, in many ways, has total control of the organization and staffing process: he designs the boxes, hires the people to fill the boxes, and can change either the people or boxes until the human organization performs in the manner he intended. A leader, whatever her position of power, cannot wave a magic wand and order her people to "believe!" She must be able to articulate the vision in such a way that her followers will *want* to believe and then *will* believe. This is indeed a very rare talent.

Getting people to comprehend a vision of an alternative future is a communications challenge of a magnitude greater than anything the manager does. Martin Luther King, Winston Churchill, and John F. Kennedy were masters of the art; so were or are Franklin Roosevelt, Adolf Hitler, Abraham Lincoln, Lee Iacocca, Mary Kay Ash, and Charles Schwab.

Managers ensure that their organizations achieve their objectives by using rational systems of measurement and control. The planning process establishes realistic production targets; the organizing and staffing process creates the man/machine systems to meet those targets; and the control systems measure output at various stages in the process and make changes in machines and people to correct deviations between planned and actual output. Tasks are structured so that normal people behaving in normal ways can accomplish highly routine jobs. They are encouraged to perform in accordance with their job description through a system of rewards and punishments.

If a plant is functioning properly, it can be a very boring place to work: there are no challenges that stimulate the intellect or get the creative juices going. In contrast, getting an organization to achieve grand visions and "go where no man has gone before" requires that the leader energize his followers to move in the direction of the vision. In order to energize them, he will have to inspire and motivate them; systems of rewards and punishment will only buy vicious compliance.

In addition to clearly articulating the vision so that their followers identify with it and believe it, effective leaders motivate their followers by continuously explaining how achieving this vision will satisfy the followers' needs and continuously bolstering their self-esteem through recognition and praise.

The Skills of the Effective Leader

Surveys conducted by Robert E. Kelley revealed the following:

- Two out of five bosses have questionable abilities to lead.
- Only one in seven leaders is perceived by his or her followers as a role model.

- Less than half of the leaders are able to instill trust in their subordinates. Nearly 40 percent of the leaders have "ego problems," feel threatened by talented subordinates, have a need to act superior, and do not share the limelight.[3]

Clearly, effective leadership is not a commodity that is in abundant supply. It is appropriate, therefore, that you understand which skills effective leaders have and determine where you need to improve. Perhaps with that knowledge you'll be able to avoid being one of Kelley's statistics.

In order to create the vision for your business—a realistic and credible picture of what a future might be—you need to be aware of what is happening in your industry and what trends are likely to influence technology and markets in the future. You need the skill to gather and assimilate the vast amount of information that is generated, discuss it with other leaders and influencers in the industry, and then discern patterns and structures and formulate hypotheses and theories that make the present and future worlds understandable. This effort requires a combination of intellectual creativity and social skills. If your vision is to be credible, it must be consistent with both current reality and the likely future reality that current trends portend.

Leaders need to be technically competent in the subject areas on which their vision is constructed. If they don't know what they're talking about, they will quickly lose credibility among their prospective followers. Understanding the "big picture"—recognizing patterns and relationships, making sense of seemingly disjointed events, and thinking and speaking in the abstract—while essential, will not be sufficient. In order to persuade her followers that she is truly in touch with reality, the leader must be able to operate where "the rubber meets the road": at the detail level, where the work of carrying out the vision must be done. Lee Iacocca's intimate familiarity with the automobile industry, gained over a forty-year period, was a critical factor in his ability to create the constituency that helped him revitalize Chrysler.

In order to create followers to help achieve her vision, a leader must articulate and communicate the vision, her rationale for it, and her strategy for achieving it in such a way that followers will be attracted to the vision and want to share the leader's future reality.

No aspiring leader—business, political, or social—will ever be effective unless she is skillful in the use of stagecraft, theater, symbols, and oratory to communicate her vision in the various media through which her followers may be influenced.

History and literature abound with examples of leaders with such gifts of communication that they were able to convince millions of people to accept their vision and the related strategy to achieve it. Here are some examples:

> I have a dream that one day on the red hills of Georgia the sons of former slaves and the sons of former slaveowners will be able to sit down together at the table of brotherhood. . . .
>
> I have a dream that my four little children will one day live in a nation where they will not be judged by the color of their skin, but by the content of their character. (*from a speech by Martin Luther King at the Civil Rights March on Washington, August 28, 1963*)

> We shall not flag or fail. We shall go on to the end. We shall fight in France, we shall fight on the seas and oceans, we shall defend our island, whatever the cost may be. We shall fight on the beaches, we shall fight on the landing grounds, we shall fight in the fields and in the streets, we shall fight in the hills; we shall never surrender. (*from a speech by Winston Churchill delivered to the House of Commons on the fall of Dunkirk, June 4, 1940*)

> Today we meet in the aftermath of the Falklands battle. Our country has won a great victory, and we are entitled to be proud. This nation had the resolution to do what it knew had to be done—to do what it knew was right. We fought to show that aggression does not pay, and that the robber cannot be allowed to get away with his swag. . . .
>
> The lesson of the Falklands is that Britain has not changed and that this nation still has those sterling qualities which shine through our history. This generation can match their fathers and grandfathers in ability, in courage, and in resolution. We have not changed. When the demands of war and the dangers to our own people call us to arms, then we British are as we have always been—competent, courageous, and resolute. (*from a speech delivered by British Prime Minister Margaret Thatcher at a rally, July 3, 1982*)

> Let the word go forth from this time and place, to friend and foe alike, that the torch has been passed to a new generation of Americans, born

in this century, tempered by war, disciplined by a hard and bitter peace, proud of our ancient heritage, and unwilling to witness or permit the slow undoing of those human rights to which this nation has always been committed, and to which we are committed today at home and around the world.

Let every nation know, whether it wishes us well or ill, that we shall pay any price, bear any burden, meet any hardship, support any friend, oppose any foe to assure the survival and the success of liberty. *(from the inaugural address of John F. Kennedy, January 20, 1961)*

In addition to articulating their message, effective leaders continuously interpret developments in society and industry to help their followers understand the significance and implications of these developments for their careers and lives. Franklin Roosevelt's radio fireside chats are an excellent example of the use of this technique.

Effective leaders have the ability to inspire trust from their followers. Trust is the glue that connects followers to their leaders. Trust implies integrity, credibility, and consistency on the part of the leader. It requires that the leader be able to empathize with his followers—not just state that he understands them, but actually be able to experience emotionally their feelings and frustrations.

In order to be a leader, you need the endurance to cope with the never-ending demands on your time, the stresses and strains caused by the ever-changing environment, and the inevitable criticisms of your policies, actions, and person. Effective leaders are able to "suffer the slings and arrows of outrageous fortune." They have learned how to manage stress and maintain balance in their life. They have high self-esteem and maintain a positive attitude as they pursue their objectives. They persevere without becoming obstinate.

Effective leaders have developed the skill to manage themselves. They are realistic about their strengths and weaknesses, and they can distinguish between situations in which they must personally "carry the ball" and when it's in the best interest of the enterprise to hand the ball off to some other member of the team. They've developed sufficient self-esteem to admit their own errors freely and to accept advice and criticism without feeling threatened. They recognize that their followers are partners, and that for the partnership to work, they need to tell the truth and listen to their partner's ideas. They reinforce their followers' innovation and creativity and are generous in sharing the rewards achieved by the enterprise among all of those who contribute to its success. The leader understands that authority, responsibility, accountability, relative pay, perks, and benefits are always going to be issues in any organization, and he has learned to be sensitive to the needs, wants, and expectations of his followers.

Because he is able to manage himself, the leader understands the dark side of being a leader and the various internal and external forces that frequently destroy trust, credibility, and effectiveness. Specifically, these include the following:

- The tendency for leaders to become corrupted by power, as described by Lord Acton in his famous aphorism: "Power corrupts, and absolute power corrupts absolutely."
- The tendency for leaders to exhibit hubris (excessive pride, self-importance, and self-entitlement) in the mistaken belief that a series of successes is invariably followed by more success.
- The tendency of leaders to succumb to soaring ambition and seek possessions, positions, and glory beyond their capability.
- The tendency of leaders to persist along a given course in order to justify their initial decision in selecting that course.

The stories of great leaders who are destroyed as a result of hubris, stubbornness, blind ambition, or abuse of power are grist for the mill of biographers, dramatists, and novelists. Shakespeare chronicles the demise of Marc Antony, the Roman tribune, who deserted his troops in the battle of Actium in order to follow Cleopatra and brought disgrace and death upon himself.

Henry Ford created the powerhouse of Ford Motor Company shortly after World War I based on the concept of producing a standardized automobile—the Model T—in sufficient quantities that the average citizen could afford one. His single-mindedness allowed Ford to achieve a 66 percent market share and unchallenged leadership. But the same single-mindedness, combined with hubris that the success would continue, converted Ford from a brilliant entrepreneur to a despot who would not change his strategy to meet the challenge of General Motors. As a consequence, Ford's market share plummeted to 20 percent, and General Motors established dominance in the automobile market.

You may remember reading about Jim Bakker, the formerly high-living leader of the "Praise the Lord" TV ministry whose lavish spending habits (air-conditioned doghouses, $500 shower curtains) and sexual peccadilloes led to his defrauding the public of $3.7 million, for which he was convicted and had to trade his pulpit for a prison cell. And then there's the case of Robert Maxwell, the English media entrepreneur who built a multibillion-dollar empire of newspapers, publishing houses, and radio and TV stations. Maxwell disappeared from his yacht in November 1992 under very mysterious circumstances; in his wake he left an empire that was in financial shambles. It was soon revealed that Maxwell had siphoned $750 million out of the pension fund of the *Daily Mirror* (a British tabloid that he owned), pillaged the treasuries of two public companies that he controlled, shifted large sums in and out of family trusts located in Liechtenstein, and illegally boosted the price of shares of his flagship enterprise, Maxwell Communications Corporation, in order to prop up their collateral value for the bank loans they secured. In addition, he manipulated the shares of stock in Berlitz International (owned by Maxwell Communications), by pledging them to nine different parties. His sons, who were suspected of having aided their father in structuring illegal transactions, were soon ensnared in a criminal investigation and filed bankruptcy.

Within a month of his disappearance, the British financial, political, and social community that had feted Maxwell and cheered his exploits for thirty years, along with thousands of loyal followers, were referring to him as a "rogue," "crook," "bully," "thief," and "megalomaniac." All his wife of forty-seven years could say was, "I'm confused. . . . When I read this deluge about my husband, I think I'm reading about a man I never knew."

The Leader's Gyroscope: Autonomy, Integrity, High Self-Esteem

The three most important characteristics that will allow a leader to stay the course in pursuit of her vision and avoid the snares of hubris, tyranny, and blind ambition are autonomy, integrity, and high self-esteem.

Autonomy

Autonomy refers to the capacity to assess reality accurately and integrate this assessment with internal cues (or "gut feelings") to develop a course of action that makes sense. It pertains to the extent to which the source of self-approval lies within the self, rather than being dependent on the social environment.

The American stereotype of the autonomous individual is one who has his feet solidly placed on the ground, knows what he wants, and looks forward to achieving it. The image of Gary Cooper standing alone in the middle of the town in the movie *High Noon* is the quintessence of this autonomous individual. An autonomous individual enjoys an inner freedom; his decisions need only conform to his own sense of what is right, not to that of his peers, friends, relatives, business associates, vendors, or others. He doesn't worry about "what people will think" if such concerns will deter him from reaching his goal. Consequently, he can make the really hard choices—those that others may shrink from.

Integrity

Integrity refers to the ability of the leader to maintain a sense of wholeness or unity by integrating her standards, convictions, and behavior. An integrated individual is one who thinks, speaks, feels, and acts in a consistent and unified manner that is consistent with her beliefs, personality, and character; her thoughts, feelings, words, and actions are all focused toward the same end. The opposite of an integrated individual is a disorganized individual who speaks exactly opposite to what she is thinking, acts in an inconsistent, and unpredictable manner, and feels perpetually anxious.

High Self-Esteem

High self-esteem implies that an individual has the confidence to make the choices and decisions that will guide his life and believes that he is a worthy and valuable human being. This confidence comes from dealing successfully with what life has to offer. If he doesn't possess the skills at the time to deal with a problem, he will acquire them. If he doesn't have the expertise to evaluate a situation, he will hire someone who does. And if he has to make a difficult emotional decision, he'll be able to make the decision and deal with the consequences of that decision in an appropriate and mature manner. If life deals bad cards, he knows that he'll be able to make the best of the situation that evolves.

Individuals who are fortunate to possess high self-esteem will, when confronted with the vicissitudes of life, remain relatively untouched emotionally and will continue to persevere in their quest. They continue despite a lack of positive reinforcement, understanding, or approval of significant others, and often in the face of hostility and opposition. They won't judge themselves harshly if they suffer a humiliating defeat, nor will they succumb to pride if blessed with a glorious victory. Neither the roar of approval nor the hiss of disdain that emanates from the crowd affects their opinion of themselves. Their only concern is that they live up to the realistic standards they have set for themselves.

Autonomy, integrity, and high self-esteem are like a well-calibrated gyroscope that keeps the executive in balance. Like the gyroscope, which has the capacity to keep a ship or plane on a given course despite radical changes in the environment, the leader needs an internal mechanism to keep upright. When they are present in the executive's personality, autonomy, integrity, and high self-esteem reinforce each other during a crisis. They allow for the freedom to make real choices and to draw upon one's personality. A business crisis is a test of the executive's capacity to remain unified under pressure in situations that can produce disintegration.

Without these traits, the executive may fail to be objective or even aware of the challenges around her. If she has a sufficient amount of integrity, she has the capacity to be sufficiently objective and realistic. To some, such an executive may appear cold, indifferent, and overly controlled; she appears to fear no one and to blame no one.

Evaluating Leadership: A Look Back in Time

The term *suspended disbelief* is used by writers of fiction to describe the psychological state required of a reader in order for that reader to be accessible to the writer. It means that the reader must suspend the natural tendency to be skeptical of the writer's efforts to weave a story. Without suspended disbelief gothic, horror, science fiction, and other writing genres that defy human experience would have no market.

So suspend your disbelief for a brief time and imagine that you're an international banker who has the capability to travel through time and space to do business. Your superiors at the International Bank of Space and Time have provided you with a loan proposal that has survived a preliminary screening. Your assignment is to conduct a due diligence investigation and report back to the loan committee with your recommendations as to whether the borrower should be funded. The prospective borrower is William Bligh, Admiral, Royal Navy, Ret.; the purpose of loan is to finance a travel business which will provide transportation to and from Tahiti and accommodations in Tahiti; the target funding date: January 1813.

Your staff has compiled a brief dossier on the applicant.

You review it in preparation for your interview.

DATE OF THIS REPORT: 1813

NAME: William Bligh

BORN: 1754

AGE: 61

RELATED EXPERIENCE:

1762–1812   Royal Navy (Retired) Rose to the rank of Rear Admiral. His career has in general been quite distinguished, except for a few incidents (noted below) that give rise to some concern on the part of the Bank.

1776–1779   Because of his reputation as a navigator and cartographer, was recruited by Captain James Cook for the expedition to find the elusive northwest passage between Europe and Asia. Cook was killed by natives during a provisioning stop on the island of Hawaii, which he had discovered during the voyage.

1781   Received his commission as lieutenant.

1783–1787   Employed in the merchant service transporting cargoes from the West Indies to England; served as a company's agent in Jamaica.

1787–1789   Appointed to command the HMS *Bounty* with orders to collect breadfruit trees in Tahiti and transport them for transplanting in the West Indies, where they would serve as a cheap source of food for the Negro slaves. During a five-and-a-half-month stop in Tahiti, 1,015 plants were loaded on the *Bounty*. Twenty-four days after the *Bounty* set sail for the West Indies, the ship was seized by mutineers led by master's mate Fletcher Christian (third in the line of command), who was in fact Bligh's protege.

Bligh and eighteen others were set adrift in a twenty-three-foot-long open boat with no firearms and very limited provisions. Bligh and his men were able to reach Timor in the East Indies forty-nine days later, after an extraordinary voyage of 3,618 miles. Only one man was lost during the voyage: the quartermaster, John Norton, who was murdered by natives.

This was the longest journey ever recorded in an open boat. The daily rations during the trip were limited to an ounce of biscuit and a quarter pint of water; these were supplemented occasionally when the men were able to catch a bird or a fish. During the trip Bligh doled out the food, charted the course, steered the boat, maintained a log, and kept the men's spirits up with lectures about the areas through which they were sailing.

This mutiny was extensively reported in the press. Bligh was praised for the navigation and leadership skills he exhibited in bringing his longboat to safety, but he also was vilified by the proponents of seamen's rights for being a sadistic tyrant whose inhumanity to his crew made the mutiny on the *Bounty* inevitable. Bligh was completely exonerated in a court-martial, and several of the mutineers were executed in England.

1792–1793   Commanded a breadfruit-tree mission to Tahiti that was completed successfully and without major incident.

1797–1801   Commanded warships with distinction at the battles of Camperdown (1797) and Copenhagen (1801). Bligh was commended personally by his immediate commander, naval hero Admiral Horatio Nelson, for his role in the battle of Copenhagen.

1805–1808   Was appointed governor of New South Wales in Australia; however, the deputy governor led a mutiny in 1808, arrested Bligh for "oppressive behavior," and returned him to England. The mutineers were subsequently tried and found guilty of conspiracy, and Bligh was exonerated.

FAMILY: Married to Elizabeth Betham (now deceased) in 1781, six surviving children.

ORGANIZATIONS: Fellow of the Royal Society

PUBLICATIONS: "A voyage to the South Sea Undertaken by Command of His Majesty for the Purpose of Conveying the Bread-Fruit Tree to the West Indies in His Majesty's Ship the Bounty Commanded by Lieutenant William Bligh, and an Account of the Mutiny on Board H.M.S. Bounty and the Subsequent Voyage of Part of the Crew, in the Ship's Boat, from Tofoa, One of the Friendly Islands, to Timor, a Dutch Settlement in the East Indies (1792)"

AWARDS: Presented with a Gold Medal by the Royal Society for Promoting Arts and Commerce for his role in bringing breadfruit to the West Indies.

The staff work indicates that the project proposed by the prospective borrower is acceptable. Moreover, the five-C analysis of character, capacity, collateral, capital, and conditions indicates that the project could be recommended to the loan committee. After reviewing the file on this project, you decide that the major uncertainty associated with this prospective borrower is his leadership ability, especially in a business environment. Although he's had a distinguished career in the military, some of the information in the file causes you concern. You therefore decide to focus on the leadership issue in your forthcoming interview, particularly his ability to inspire and motivate others to help achieve his business objectives.

226 • *Romancing the Business Loan*

You review the bank's written policy, which outlines demonstrated leadership ability on the part of the borrower as a prerequisite for a strong recommendation and the absence of demonstrated leadership ability as sufficient grounds for rejecting a borrower. It states that effective leaders will demonstrate the following positive characteristics:

1. The ability to formulate and create a future vision of the enterprise that is consistent with the unmet needs of the management and employees.
2. The ability to articulate and communicate this vision in a manner that inspires and motivates the management and staff to devote all of their energies toward meeting the objectives necessary to realize the vision.
3. The ability to "stay the course"—to keep the vision in focus despite the adversities and criticism that invariably impede the implementation of any plan.
4. The ability to "reality check" the vision constantly in light of changed circumstances and to make adjustments in the goals, strategy, or tactics to ensure that the vision remains credible.
5. The ability to select competent, loyal, and intelligent subordinates to help plan and execute the actions that are required to realize the vision.

The policy also states that effective leaders will not be prone to exhibit any of the following negative characteristics:

1. Abuse their positions of power.
2. Be arrogant and exhibit behavior indicating that they believe they are entitled to wealth and success.
3. Have goals that are unrealistic in light of their resources and capabilities.
4. Be stubborn, insensitive, and exhibit a lack of empathy.

You are now prepared for your due diligence interview with the applicant. You look up his current address in space/time and find it to be Manor House, Faningham in Kent, 1813; you ask the bank's travel department to make arrangements. Confident that you understand all aspects of the situation, you embark on your due diligence trip.

Several days later, you're in your office preparing your report for the loan committee, which is to meet the next day. Prior to writing up your recommendations, you review your notes, including the following excerpt from the interview.

BANKER: We're very positive about the Tahitian project. The market forecasts you've prepared indicate there is a large demand for a full service, five-star resort and comfortable, safe cruise vessels for transporting the passengers. Your name and reputation will ensure that the project will excite the imagination of the whole of Europe.

BLIGH: Ah, yes. That pleases me a great deal. With the recent death of my dear Elizabeth, I need something to work on that will make use of my talents—and is not associated with battle and death. I have seen too many good men die. I want to live out my life bringing pleasure and joy to people rather than pain and suffering.

BANKER: There are some items that came up during the staff work that I'd like to discuss with you.

BLIGH: I fully expected it, so proceed.

BANKER: You've been described in the press as having an overzealous and overbearing manner, as unduly tyrannical, possessed of an abusive and insulting tongue, with a propensity for temper tantrums. Furthermore, it is said that your appellation among your peers is—

BLIGH   (*interrupting*) "That *Bounty* bastard"?

BANKER: Yes. Perhaps you can give me your side.

BLIGH: Well, of course, this was all exhaustively dealt with in the court-martial, and I was completely exonerated of any wrongdoing associated with the mutiny on the HMS *Bounty*.

BANKER: I've read the proceeding. But I'm more interested in your comments.

BLIGH: I do have a terrible tongue and temper, which I zealously work to control. God, I wish I could cure it! But those who have served with me and my friends and colleagues know that shortly after I explode, I recover quickly and bear no grudge. As for my reputation with my men, I am sure you will find it no worse than that of other ship captains. Many of them say I was a father to every man on the ship.

BANKER: Fletcher Christian's brother, Edward, has stated that his interviews with the *Bounty* crew prove your cruelty, sadism, and the excessive lashings you ordered made the mutiny on the *Bounty* inevitable.

BLIGH: Poppycock! The number of punishments was absolutely in line with those ordered by other ships' captains on voyages of similar length.

BANKER: Then what caused the mutiny? You were totally surprised. In fact, you wrote in your journal the night before the mutiny: "Thus far the voyage has advanced in a course of uninterrupted prosperity, and has been attended with many circumstances equally pleasing and satisfactory."

BLIGH: Yes, I was surprised. There was no hint of mutiny. The precipitating event, I believe, was my calling Mr. Christian a hound and a scoundrel for stealing cocoanuts, which he admitted. I asked him to dinner that night to apologize, but he sent his regrets, stating that he was ill. (*pause*) But I believe the underlying cause was that several of the crew had discovered their paradise in Tahiti. Most seamen come from overcrowded, unsanitary homes whose previous idea of happiness was a smelly waterside tavern in which they could drink themselves stupid and finish the evening in the arms of a coarse-mouthed doxy. We showed them a life-style in Tahiti—with its beautiful weather, clear ocean, and pristine beaches—where they enjoyed rich meats, luscious fruits, and the warm-scented, willing arms of Tahitian maidens. For most seamen a life on Tahiti was going to be much happier than any they could possibly experience in England. Many had developed close attachments to their "wives" and other natives. The king, I learned later, had offered many of them tracts of land to cultivate should they stay. Frankly, I did not anticipate the extent to which the five and one-half months of dissipation and ease on Tahiti would undermine the ship's discipline. I believe that was the true cause of the mutiny on the *Bounty*, and I am accountable for having neither expected nor planned for it.

BANKER: I note that you didn't bring charges against John Freyer, your second in command, for questioning your authority during your harrowing trip to Timor.

BLIGH: Damned ingrate! He was always grousing and causing me problems. But he was hungry, tired, and frightened—it was understandable, but not excusable. Nothing would be served by my sullying Freyer's record. We had all had our fill of hardship.

BANKER: I want to thank you, Admiral, for your candor. You've been very helpful. I have everything I need to make my report.

BLIGH: Well, good day, then.

Your recommendation reads as follows: "On the basis of the staff work, the background check, and my interview with the borrower (which is attached), I recommend that the borrower's loan application be approved. Admiral Bligh is an individual with stellar character and outstanding leadership qualities. But for yellow journalism and the efforts of Edward Christian to besmirch his name in order to clear that of his mutinous brother, Admiral Bligh would be regarded as a true naval hero."

Your banker wants borrowers who have the leadership qualities of Admiral Bligh, who is tenacious, intelligent, courageous, and inspirational. He or she wants someone who will not fold when the tough times come, take advantage of employees when resources are scarce, or be mean-spirited when under stress. Do you doubt that Admiral Bligh would literally move heaven and earth to pay back the bank's loan? You now have your model. Persuade the banker that you have the leadership qualities of an Admiral Bligh, and you can expect to move to the very top of his or her list of loan applicants.

12

Staying at the Top of Your Game and Keeping Your Banker Happy

PATIENT: Doctor, I can't get any sleep. I'm worried. I owe the bank $100,000, and I can't pay.

PSYCHIATRIST: Call your banker immediately and tell him you cannot pay the $100,000. He won't be able to sleep, but you will.

Congratulations! The bank has provided the funds. You have one day to enjoy the euphoria of that large line of credit; then you need to get busy making your plan a reality. Achieving this goal will be greatly facilitated if you continuously do two things: (1) stay fully engaged in the management of your business, and (2) keep your banker happy.

In this chapter I will show how the six skills we discussed in chapters 6 through 11, which will enhance your ability to charm your banker, will also keep you at the top of your game in managing your company. Finally, I will review the behaviors and actions that are absolutely essential to maintaining the interest and support of your banker for many years.

Bankers know that 90 percent of business failures are due to bad management. Bad management falls into three categories: (1) the failure of management to anticipate the future environment in which it will compete, (2) the failure of management to learn from its experiences in similar business situations, and (3) the failure of management to adapt to a changing environment. Therefore, throughout the life of your loan, your banker will be watching your business for evidence of these failures. To maintain your loan, you must establish your ability to anticipate, learn, and adapt.

Table 12–1 shows a matrix consisting of the "banker's six" key borrower's characteristics identifying the rows and the three primary types of management strengths heading the columns. At each intersection where possessing the attribute designated by the row will prove the managerial strength identified by the column, I have placed an asterisk (*).

As you can see, there is an asterisk at most of the intersections, meaning each of the attributes that will help you romance the loan will also provide insurance against your business succumbing to three leading causes of business demise.

Let's see how.

Anticipating

Organizations fail to anticipate because leaders don't ask, followers don't tell, and both leaders and followers readjust their perceptions of reality to fit their fantasy that the future will behave in accordance with their hopes. The leader may not ask because he or she is not fully engaged in the business, finds interaction with subordinates frustrating and unsatisfying, and wants to avoid confrontation. Subordinates may not tell because they are intimidated by the

TABLE 12–1
Keeping the Business Loan

The Banker's Six	Ability to		
	Learn	Anticipate	Adapt
Having a stellar character		*	*
Being financially literate	*	*	*
Having diplomatic skills			*
Being an effective strategist	*	*	*
Keeping good company	*	*	*
Being an effective leader	*	*	*

leader, whose strong personality and abrasive manner may make discussion about sensitive matters extremely difficult. Leaders and followers frequently embrace the self-protecting coping mechanism of denial as a means of avoiding having to deal with serious issues: they spend their time and energy in mutual reassurance rather than planning for the unpleasant reality.

Formulating strategy (in conjunction with your senior managers, professional advisers, and members of your board), participating in preparation of business plans that incorporate financial projections, and interacting with your followers and industry colleagues and experts as a leader of your business create the continuous need for you to identify, evaluate, and decide how to cope with threats and opportunities. Thus, the prerequisite for anticipating is structured into the "banker's six" in the constant demand that senior management focus on, rather than ignore or avoid, aspects of the company's environment that could have either beneficial or detrimental effects on future performance. Denial, avoidance, and complacency—the building blocks of failure to anticipate—cannot flourish in this type of atmosphere.

Learning

If you possess the attributes that are associated with an effective leader, you will be ruthless and persistent in your search for the truth. You'll be predisposed to analyze carefully the performance of every aspect of your company, and you won't allow yourself to be diverted from gaining a full understanding of why the performance that was projected has not been achieved. You will oppose any efforts on the part of others to obfuscate, dissemble, or act disingenuously to deter you from discovering the facts and circumstances that will allow you to formulate actions to correct problems.

If you keep company with competent professionals and have a board of directors or advisory board composed of seasoned businesspeople, you will greatly expand your knowledge and understanding of the business world through those associations. You can expect the members of your board, in fulfilling their fiduciary duty, to insist that you report periodically on the performance of the company, and they will continuously challenge you to explain and justify your actions. The members of your board, as well as the professionals you retain, have a valuable stake in your education. A portion of their income and, more importantly, their reputation is linked to your success and the success of your business. (After all, they too are judged by the company they keep.) You can expect them to identify areas in which your experience, skills, and education may be lacking and to assist you in filling those voids.

Since you are financially literate, you will never feel intimidated by the thick reports that are prepared by your financial department. You'll be able to understand them thoroughly and to discuss their intricacies with your chief financial officer and the members of your board. You will always be fully cognizant of how the operations of any department or activity affect the performance of the overall business, and of how changes in any aspect of operations will affect the future financial performance.

Since you manage your business in accordance with a strategic plan, you will always be focused on how taking advantage of an opportunity or responding to a perceived threat will further or hinder the realization of your plan. In periodic meetings with your senior managers, you'll inquire as to their contributions in implementing the plan and what deficiencies they perceive in their efforts or those of any other manager. In the yearly meetings with your board and senior managers, you will thoroughly review every aspect of the strategic plan, and of the past year's efforts to implement it, to learn which aspects of the plan or implementation should be changed. The periodic meetings to review progress and update the plan will create a forum for you to learn continuously about the strategic aspects of your business; they will also force you to pursue diligently the improvement of your competitive advantage.

Adapting

Clausewitz, the great Prussian military strategist, observed that war is the province of chance, and chance will throw up opportunities as often as it will present adversity. Whereas failures to anticipate and to learn are jointly the responsibility of the organization and its leader, failure to adapt can be laid at the door of the leader.

Being an effective leader, you recognize that it is your responsibility to be vigilant in spotting both threats and opportunities, as well as to take appropriate measures to neutralize the threats and capitalize on the opportunities. Since you are financially literate and a strategist, you have the ability to comprehend the financial, operational, and strategic implications of the threats and opportunities, and you can discuss them intelligently with the professionals and board members with whom you will consult. You will call upon your advisers to help you analyze the problems, review the various options, and arrive at the very best decision. You recognize that rapid changes inevitably create conflicts with and among the various stakeholders of the business—the employees, key managers, investors, and suppliers, all of whom have a vested interest and some degree of control over the business. You will use your diplomatic and negotiating skills to accommodate these varied interests and positions and, hopefully, avoid litigation whenever possible. And because you have an unblemished character, your credibility will be unquestioned, and you will be aided by the reservoir of goodwill you have created.

Keeping Your Banker Happy

There's a tendency to emerge from a successful financing effort with an overwhelming feeling of relief similar to what you might experience after completing a must-pass course. Having completed the course with a passing grade, you bask in the afterglow, relishing the thought that you'll never have to solve another calculus problem or open another economics textbook. Borrowing doesn't work that way. Every loan you receive must be paid back in a specific period or renewed; if your business is successful, it's likely that you'll have to borrow additional funds.

The bank is under no obligation either to renew your loan or to provide you more funds. In fact, a banker may even call your loan before it is due. Things change; competitive forces, technology, and market conditions cause some companies to prosper and others to deteriorate. The bank will always be looking for ways to increase the quality of its assets by replacing clients of marginal performance with those that have good track records and show promise.

If you repeatedly fail to meet your plan milestones or experience unanticipated major losses, you may be invited to leave the bank. Being asked to take your business elsewhere is unpleasant at the very least, and it may precipitate a crisis in your company, since senior management will have to drop virtually everything to search out replacement financing.

Once you establish a satisfactory banking relationship, you will therefore want to nurture it; a satisfactory relationship is a ticket to feed at the money trough. The smart businessperson begins to prepare the next loan request the day after the current loan request funds. There are a number of actions you'll want to take, however, and several you must avoid in order to build a sound and lasting banking relationship.

The Major Don'ts

1.   Don't hide from your banker when he calls to inquire about late interest or principal payments. Call the loan officer the minute you determine that your payment will be late, explain why you will be late, and tell him when he can expect to receive your check. The bank prepares a daily report of the borrowers who are delinquent on their payments. These reports are reviewed at the time of a bank examination, and your frequent appearance on the list may result in your loan being downgraded. Downgrading of your loan may result in the bank's having to reduce its earnings to reflect the lower quality of your loan. This event will guarantee you an invitation to leave the bank.

2.   Avoid overdrawing your account, and never, *never* "play the float" or kite checks in order to solve a cash flow problem. An occasional overdraft that results from a clerical error or administrative oversight is not a big deal. Bankers expect it, and the charges for overdrafts are high enough that they adequately compensate the bank for their management time. Some companies attempt to use the float as a source of working capital, however, a practice that despite very careful and consistent management effort often fails and undercuts the credibility of the management team. Bankers view excessive overdrafts as an attempt by the borrower to draw down an unauthorized loan. The banker is reluctant to bounce checks because of the potential damage to the borrower's reputation, which may indirectly affect the borrower's ability to repay the loan.

As in the case of payment delinquencies, the bank prepares a daily list of depositors with overdrafts, and that list is circulated within the bank. Borrowers who frequently appear on the list are viewed negatively by other bank officers. This negative impression will be carried over to the loan committee when your next loan request is being considered.

3. Don't color the information you provide to the bank. Tell it like it is—the good, the bad, and the ugly. I'm always surprised that any businessperson believes that dissembling, stonewalling, or outright lying to a banker can possibly have a positive result. I recently sat in on a deposition where a retired businessman was being asked about some documents that his corporation sent to his bank several years before. The testimony was as follows:

LAWYER: Please look at these financial statements and see if they comport with your general recollection of what was happening in the business.

BUSINESSMAN: Like I told you before, there's no use looking at them because anything made out to the bank is not what the other directors got. You know that. You don't send the same kind of things to both places.

LAWYER: Are you saying you had two sets of financial statements that were different?

BUSINESSMAN: No, I'm not saying that.

LAWYER: Then what are you saying?

BUSINESSMAN: When they sent the stuff to the bank, they colored it different than the real statements. I mean, if you're losing money, you're not going to tell the bank you're losing money.

4. Don't pursue unrelated business or private ventures that will be distracting and divert your time and energies from the business that has borrowed the bank's money. If you do, you can expect that the bank's confidence in you will lessen. Veteran loan officers can point to many a failed borrower who neglected the core business in pursuit of unrelated business or personal activities.

5. Don't take the credit relationship for granted and assume that you have a pass to the bank's vault. A client of mine with an excellent banking relationship persisted in using his working capital line to purchase capital equipment, even though the loan agreement required that he obtain prior approval from the bank for

every significant capital asset purchase. He informed the bank of his actions only after the equipment was delivered, installed, and paid for. He was confident that his excellent relationship with the loan officer and his impeccable record of never missing a loan payment would protect his relationship with the bank. It did not, and he was asked to leave the bank.

The Major Do's

1. Read your loan agreement carefully, and set up internal systems and procedures to ensure that you comply with the technical requirements. A bank is a bureaucratic organization, and as such, it must maintain a paper trail to show senior management and the bank examiners that you are in compliance. Many entrepreneurs are very casual about the technical requirements of the loan agreement, such as the submittal of periodic financial statements, certificates of compliance, evidence of insurance in force, personal financial statements, and corporate resolutions. Your attention to these issues shows the banker that you are every bit the professional he thought you were when he recommended the loan.

2. Make sure that the banker hears any bad news from you before she hears it from anyone else. If your major customer is about to file bankruptcy, throwing into question the collectibility of tens of thousands of dollars in receivables, you want to be the bearer of the bad tidings. If your banker hears it from anyone else or reads about it in the press, she will always question whether you were surprised or were not forthcoming with the information; neither alternative helps your credibility.

3. Keep your banker fully informed as to your past and anticipated performance against your business plan. The bank made the commitment on the basis of the plan, and the plan establishes the benchmark against which your performance as an executive will be measured.

If you fail to meet your objectives, make sure you fully understand the reasons and take care to explain it to your banker. If you anticipate that future performance will fall below explanations, make sure you understand what assumptions or analyses were faulty or incorrect, and make sure you explain it to your banker.

The reports your banker prepares for his senior management must continue to sell your story and you; Make sure that they do.

If and when a serious problem arises that will affect your ability to perform under the loan agreement, promptly arrange a meeting with your banker. Make sure you have a plan to deal with the problem when you walk into that meeting, even if you and your staff have to work twenty-four hours a day between the time of the call and the time of the meeting. Your banker invested in your business because he believed that you were an exemplary leader. Do not prove him wrong by bringing him a problem without a plan for achieving a solution.

4. Make promises you can keep, and keep the promises you make. Your character and credibility are your most valuable assets. Making unrealistic and extravagant promises can destroy your reputation within a bank.

5. Finally, continue to charm your banker. Periodically invite her and her boss to your plant or offices and brief them as to what's going on in your industry. Explain your strengths and weaknesses compared to those of your major competitors and how your competitive position may have improved or weakened. Describe your strategy for maintaining or increasing your market share. Solicit their opinion about matters in which they are knowledgeable. They are very important to you; make sure they know that you know this. Romance is important in maintaining every close relationship.

Notes

Chapter 1

1. Ogden Nash, *A Penny Saved Is Impossible*, Little, Brown & Co., 1981.
2. John Steinbeck, *The Grapes of Wrath*, New York: Viking Press, 1939.
3. Charles Dickens, *A Christmas Carol and the Chimes*, New York: Harper and Row, 1965.

Chapter 2

1. L. J. Davis, "Chronicle of a Debacle Foretold: How Deregulation Begat the S & L Scandal," *Harper's*, September 1990, p. 50.
2. Fred R. Bleakly, "Regulators from Hell Frighten Some Banks But Also Win Praise," *Wall Street Journal*, April 27, 1993, p. A1.
3. Louis Uchitelle, "Bankers Expected to Stay Hesitant to Lend for Years," *New York Times*, July 5, 1991, p. A1.
4. Richard C. Breeden and William M. Isaac, "Thank Basel for Credit Crunch," *Wall Street Journal*, November 4, 1992, p. A14.

Chapter 3

1. Robert Morris Associates, the association of bank loan officers, publishes *Annual Statement Studies*, which contains composite financial data on manufacturing, wholesaling, retailing, service, and contracting lines of business. The statements show the statistical distribution of performance indexes for large numbers of companies in the same business. It can be ordered by writing to Robert Morris Associates, One Liberty Place, Philadelphia, PA 19103.
2. These terms are defined as follows:
Timely—time lag between creation, collection and reporting must be quick to allow for effective action;
relevant—information collected and reported must be pertinent to your particular company;
accurate—information must reflect physical realities of your business;

appropriate—management levels must each have information aggregated and organized in the detail required for their scope of control;

consistent—same assumptions and conventions must be used to prepare reports applying to various time periods.

Chapter 4

1. Anthony Sampson, *The Money Lenders: Bankers and a World in Turmoil*, New York: Viking Press, 1981.

Chapter 9

1. Steve Shagan, *Save the Tiger*, New York: Dial Dial Press, 1972.
2. Lewis Carroll, *Alice in Wonderland*, Boston: Little Simon, 1986.
3. Benjamin B. Tregoe and John W. Zimmerman, *Top Management Strategy: What It Is and How to Make It Work*, New York: Simon and Schuster, 1980.
4. Michael E. Porter, *Competitive Advantage: Creating and Sustaining Superior Performance*, New York: Free Press, 1985.

Chapter 10

1. Arthur Miller, *All My Sons*, New York: Viking Press, 1960.
2. Robert E. Kelley, *In Praise of Followership*, New York: Doubleday Currency, 1991.

Chapter 11

1. Manfred F. R. Kets de Vries, *Prisoners of Leadership*, New York: John Wiley & Sons, 1989.
2. John P. Kotter, "What Leaders Really Do," *Harvard Business Review*, May/June 1990, p. 104.

Bibliography

Chapter 1

Bollenbacher, George M., *The Business of Banking, Surviving and Thriving in Times of Unparalleled Consolidation and Competition*. Chicago: Bankers Publishing Company, Cambridge, England: Probus Publishing Company, 1992.

Sampson, Anthony, *The Money Lenders: Bankers and a World in Turmoil*. New York: Viking Press, 1981.

Chapter 2

"The Bank Police Get a Bigger Stick," Business Week, August 31, 1992, p. 59.

"Pillars of Sand, *Time*, January 14, 1991, p. 38.

"The Future of Banking," *Business Week*, April 22, 1991, p. 72.

Bacon, Kenneth H., "Losing Ground: Bank's Declining Role in Economy Worries Fed, May Hurt Firms," *Wall Street Journal*, July 9, 1993.

Bizer, David S., "Examiners Crunch Credit" *Wall Street Journal*, March 1, 1993.

Bleakley, Fred R., "Continuing Crunch: Many Midsized Firms Still Find that Insurers and Banks Deny Loans," *Wall Street Journal*, November 16, 1992, p. A1.

Bleakley, Fred R., "Regulators from Hell Frighten Some Banks But Also Win Praise," *Wall Street Journal*, April 27, 1993, p. A1.

Bryan, Lowell L., Bankrupt: Restoring the Health and Profitability of Our Banking System. New York: Harper Business, 1991.

Crawford, Richard D. and William W. Sihler, *The Troubled Money Business: The Death of the Old Order and the Rise of the New Order*. New York: Harper Business, 1991.

Davis, L. J., "Chronicle of a Debacle Foretold: How Deregulation Begat the S & L Scandal," *Harper's*, September 1990, p. 50.

Davis, L. J., "The Problem with Banks? Bankers," *Harper's*, June 1991, p. 45.

Hector, Gary, "Victims of the Credit Crunch," *Fortune*, January 27, 1992, p. 100.

Hector, Gary, "Banking Finally Hits the Bottom," *Fortune*, April 6, 1992, p. 98.

Mayer, Martin, *The Bankers*. New York: Ballentine Books, 1974.

Mayer, Martin, *The Money Bazaars: Understanding the Banking Revolution Around Us*. New York: E.P. Dutton, 1984.

Ryan, Timothy, "Banking's New Risk: Litigation," *Wall Street Journal*, November 13, 1992, p. A14.

Slater, Robert, *The Titans of Takeover*. Englewood Cliffs, NJ: Prentice-Hall, 1987.

Smith, Geoffrey, "Rockefeller Reflects," *Financial World*, July 23, 1991, p. 6.

Uchitelle, Louis, "Bankers Expected to Stay Hesitant to Lend for Years," *New York Times*, July 5, 1991, p. A1.

Chapter 3

"Jumping into the Credit Gaps," *Business Week*, October 19, 1992, p. 94.

Rich, Stanley R. and Gumpert, David E., "How to Write a Winning Business Plan," Harvard Business Review, p. 156 (May/June 1985).

Thurstan, Philip H., "Should Smaller Companies Make Formal Plans," Harvard Business Review, p. 162 (Sept/Oct 1983).

Chapter 4

Bel Air, Roger, *How to Borrow Money from a Banker: A Business Owner's Guide*. New York: AMACOM, 1988.

Dawson, George M., *Borrowing for Your Business: Winning the Battle for the Banker's "Yes."* Dover, NH: Upstart Publishing, 1991.

Murdock, Clint, *The Buck Stops Here*. Provo, UT: Allen Group, 1983.

Pulis, Arthur G., III, *Negotiating a Bank Loan You Can Live With*. Chicago: Probus Publishing Company, 1991.

Chapter 5

Greenberg Consulting and Craig T. Norback, *The Entrepreneur's Guide to Raising Venture Capital*. Blue Ridge Summit, PA: Liberty Hall Press, 1991.

Rowe, Alan J., Richard O. Mason and Karl E. Dickel, *Strategic Management and Business Policy: A Methodological Approach*. 2nd ed. Reading, MA: Addison-Wesley, 1986.

Thomas J. Peters and Robert H. Waterman, Jr., *In Search of Excellence: Lessons from America's Best Run Companies*. New York: Harper and Row, 1982.

Chapter 6

"Armored and Dangerous: Did Bank Insiders Help Revere Take Clients for a Ride?" *Business Week*, October 1993, p. 99.

Agins, Teri, "Loose Threads: Dressmaker, Leslie Fay is an Old-Style Firm that is in a Modern Fix," *Wall Street Journal*, February 23, 1993, p. A1.

Agins, Teri, "Report Is Said to Show Pervasive Fraud at Leslie Fay," *Wall Street Journal*, September 27, 1993, p. B4.

Bleakley, Fred R., "Poor Protection: Suspicions by Rivals Open Up a Scandal at Armored Car Firm," *Wall Street Journal*, February 17, 1993, p. A1.

Bleakley, Fred R., "Armored Car Case Leads to Indictment for Bribery, Theft," *Wall Street Journal*, May 14, 1993, p. A7.

Breeden, Richard C. and William M. Issac, "Thank Basel for Credit Crunch," *Wall Street Journal*, November 4, 1992, p. A14.

Cadbury, Sir Adrian, "Ethical Managers Make Their Own Rules," *Harvard Business Review*, September/October 1987, p. 69.

Reeves, Thomas C., *A Question of Character: A Life of John F. Kennedy*. New York: Free Press, 1991.

Zipser, Andy, "Cooking the Books: How the Pressure to Raise Sales Led MiniScribe to Falsify Numbers," *Wall Street Journal*, September 11, 1989, p. A1.

Zipser, Andy, "MiniScribe's Investigators Determine That 'Massive Fraud' Was Perpetrated," *Wall Street Journal*, September 12, 1989, p. A8.

Chapter 7

Casey, Cornelius J. and Norman J. Bartczak, "Cash Flow—It's Not the Bottom Line," *Harvard Business Review*, July/August 1984, p. 61.

Churchill, Neil C., "Budget Choice: Planning vs. Control," *Harvard Business Review*, July/August 1984, p. 150.

Stancill, James McNeil, "How Much Money Does Your New Venture Need," *Harvard Business Review*, May/June 1986, p. 122.

Stancill, James McNeil, "When Is There Cash in Cash Flow?" *Harvard Business Review*, March/April 1987, p. 38.

Chapter 8

Bazerman, Max H. and Margaret A. Neale, *Negotiating Rationally*. New York: Free Press, 1992.

Cohen, Herb, *You Can Negotiate Anything*. Secaucus, NJ: Lyle Stuart, 1980.

Fisher, Roger and William Ury, *Getting to Yes: Negotiating Agreements Without Giving In*. Boston: Houghton Mifflin Company, 1981.

Freund, James C., *Smart Negotiating: How to Make Good Deals in the Real World*. New York: Simon & Schuster, 1992.

Griffin, Trenholme J. and W. Russell Daggatt, *The Global Negotiator: Building Strong Business Relationships Anywhere in the World*. New York: Harper Business, 1990.

Lax, David A. and James K. Sebenius, *The Manager as Negotiator: Bargaining for Cooperation and Competitive Gain*. New York: Free Press, 1986.

March, Robert M., *The Japanese Negotiator: Subtlety and Strategy Beyond Western Logic*. New York: Kodansha International, 1988.

Morrison, William F., *The Prenegotiation Planning Book*. New York: John Wiley & Sons, 1985.

Nierenberg, Gerard I., *The Complete Negotiator*. New York: Nierenberg and Zeif Publishers, 1986.

Ury, William, *Getting Past No: Negotiating with Difficult People*. New York: Bantam Books, 1991.

Wolf, Bob, *Friendly Persuasion: My Life as a Negotiator*. New York: G. P. Putnam's Sons, 1990.

Chapter 9

Aaker, David A., *Developing Business Strategy*. New York: John Wiley & Sons, 1984.

Birnbaum, William S., If Your Strategy Is So Terrific How Come it Doesn't Work? New York: AMACOM, 1990.

Ghemawat, Pankaj, "Sustainable Advantage," *Harvard Business Review*, September/October 1986, p. 53.

Hayes, Robert H., "Strategic Planning—Forward in Reverse?" *Harvard Business Review*, November/December 1985, p. 111.

Henderson, Bruce D., "The Origin of Strategy: What Business Owes Darwin and Other Reflections on Competitive Dynamics," *Harvard Business Review*, November/December 1989, p. 139.

Hinterhuber, Hans H. and Wolfgang Popp, "Are You a Strategist or Just a Manager?" *Harvard Business Review*, January/February 1992, p. 105.

Isenberg, Daniel J., "The Tactics of Strategic Opportunism," *Harvard Business Review*, March/April 1987, p. 92.

Mintzberg, Henry, "The Fall and Rise of Strategic Planning," *Harvard Business Review*, January/February 1994, p. 107.

Ohmae, Kenichi, "Getting Back to Strategy," *Harvard Business Review*, November/December 1988, p. 149.

Porter, Michael E., *Competitive Advantage: Creating and Sustaining Superior Performance*. New York: Free Press, 1985.

Rock, Arthur, "Strategy vs. Tactics from a Venture Capitalist," *Harvard Business Review*, November/December 1987, p. 63.

Tilles, Seymour, *How to Evaluate Corporate Strategy from Strategic Management*, edited by Richard G. Hamermesh. New York: John Wiley & Sons, 1983.

Tregoe, Benjamin B. and John W. Zimmerman, *Top Management Strategy: What It Is and How to Make It Work*. New York: Simon and Schuster, 1980.

Chapter 10

Benson, Benjamin with Edwin T. Crego and Ronald H. Drucker, *Your Family Business: A Success Guide for Growth and Survival*. Homewood, IL: Dow Jones-Irwin, 1990.

Fox, Harold W., "Quasi-Boards: Useful Small Business Confidants," *Harvard Business Review*, January/February 1982, p. 158.

Goldstick, Gary, *Business Rx: How to Get in the Black and Stay There*. New York: John Wiley & Sons, 1988.

Chapter 11

Allen, Kenneth S., *That Bounty Bastard—The True Story of Captain William Bligh*. New York: St. Martin's Press, 1976.

Bennis, Warren and Burt Nanus, *Leaders: The Strategies of Taking Charge*. New York: Harper and Row, 1985.

Bennis, Warren, *On Becoming a Leader*. Reading, MA: Addison-Wesley, 1989.

DePree, Max, *Leadership Is an Art*. East Lansing: Michigan State University Press, 1987.

"Judgment Day: The Jury Nails Jim Bakker on all 24 Counts of Fraud," *Time*, October 16, 1989, p. 65.

Kelley, Robert E., "In Praise of Followers," *Harvard Business Review*, November/December 1988, p. 142.

Kelley, Robert E., *The Power of Followership*. New York: Doubleday Currency, 1991.

Kets de Vries, Manfred F. R., *Prisoners of Leadership*. New York: John Wiley & Sons, 1989.

Klein, Edward, "The Sinking of Captain Bob," *Vanity Fair*, March 1992, p. 180.

Kotter, John P., "What Leaders Really Do," *Harvard Business Review*, May/June 1990, p. 104.

Nanus, Burt, *The Leaders' Edge: The Seven Keys to Leadership in a Turbulent World*. Chicago: Contemporary Books, 1989.

Zaleznik, Abraham, "Managers and Leaders: Are They Different?" *Harvard Business Review*, March/April 1992, p. 126.

Chapter 12

Cohen, Elliott A. and John Gooch, *Military Misfortunes: The Anatomy of Failure in War*. New York: Vintage Books, 1991.

Index

Merchant of Venice, The (Shakespeare), 4
Merrill Lynch, 21, 180
Milken, Michael, 15, 19
Miller, Arthur, 191
MiniScribe, 101–2
Mixed expenses, 120
Money market funds, impact of, 21–22

National City Co., 15
Negotiation process
 documenting the deal, 163–64
 establishing alternatives, 147–48
 establishing wants, expectations, and needs, 145–47
 identifying all the issues, 144–45
 implementing the deal, 164–65
 interaction phase, 157–58
 leverage, 149–55
 reaching agreement, 160–63
 reasons for aborted negotiations, 165–67
 strategies, 155–56
 steps in, 143–44
 tactics, 158–60
Negotiator, how to become an effective, 167–69
New York Times, 33
Nordstrom, 179, 181

Operations versus strategy, 174–78
Persuasion, 159
Peters, Thomas J., 75
Pickens, T. Boone, 19
Porter, Michael, 179
Power of Followership, The (Kelley), 197
Price Club, 180
Principal, banker's role in participating as a, 14–15
Problem solving, 159
Professional help
 attorneys, 199–202
 board of directors, 196–97
 certified public accountants, 202–4

consultants, 204–6
cost of, 207–9
management staff, 197–99
Profitability ratios, 115, 116
Profit and loss forecast, 43
Projected balance sheet, 133–37
Projected income statement, 126–28
Prudence, 94

Quality control, 206–7
Quick ratios, 115, 116

Raffia, Howard, 160
Rationality, 167
Ratios
 asset/liability management, 116, 117
 debt-to-worth, 67–68, 115, 116
 financial analysis and use of, 110–19
 liquidity, 115, 116
 profitability, 115, 116
 return on investment, 115, 116, 117
 working capital, 116, 117
Real estate, bank investments in commercial, 24
Real estate lenders, 46
Regulations, impact of S & L scandal on, 32–33
Research and development (R & D) expenses, 126, 127
Resolution Trust Corp., 30
Restructuring firms, 44
Return on assets, 115, 116
Return on investment (ROI), 115, 116, 117
Revere Armored Inc., 102
Robert Morris Associates, 77, 110
Rockefeller, David, 24

Sales forecast, 126
Sales-to-working-capital ratio, 68, 124
Save the Tiger, 171–73
Savings and loan (S & L) scandal
 cost of, 25–26
 description of, 25–30
 impact of, 30–36